INTRODUCTION

Professor Biography i
Course Scope 1

LECTURE GUIDES

LECTURE 1
The Land of Canaan 5

LECTURE 2
The Arrival of the Israelites 20

LECTURE 3
Jerusalem—An Introduction to the City 35

LECTURE 4
The Jerusalem of David and Solomon 51

LECTURE 5
Biblical Jerusalem's Ancient Water Systems 66

LECTURE 6
Samaria and the Northern Kingdom of Israel 82

LECTURE 7
Fortifications and Cult Practices 96

LECTURE 8
Babylonian Exile and the Persian Restoration 111

LECTURE 9
Alexander the Great and His Successors 127

LECTURE 10
The Hellenization of Palestine 140

Table of Contents

LECTURE 11
The Maccabean Revolt 155

LECTURE 12
The Hasmonean Kingdom 169

LECTURE 13
Pharisees and Sadducees 184

LECTURE 14
Discovery and Site of the Dead Sea Scrolls 199

LECTURE 15
The Sectarian Settlement at Qumran 214

LECTURE 16
The Dead Sea Scrolls and the Essenes 228

LECTURE 17
The Life of the Essenes 242

LECTURE 18
From Roman Annexation to Herod the Great 254

SUPPLEMENTAL MATERIAL

Maps 269
Timeline 273
Glossary 278
Biographical Notes 293
Bibliography 303

The Holy Land Revealed

Jodi Magness, Ph.D.

PUBLISHED BY:

THE GREAT COURSES
Corporate Headquarters
4840 Westfields Boulevard, Suite 500
Chantilly, Virginia 20151-2299
Phone: 1-800-832-2412
Fax: 703-378-3819
www.thegreatcourses.com

Copyright © The Teaching Company, 2010

Printed in the United States of America

This book is in copyright. All rights reserved.

Without limiting the rights under copyright reserved above,
no part of this publication may be reproduced, stored in
or introduced into a retrieval system, or transmitted,
in any form, or by any means
(electronic, mechanical, photocopying, recording, or otherwise),
without the prior written permission of
The Teaching Company.

Jodi Magness, Ph.D.

Kenan Distinguished Professor
for Teaching Excellence in Early Judaism
University of North Carolina at Chapel Hill

Professor Jodi Magness holds a senior endowed chair in the Department of Religious Studies at the University of North Carolina at Chapel Hill: the Kenan Distinguished Professor for Teaching Excellence in Early Judaism. Professor Magness received her B.A. in Archaeology and History from the Hebrew University of Jerusalem (1977) and her Ph.D. in Classical Archaeology from the University of Pennsylvania (1989). From 1990 to 1992, Professor Magness was a Mellon Postdoctoral Fellow in Syro-Palestinian Archaeology at the Center for Old World Archaeology and Art at Brown University. From 1992 to 2002, she was Associate and then Assistant Professor of Classical and Near Eastern Archaeology in the Departments of Classics and Art History at Tufts University.

Professor Magness's book *The Archaeology of Qumran and the Dead Sea Scrolls* (Eerdmans, 2002) won the 2003 Biblical Archaeology Society's Award for Best Popular Book on Archaeology for 2001–2002 and was selected as an Outstanding Academic Title for 2003 by *Choice: Current Reviews for Academic Libraries*. Her book *The Archaeology of the Early Islamic Settlement in Palestine* (Eisenbrauns, 2003) was awarded the 2006 Irene Levi-Sala Prize for Books in the Archaeology of Israel in the nonfiction category.

Professor Magness's other books include *Jewish Daily Life in Late Second Temple Period Palestine* (Eerdmans; forthcoming); *Debating Qumran: Collected Essays on Its Archaeology* (Peeters, 2004); *Hesed ve-Emet: Studies in Honor of Ernest S. Frerichs* (coedited with Seymour Gitin; Scholars Press, 1998); and *Jerusalem Ceramic Chronology circa 200–800 C.E.* (Sheffield Academic, 1993). She is currently at work on *The Archaeology of the Holy Land 586 B.C.–640 C.E.* (under contract with Cambridge University Press). In addition, Professor Magness has published numerous articles in journals and edited volumes. Her research interests, which focus on Palestine in the Roman, Byzantine, and early Islamic periods, include ancient pottery, ancient synagogues, Qumran and the Dead Sea Scrolls, and the Roman army in the East. Professor Magness has participated in 20 different excavations in Israel and Greece, including codirecting the 1995 excavations in the Roman siege works at Masada. From 2003 to 2007, she codirected excavations in the late Roman fort at Yotvata, Israel. In June 2011, she will begin a new excavation project at Huqoq in Galilee.

In 1997–1998, Professor Magness was awarded a fellowship from the American Council of Learned Societies and a fellowship in Byzantine Studies at Dumbarton Oaks in Washington DC for research on *The Archaeology of the Early Islamic Settlement in Palestine*. In 2000–2001, Professor Magness was awarded a National Endowment for the Humanities Fellowship for college teachers and a Skirball Visiting Fellowship at the Oxford Centre for Hebrew and Jewish Studies for research on *The Archaeology of Qumran and the Dead Sea Scrolls*. In spring 2005, she received a Fulbright lecturing award through the United States–Israel Educational Foundation to teach two courses at the Institute of Archaeology at the Hebrew University of Jerusalem. In 2007–2008, Professor Magness was awarded a fellowship at the School for Historical Studies at the Institute for Advanced Study in Princeton, New Jersey, for research on *Aspects of Jewish Daily Life*. In 2008, she received a national teaching honor: the Archaeological Institute of America's Award for Excellence in Undergraduate Teaching. Most recently, Professor Magness was awarded a Chapman Family Faculty Fellowship for 2010–2011 at the Institute for Arts and Humanities at the University of North Carolina at Chapel Hill for work on *The Archaeology of the Holy Land, 586 B.C.–640 C.E.*

Professor Magness is a member of the Managing Committee of the American School of Classical Studies at Athens and the Program Committee of the Society of Biblical Literature. She has also been a member (and past vice-president) of the board of trustees of the W. F. Albright Institute of Archaeological Research in Jerusalem, the governing board of the Archaeological Institute of America (AIA), and the board of trustees of the American Schools of Oriental Research. She also served as president of the North Carolina Society of the AIA and the Boston Society of the AIA. ∎

The Holy Land Revealed

Scope:

This course covers the ancient history of what many people know as the Holy Land, a geographic area that includes modern Israel, Jordan, and the Palestinian territories. The course also looks at other regions in the ancient Near East, including Asia Minor (modern-day Turkey) and Mesopotamia (encompassing modern Iraq and much of Iran). The timespan we will cover begins with the First Temple period (c. 960 B.C.–586 B.C.) and takes us through the Second Temple period, the time of Jesus, and the destruction of the temple (c. 516 B.C.–A.D. 70) Our historical sources for these periods of ancient history include the Hebrew Bible and related religious works, the Dead Sea Scrolls, the writings of Josephus and Philo, the New Testament, and the Mishnah and Talmud. We will also explore the archaeology of the ancient Near East, which will complement our study of the historical sources by giving us a more complete picture of ancient societies.

In Lecture 1, we begin with a look at the original inhabitants of ancient Palestine—the Canaanites—and we discuss the extent to which the Hebrew Bible can serve as a reliable source of information about the history of the Holy Land. In Lecture 2, we talk about the arrival and settlement of the Israelite tribes in Canaan; we'll see these events described in the Hebrew Bible and consider the degree to which those events are corroborated or not by archaeological evidence. In Lecture 3, we review the history of Jerusalem from biblical accounts, beginning with David and Solomon and going down to the destruction of the city by the Babylonians in 586 B.C. In Lecture 4, we then compare the archaeological remains we have from Jerusalem in this period with descriptions in the Hebrew Bible. Lecture 5 offers a detailed look at the water systems that supplied ancient Jerusalem and gives us some idea of the difficulties faced by 19th-century archaeological explorers.

With Lecture 6, we move outside of Jerusalem and look at the northern kingdom of Israel, which had split from the united monarchy after the death of Solomon in about 930 B.C. Among the problems that developed between the northern and southern kingdoms was a division over how to worship the God of Israel, Yahweh. As we'll see, evidence of this division can be found in the archaeology of the kingdom of Israel at the Tel Dan site and elsewhere. In Lecture 7, we turn from the political events that affected the kingdoms of Israel and Judah to the everyday lives of some of their citizens, focusing specifically on fortifications and cultic practices. In the next lecture, we continue our story with the Babylonian destruction of the kingdom of Judah in 586 B.C. and the Babylonian Exile, ending with the return of the Judeans from exile under Persian rule. In Lecture 9, we discuss the conquests of Alexander the Great and the effect of Hellenization, that is, the spread of Greek culture in the wake of Alexander's conquests. In Lectures 10 and 11, we look at the impact of Hellenization on the non-Jewish peoples in the area of ancient Palestine and the Jewish population of Judea. Lecture 11 also covers the Maccabean revolt and the establishment of an independent Jewish kingdom ruled by the Maccabees and their successors, the Hasmoneans. In Lecture 12, we continue the story of the Hasmoneans until their takeover by the Romans, then consider one of the important neighboring peoples of the Hasmoneans, the Nabateans.

Lecture 13 turns to some of the Jewish groups that emerged in opposition to the Hasmoneans, specifically the Sadducees and the Pharisees. Lecture 14 begins a series of four lectures concerning another sect that emerged during the Late Second Temple period, the Essenes, and the scrolls left behind by their community at Qumran. We discuss the discovery of the Dead Sea Scrolls, tour the settlement at Qumran, and look at some of my own research on the archaeology there.

The sectarian settlement at Qumran was established during the Hasmonean period and was occupied through the period of the Roman takeover and the reign of Herod the Great. In Lecture 18, we consider the important transition from the Hasmonean period to the reign of Herod. As we'll see in Lectures 19 and 20, Herod may have been a ruthless king, but he is known among archaeologists as the single greatest builder in the history of Palestine. We'll see his rebuilding of the Second Temple and the area of the Temple Mount in Jerusalem and his construction of another important city, Caesarea Maritima. Having looked at the archaeological landscape created by Herod, in Lecture 21, we talk about his final days, his death, and the events after his death, leading up to and including the governorship of Pontius Pilate.

In Lectures 22 and 23, we study the smaller towns and villages, such as Bethlehem and Nazareth, that formed the backdrop to the life of Jesus. We also attempt to understand the socioeconomic environment of Galilee, which was polarized between an elite upper class and the majority of the population who lived at the subsistence level. Although Jesus apparently spent most of his life in Galilee, much of the information we have about him concerns his final days in Jerusalem. In Lecture 24, we review what is known from archaeology to learn what Jerusalem looked like in those last days. In Lectures 25 and 26, we explore the topic of ancient Jewish tombs and burials, setting the stage for a discussion, in Lecture 27, of Gospel accounts of the death and burial of Jesus and his brother, James.

The death of James highlights the instability in the Holy Land from the time of Herod's death until A.D. 66, when the First Jewish Revolt broke out against the Romans. As we'll see in Lecture 28, this revolt officially ended with the destruction of Jerusalem and the Second Temple in A.D. 70, but in Lectures 29 and 30, we follow the continued fighting of the Jews against the Romans, specifically in the fortresses of Herodium, Peraea, and Masada. In the decades after 70, the Jews lived in expectation of rebuilding the temple, but the decision of Emperor Hadrian to rebuild Jerusalem as a pagan city led to the outbreak of additional revolts. Lecture 31 looks at these rebellions, culminating in the Second Jewish Revolt, or the Bar-Kokhba Revolt, the end of which seems to mark the parting of the ways between Judaism and Christianity. In Lecture 32, we explore Hadrian's rebuilding of Jerusalem as Aelia Capitolina before moving on, in Lecture 33, to the Byzantine period to consider how Christianity literally transformed the appearance of the Holy Land. In Lecture 34, we look at what happened to the Jewish population of Palestine during the course of this transformation, and in Lecture 35, we see the impact of the arrival of Islam. Finally, we close this lecture series with an overview of scientific archaeological excavation and a look at the promise of even greater understanding of the past held by advances in technology, genetics, and other sciences. ■

The Land of Canaan
Lecture 1

Where archaeology and history diverge is in the types of information that they use for understanding the past.

In this first lecture, I will begin with some very key concepts, some chronologies, and some terms of dating. To start, the term "Holy Land" is not the only name for this piece of territory. The area is also called **Palestine**, the Land of Israel (or in, Hebrew, Eretz Israel), and Canaan. Basic chronological terms include the "First Temple period," which begins with the building of the temple by Solomon c. 960 B.C. and ends in 586 B.C. with its destruction by the Babylonians, and the "Second Temple period," which begins with the consecration of the Second Temple in 516 B.C. and ends with its destruction by the Romans in A.D. 70.

Much of our information will come from historical or literary sources, such as the **Hebrew Bible**, the **Apocrypha** and Pseudepigrapha, and the Dead Sea Scrolls. We will rely very heavily on a famous ancient Jewish historian called Josephus, as well as Philo of Alexandria and other written sources. We will also use a lot of archaeology, which differs from history in its method. Historians study written documents to understand the past; archaeologists study human material culture, the things that people have left behind. Archaeology compliments the picture of the past that we get from literary or written sources and, in periods for which we have no historical records, gives us some of our only information about the past.

> **Historians study written documents to understand the past; archaeologists study human material culture, the things that people have left behind.**

One of the conventions that archaeologists have is dividing the past into a sequence. For our purposes, historic periods start with the 5th century B.C., when people began to keep records of history; periods before that are prehistoric. Archaeologists have divided prehistoric time in the Mediterranean basin into the sequence: Stone Age, Bronze Age, and Iron

Age. Until the invention of radiocarbon dating around 1950, there was no real way to get dates for the prehistorical remains that we dug up. To solve this problem, archaeologists tied their chronologies to Egypt, because Egypt is the only country with a continuously dated calendar going back almost 5,000 years.

The very early inhabitants of the Holy Land, whom we call Canaanites, settled in Palestine around 5,000 years ago and eventually developed a culture based around fortified city-states, of which we do have archaeological remains. The mounds, or tells, where these cities existed contain material traces of Canaanite culture, especially of their religion. Jerusalem was one of these cities. Excavations in Jerusalem have unearthed pottery and remains of houses and tombs that date back to the beginning of the Bronze Age, and we also have correspondence between the Egyptian pharaohs and the local kings in the area of Jerusalem.

Jerusalem's Temple Mount, the religious heart of the city.

How reliable is the Hebrew Bible as a source of information about this ancient time? What makes this question difficult to answer is that the Hebrew Bible was composed and edited through many centuries, and often it refers to events that occurred centuries or millennia before they were written down. We must remember these things when we use the Hebrew Bible as a source of information.

By the end of this course of lectures, you will understand not just many different pieces of information but also the kinds of critical tools and methods that archaeologists and scholars use to evaluate the validity of historical claims presented to the public. ■

Important Terms

Apocrypha: Books included in the Catholic canon of sacred scripture but not in the Jewish and Protestant canons (examples: Tobit and Ecclesiasticus).

Hebrew Bible: Roughly corresponds with the Old Testament.

Palestine: Modern Israel, Jordan, and the Palestinian territories (ancient Canaan).

Questions to Consider

1. How do the differences between history and archaeology affect our understanding of the past?

2. How would you respond to the argument that the Hebrew Bible contains no historically reliable information at all?

The Land of Canaan
Lecture 1—Transcript

My name is Jodi Magness and I'm a professor at the University of North Carolina at Chapel Hill. My appointment is in the Department of Religious Studies, specifically in early Judaism, which means Judaism of the Second Temple period. But in fact, by training, I am an archaeologist, a classical archaeologist, which means that I'm trained in the archaeology of ancient Greece and Rome.

How did I come to be in a Department of Religious Studies? Well it's because all of my work in research focuses on the Holy Land, mostly in the time of Jesus. So because of this overlap I hold this unusual appointment. I've actually wanted to be an archaeologist since I was 12 years old thanks to a teacher that I had in seventh grade who introduced us to world history, and I fell in love with ancient Greece at that time and have sort of been on one track ever since.

I, myself, have worked on archaeological excavations in Israel and in Greece, including co-directing my own excavations at a number of sites such as the Roman Siege-Works at Masada, which we're going to be talking about later in this course. In fact, I am very excited about this course because it gives me an opportunity to introduce to you the subject of my lifetime passion, which is the archaeology of the Holy Land.

I'm going to start this first lecture by introducing you to some very key concepts, some chronologies, some terms of dating, and then we will, towards the end of the lecture, talk about the earliest inhabitants of the Holy Land, the Canaanites. First of all, to start with some key definitions, I'd like to start with the term the Holy Land.

This term Holy Land is actually a very Christian term and a Christian concept, and it is true we will spend a lot of time over the course of these lectures talking about Christianity and Jesus in the Holy Land. But what are some of the other terms for this piece of territory? It's actually a piece of territory that due to political reasons is quite controversial. For example, sometimes we refer to this piece of territory as Palestine, in fact, over the course of our lectures I will be using the term Palestine quite a bit. I will use it not in the modern politically-loaded sense of the word, but actually in a more ancient sense of the word to refer to the territory of modern Israel, Jordan, and the Palestinian territories.

Of course some people don't feel comfortable referring to this territory as Palestine, and so sometimes you will hear a different term used, that is the term Land of Israel, which is actually an ancient biblical term in Hebrew Eretz Israel. Of course, sometimes this land is called Canaan after the earliest inhabitants who we'll be talking about a little bit later in this lecture.

The area of ancient Palestine is part of a much larger geographical region called the Ancient Near East. The Ancient Near East encompasses the area of modern Turkey, Syria, Palestine, down to Egypt, through Jordan, across to Iraq and into the area of modern Iran.

For antiquity, we refer to this as the Ancient Near East or the Near East, but it basically corresponds with the same geographical region that today we call the Modern Middle East. This is actually a very interesting thing. Why do we refer to it as the Near East for ancient periods but the Middle East for modern periods? It all has to do with perspective, because in antiquity our sources who wrote about this territory were mostly writers or authors living in the area of Greece and Italy. From their perspective, this was the Near East, but in the modern world, our perspective has moved farther away to Western Europe and North America. So today, in modern times, we refer to this as the Middle East, but in terms of the actual geographical extent is pretty much identical with the Ancient Near East.

I also want to point out a couple of key geographical regions within the Ancient Near East, the area today that is occupied by the country of Turkey, is a land mass that is sometimes referred to as Asia Minor. Sometimes Turkey is referred to as the area of Anatolia, both of these are ancient terms, and we will be using the term Asia Minor over the course of our lectures to refer to the area of modern Turkey.

Another geographical term that's very common is Mesopotamia. Mesopotamia is a Greek word that literally means the land between the rivers, referring to the land, the territory between the Tigress and Euphrates Rivers. Mesopotamia is not a country, it is a geographical territory, just as we use the term "North America" to refer to a geographical territory and within that area of North America today there are different countries, and so in the area of ancient Mesopotamia there were different countries over the course of time, for example Babylonia and Syria, which we will be mentioning in our lectures. Today of course the area of Mesopotamia is occupied by the modern country of Iraq. The area to the east of that, the area to the east of Mesopotamia in antiquity, was ancient Persia, which today corresponds pretty much with the area of modern Iran.

Let's now define some basic chronological terms, some periods that we're going to mentioning over the course of our lectures. First of all we're going to be talking, at the beginning of the course especially, about the First Temple and the First Temple period. The First Temple refers to Solomon's Temple, the temple built by Solomon on the Temple Mount in Jerusalem, which was built approximately 960 B.C. and stood until 586 B.C. when it was destroyed by the Babylonians. So that period from approximately 960 to 586 B.C. is what we refer to as the First Temple period.

A little while later a second Jewish temple was built on the site of the Temple Mount where Solomon's Temple had previously been, we call that temple the Second Temple. It was consecrated in 516 B.C. and was destroyed by the Romans in the year 70 A.D., and so that period, 516 B.C. to 70 A.D., is the Second Temple period. We will be spending a lot of time talking about the Time of Jesus, which corresponds with what we call the Late Second Temple period, specifically the late 1st century B.C. and 1st century A.D.

We will also spend a lot of time talking about the area of the Temple Mount in Jerusalem and the site of the two ancient Jewish temples, and we can still see in the old city of Jerusalem today the area of the Temple Mount, this big open plaza, that had originally these two successive temples sitting on it where today the Dome of the Rock and the al-Aqsa Mosque are located, and we can see today the western side of the wall that surrounded the Temple Mount, which is today venerated by Jews as the Wailing Wall, or the Western Wall.

What sources of information will we be using over the course of our lectures? Well a lot of our information is going to come from historical or literary sources, and these historical and literary sources are very diverse, and they are going to include the following. They are going to include the Hebrew Bible. That is what many people call the Old Testament, which includes the Torah, which many people refer to as the Pentateuch or the Five Books of Moses. When I cite biblical passages I will be using the New Revised Standard Version. We will also be using the Apocrypha and Pseudepigrapha, the Dead Sea Scrolls, and we'll be spending quite a bit of time talking about the community that deposited those scrolls in the caves by the shore of the Dead Sea. We will be relying very heavily on a famous ancient Jewish historian called Flavius Josephus. We will be using to a lesser degree Philo of Alexandria. We will of course also be using the New Testament, and we will be using the Mishnah and Talmud to a lesser degree, that were compiled by rabbis between the 2nd and 5th centuries A.D.

All of those are going to be various sorts of historical and literary sources of information that we will be drawing upon. We will be also using a lot of archaeology in this course; that is we will be drawing a lot on archaeological information. I want to, here, highlight and contrast the similarities and differences between archaeology and history, specifically what is the difference between archaeology and history.

Both disciplines study the past; that is both disciplines attempt to give us an understanding or a picture of the past. In that, archaeology and history are very similar. Where archaeology and history diverge however is in the types of information that they use for understanding the past. Specifically historians study written documents to understand the past, so whatever sources of literature or writings have come down to us over the course of time, those are studied by historians.

This means that history gives us a very particular kind of understanding of the past because, of course, in antiquity most people didn't know how to read and write. The people who knew how to read and write generally were the upper classes of society, the elite, and so generally the historical sources that we have to tell us about the past give us the perspective of those upper classes, the wealthier classes, and not so much the perspective of the poorer classes of society, and certainly not the perspective of some members of society like women, for example, or maybe slaves or children.

What is archaeology in distinction to history? Archeology is the study of human material culture, the material culture, things that people have left behind. When archaeologists go to excavate an archaeological site, they dig up all sorts of different things that people have left behind. It is true that when archaeologists excavate a site we find the remains of things like palaces and citadels, but side by side with that, archaeologists also dig up the remains associated with the poorer classes, associated with women, associated with children. In other words archaeology compliments the picture of the past that we get from literary or written sources and in cases, in periods for example when we have no historical or literary sources about a particular time or a place, archaeology gives us some of our only information about the past. And so both because of my own particular background and interest and because archaeology gives us so much valuable information about the Holy Land, we will be incorporating archaeological information to a very large degree over the course of the lectures that we will be having.

One of the things that I want to explain in terms of basic definitions is periodization, because one of the conventions that archaeologists have is dividing the periods that we study into sort of a sequence. If you look at countries around the Mediterranean; that is the area that we call the Old World, you will find first of all a division into prehistory versus history, prehistoric periods versus historic periods.

Prehistory versus history isn't exactly what you might think. That is, it is true that writing was invented in the ancient Near East in Egypt and in Mesopotamia, about 5,000 years ago in about 3,000 B.C. For our purposes historic periods are considered to start not 5,000 years ago, but rather around let's say the 5th century B.C. Why the 5th century B.C.? Because it wasn't until then that we begin to get the idea of writing history in the sense of the modern definition of history, keeping records of history in the sense of the modern word, and this begins to be done first by the ancient Greeks, around the 5th century B.C.

The periods before that in the Mediterranean world are considered prehistoric in the sense that there is no history writing in the sort of modern sense of the word. What archaeologists have done then is to divide the prehistoric periods into a sequence called Stone Age, Bronze Age, Iron Age. I'm sure you have all heard of these terms. Notice a very interesting thing, that these terms reflect a judgment based on a sequence of materials that are used to make tools where the earliest and "most primitive" period is the Stone Age. Then humans advance and begin to use bronze, and you get to the Bronze Age, and then the latest and most sophisticated technology for working tools is iron, and then you get to the historic periods.

This tripartite chronology was actually worked out in the 19th century at the height of the industrial revolution when human progress was measured in terms of technology and materials that were used to make tools, and we still use this terminology today. In addition, these periods are further subdivided by scholars and very interesting the Bronze Age in particular is divided into a sequence of Early Bronze, Middle Bronze, and Late Bronze, so EB, MB, and LB, for those in the know. There is actually a very interesting reason for this division too, and that is up until the invention of radio carbon dating around 1950, after World War II ended, when with radio carbon dating you can basically take an organic material and send it to a lab and get back a date. Up until the invention of radio carbon dating, there was no real way to get dates for the remains that we dug up that were earlier than historical periods. So, one of the problems in the Mediterranean basin before 1950 was trying to date the layers that you were digging up, the remains that you were digging up, in a period before the introduction of radio carbon dating.

What everybody did to solve this problem before the 1950s was to try and tie their chronology to Egypt, because Egypt is the only country in the Mediterranean with a continuously-dated calendar going back almost 5,000 years where they kept the dates of the reigns of the different pharaohs. So if you could tie yourself to Egypt, if for example you found a scarab at the site you were digging at, you could tie your chronology to Egypt and you could get a date in that way, and so the division of the Bronze Age in the Old World mirrors the division of Egyptian chronology where the early Bronze Age is basically equivalent to the Old Kingdom in Egypt, the Middle Bronze Age to the Middle Kingdom, and the Late Bronze Age to the New Kingdom.

We're going to be talking at the beginning of the course in particular about a period that is often described as the Biblical period in the Holy Land. By Biblical I mean not the New Testament period, but rather the Old Testament period. Usually when archaeologists refer to biblical archaeology in the Holy Land or they refer to the Biblical period they are referring specifically to the Old Testament period and that would then include what we call the Bronze Age, which is the Canaanite period, the period when the Canaanites were the inhabitants of the country, and the Iron Age, which is the Israelite period, the period when the Israelites come in and settle down.

In terms of absolute dates, the Bronze Age dates approximately 3000 to 1200 B.C., and the Iron Age dates approximately 1200 to 586 B.C., and that date 1200 for the beginning of the Iron Age is really a big watershed for the division between the Bronze Age and the Iron Age all around the eastern Mediterranean. This period of the Biblical period and in particular the Iron Age encompasses or includes the First Temple period, which as we already mentioned dates approximately 960 to 586 B.C.

Let's now talk about the arrival of the Canaanites. We're going to start with these very early inhabitants of the Holy Land, which is basically somewhere around 3000 B.C., around 5000 years ago these people who the Bible calls the Canaanites entered Palestine and settled down, and hence we refer to the country as Canaan. When the Canaanites first settled in the country they established small villages around the country, and over the course of the next several hundred years some of those villages began to grow into towns and eventually some of those towns grew into cities.

What we end up with eventually is Canaanite civilization being an urban civilization, an urban culture, based around city-states, and the eventual configuration of what we have in Canaan then are a series of independent city-states around the country where at the core of each one of these city-states is a fortified city which controls a certain territory around it. These city-states were all independent from each other, and sometimes were in conflict with each other, but never were they united under the rule of a single ruler in the way that Egypt for example was unified under the rule of a pharaoh.

We have remains of these Canaanite city-states at various sites around the country that have been excavated, and I'm going to mention only a few. At the very northern end of the country is a large site called Hazor. If we move south of Hazor, not far from Haifa on the coast, is a site called Megiddo. If we continue south of that we get to the middle of the country and a site called Gezer, and if we continue south from Gezer to the southern part of the country, we get to the site of Lachish (or La-heesh). We will be talking about all of these Canaanite city-states and more either as part of the Canaanite period or later settlements at these sites over the course of the series. Since Canaanite civilization was an urban culture and these city-states were fortified, we do have archaeological remains of fortifications. I show for example the Middle Bronze Age Gate at Gezer, a kind of fortification that we will be talking about in another lecture.

One of the most important Canaanite city-states which remained important for centuries afterwards is Megiddo, which eventually comes to be identified with Armageddon, and Megiddo was so important because of its location. All throughout antiquity and even up until today the major north-south thoroughfare through Palestine was along the coast, the coastal plane, because it's flat. If you go inland you get into hill country and it becomes harder to traverse.

All throughout antiquity if you wanted to go from Egypt in the south to Syria in the north, you had to go along the coastal road, and when you got to the area of Haifa you then hit a mountain ridge, the Carmel Mountains, which jut out into the sea where you simply cannot continue. At that point then what you have to do is go through one of the mountain passes. Megiddo guards the outlet of one of the major mountain passes and therefore had a very important strategic location, and then from that point once you've gotten to Megiddo, you've crossed the mountain pass, you're in the Jezreel Valley, you can then cut across towards the Jordan Valley, Sea of Galilee, and head north towards Syria.

Another one of the major biblical sites was the large fortified mound at Hazor, which consists of a fortified upper city and then a large fortified lower city, and these are clearly visible for example in aerial photographs. The Canaanites of course were not Israelites, they were—I hate to use the word Pagan because it's so loaded—what we would call a Pagan population that worshiped different gods. Of course then we see this reflected also in the archaeological remains of their city-states, for example at Hazor Yigael Yadin, the excavator, found the remains of a late Bronze Age shrine that clearly was dedicated to the Moon god. Why do I say "clearly"? Because there is a stone found in the shrine that is carved with two hands raised with a crescent moon above and a disk in the middle and a seated figure of a man who has a crescent carved on his chest.

Notice by the way very characteristic of these Canaanite shrines and something that we will see later among the Israelites as well is the idea of building a shrine representing deities simply by standing stones, either with carvings on them or quite frequently just plain standing stones. These kinds of standing stones are what we call stelae, the singular is stele, and they're very, very common in this part of the world in the area of ancient Palestine.

Also notice by the way that one of the objects found in this shrine was a large stone slab carved in the shape of a lion, which is what we call an orthostate, this big stone slab carved as a lion, which was presumably placed at an entrance into the sanctuary, into the shrine, which literally then guards the entrance.

So we have this idea that you have different shrines dedicated to different gods in these Canaanite city-states and this now brings us to Jerusalem, a city that we're going to be spending a lot of time talking about, and in fact, the earliest settlement in Jerusalem goes back to the beginning of the Bronze Age. At the beginning of the Bronze Age, at the beginning of the Canaanite period, Jerusalem was first settled, so we're talking about 5,000 years ago. We know this because archaeological excavations in Jerusalem have brought to light pottery and some fragmentary remains of houses and tombs that date all the way back to the beginning of the Bronze Age. So we know that the city was settled.

We also know that there was settlement in Jerusalem in the Bronze Age because we have documents that refer to Jerusalem. Specifically we have documents that date to the Bronze Age from Egypt which represent correspondence between the Egyptian pharaohs and the local kings in the area of Jerusalem. In fact, these documents give us the early name of the city of Jerusalem, which was Yerushalem.

Many people today think that the name Jerusalem, Yerushalayim in Hebrew, comes from the word shalem meaning peace. This is actually not the case; this is a later understanding of the name Jerusalem. Originally the name Yerushalem probably meant "foundation of the god Shalem," in other words, referring to the deity who was the patron deity of the city. In fact it was very common in antiquity for cities to be named after the patron deity.

For example Jericho, Jericho in Hebrew, was apparently named after the Moon God Yereha, who is Moon God in Hebrew, and apparently Jericho took its name from the patron deity the Moon Deity. This very early population of Jerusalem is what the Bible calls the Jebusites, and we actually don't know whether these Jebusites mentioned in the Bible are related to Canaanites or whether they are an unrelated population.

As I mentioned a little while ago, we will be using different kinds of literary and written sources for information, and one of the sources that we will be using is the Hebrew Bible. This is a perfect time now to bring up the problem of how reliable is the Hebrew Bible as a source of information? The answer to that question will vary depending on who you ask. That is scholars will differ in their assessment of how reliable the Hebrew Bible is as a source of historical information.

The first thing to point out is that the Hebrew Bible is not a historical document in the sense that it was not written as a historical document in our sense of the word. It was written to fulfill different purposes. That does not mean that the Hebrew Bible doesn't contain any historical information, but it means that it was not written for that purpose. So when you evaluate the Hebrew Bible you first of all have to understand the purposes of the writers of the Hebrew Bible.

What makes this question how reliable is the Hebrew Bible as a source of historical information, what makes this such a difficult question to answer is the fact that the Hebrew Bible is an extremely complex document. It is first of all not "a" document, it is a series of different works that were composed over the course of many centuries beginning probably—and this is the source of debate among scholars—but beginning probably in the late 8th and 7th centuries B.C. and then continuing all the way down until well Daniel actually is the last one, and we're now talking middle of the 2nd century B.C. there, so you have a very long process of composition of these various books or works in the Hebrew Bible.

Not only did the composition of these works take place over a long period of time, but once the works were composed, they were edited and re-edited over the course of time. So what we end up with today is a work that was written and edited and re-edited over a very long period that is a very complicated process. Now another problem is that if we look at the Hebrew Bible as a source of information and in particular if we look at the Pentateuch, the Five Books of Moses, we have an even bigger problem, because if you look at the earlier books of the Pentateuch, for example Genesis or even Exodus for example, these books describe events that occurred long before the Hebrew Bible began to be edited and written down even by the most optimistic estimates.

What we end up with is a gap between the time when the Hebrew Bible is first edited and written down, let's say maybe late 8th, 7th century B.C., and events that are described in these earlier books. So if we're talking about creation account and the Garden of Eden or we're talking about Noah's Ark or we're talking about the patriarchs or even if we get all the way down to the time of the Exodus, let's say, we're talking about events that occurred centuries or millennia earlier, if they occurred at all, that occurred centuries or millennia earlier than the time they were written down.

This is exactly the problem, because we have no way of verifying that those events actually occurred and that they were then remembered in an authentic way and reported, presumably orally, over the course of many generations until they're finally written down. In other words, what I'm trying to say here is that the farther back you go in time from the time the Hebrew Bible is first edited and written down, the further back you go in time the less reliable it is thought to be as a source of historical information. So this is one of the things that we must keep in mind when we use the Hebrew Bible as a source of information.

A lot of the events reported in the Hebrew Bible are covered in the popular media in various ways, TV programs devoted to things like Noah's Ark, the discovery of Noah's Ark, or for example the Exodus of the Israelites from Egypt, these are all topics that are covered by a lot of popular programs in the media. One of the things people always want to know is well how accurate is that media programming?

What I'm hoping for us, over the course of these lectures, is that by the time we get to the end you will have gained not just understanding of lots of different facts of information, pieces of information and factoids and things like that, but you will gain an understanding also of the kinds of critical tools and methods that as archaeologists and as scholars we use to evaluate the validity of the claims. What I'm hoping is that this course will not just introduce you to the Holy Land, which in itself is fascinating of course, but that also you will come away with a bigger picture and an understanding of critical methodology and critical evaluation of material that is presented to the public.

The Arrival of the Israelites
Lecture 2

> In fact many scholars now believe that the Exodus, if it ever occurred, occurred not in the way that is described in the Bible, but as a much smaller event, that is perhaps as a small number of people leaving Egypt wandering perhaps to some extent in the desert eventually entering the land of Canaan and joining up in Canaan with other people.

In this lecture, we'll continue talking about the arrival of the Israelite tribes in Canaan and their settlement there, how these events are described in the Hebrew Bible, and to what degree those descriptions are corroborated or not by archaeological evidence.

The Canaanites settled in Canaan at the beginning of the Bronze Age, roughly around 3000 B.C. With time, their villages grew into towns and, in some cases, large fortified cities. By the late Bronze Age—the 14th and 13th centuries B.C.—Canaan consisted of fortified city-states. It's precisely during this period that the Israelite Exodus from Egypt supposedly took place. In the last lecture, we talked quite extensively about the degree to which the Hebrew Bible can be used as a reliable source of information. To what extent is the account of the Exodus corroborated by archaeology?

On the Merneptah stele is a reference to Israel as a people: "Israel is laid waste, his seed is not."

The problem is that, if there was an exodus from Egypt, this is the sort of event that would leave little if any traces in the archaeological record. The Exodus involved people wandering around in a nomadic or semi-nomadic fashion through the desert. They were not building settlements or cities or leaving the kind of remains that would be traceable in the archaeological record.

However, we do have an important piece of information about the early Israelites that comes from the time the Exodus would've taken place. This is a large standing stone called the **Merneptah stele**, named after an Egyptian pharaoh, Merneptah, and commemorating his victories. On the Merneptah stele is a reference to Israel as a people: "Israel is laid waste, his seed is not." This reference in no way corroborates the biblical story of the Exodus, but it indicates the existence of a people called Israel at the time they would have arrived in the land of Canaan.

In around 1200 B.C., the system of city-states in Canaan collapsed. At this time, many peoples were moving about the eastern Mediterranean world, and cities and kingdoms were destroyed. This collapse coincided with the Israelite tribes' entry into Canaan and settlement in the hilly center of the country. At exactly the same time, other peoples also moved into the area, such as the **Moabites** and the **Philistines**, who settled more arable and richer parts of Canaan and became enemies of Israel.

Archaeological evidence sometimes supports the biblical account of the settlement and sometimes does not. For Jericho, there isn't evidence at this time of walls that could collapse, but there is evidence of destruction by fire at the site of the northern Canaanite city Hazor. Archaeology alone, however, cannot tell us who destroyed that city.

The Hebrew Bible indicates that violence did not end with the settlement; indeed, the Bible is filled with stories about wars and battles, especially between the Philistines and the Israelites. In these accounts appear important figures, such as Samson, Saul, David, and Goliath. It is Saul's death in a battle with the Philistines that enables David to become the next king and leads to the creation of a united kingdom under David and his son Solomon. ∎

The death of King Saul set the stage for the creation of a united Israel.

Important Terms

Merneptah stele: Monumental stone inscription of the pharaoh Merneptah, which contains the first reference to the people "Israel" (1209 B.C.).

Moabites: Iron Age inhabitants of the area south of Ammon and north of Edom.

Philistines: People of Aegean origin who settled the southern coast of Palestine in the early Iron Age.

Questions to Consider

1. To what extent does archaeology support the biblical account of the early Israelite settlement in Canaan, and what does archaeology tell us about the nature of that settlement?

2. Why does it (or should it) matter whether archaeology supports the biblical account of any event?

The Arrival of the Israelites
Lecture 2—Transcript

In our last lecture, we talked about the original inhabitants of ancient Palestine, the Canaanites, and we also talked about to what extent the Hebrew Bible is a reliable source of information about the history of the Holy Land. In this lecture, I'd like to pick up and talk about the arrival of the Israelite tribes in Canaan and their settlement in the land of Canaan, and also talk about the events as described in the Hebrew Bible and to what degree those events are corroborated or not by archaeological evidence.

The Canaanites settled in Canaan in the land of Israel in the Bronze Age, at the beginning of the Bronze Age, roughly around 3000 B.C. During the course of the Bronze Age, their settlements, their villages, grew into towns and some of them grew into large fortified cities so that by the late Bronze Age, by let's say the 14th and 13th centuries B.C. Canaan consisted of a series of fortified city-states, many of which were often at war with each other.

This period of the late Bronze Age is, in fact, a very interesting period around the eastern Mediterranean because during this period there were a series of powerful kingdoms and empires around the eastern Mediterranean. For example, in Greece we have the Mycenean kingdoms, which in some respects are analogous to what we have in Canaan in the sense that the Mycenean kingdoms were a series of separate independent fortified kingdoms which often were at war with each other and were not united under the rule of a single monarch or king.

In Anatolia, that is the area of Asia Minor, modern Turkey, we have a powerful kingdom that is called the Hittite kingdom or the Hittite Empire. In Egypt the late Bronze Age is the period of the New Kingdom. So literally in the late Bronze Age, the eastern Mediterranean is ringed by a series of powerful kingdoms and city-states. Not only that, but these various kingdoms and city-states were in contact with each other.

We know for example that they traded extensively with each other because various kinds of pottery and other examples of archaeological artifacts have been found imported and exported from various places around the

Mediterranean. For example, at Tel Dan a Mycenean chariot krater, that is a large sort of a vase used for mixing wine and water that was imported from Mycenean Greece, was found and presumably was acquired by somebody with a lot of money who lived at Tel Dan, a Canaanite city-state in the very northern part of Canaan.

We also know that these city-states and kingdoms were in contact with each other because we have actual examples of correspondence of letters that their kings and rulers sent back and forth to each other. Some of the most famous and important examples of these are texts that were found in Egypt and these texts interestingly are written not in hieroglyphs, not in the native script of Egypt, but are written in cuneiform on little clay tablets.

What exactly is cuneiform? Cuneiform, which probably is not as familiar to most people as hieroglyphs, is a script that is a kind of an alphabet that was made by taking a sharpened reed, that reed was sharpened so that the tip was wedge-shaped, and then making impressions with the wedge-shaped tip into a soft clay tablet. And the impressions formed by the tip make the symbols in this script which is called cuneiform. In fact, cuneiform comes from the Latin word cuneus, which means wedge, because the symbols are wedge-shaped.

Cuneiform actually refers not to the language, but to the alphabet or script. And by that I mean it refers to the actual letters rather than the language that the script was written in. An analogous example would be today we write different languages, English, German, French, Spanish, Latin, in the same alphabet, in the same script, but they're different languages. So different languages in antiquity were written using cuneiform script and in the late Bronze Age cuneiform was used for all of the correspondence, the international correspondence between these kingdoms and empires around the eastern Mediterranean. So one of the things that we have surviving, especially from Egypt, are examples of cuneiform tablets which represent the correspondence between these various kings and empires.

It's precisely during this period, that is during the late Bronze Age, the 14th, 13th centuries B.C., that the Israelite Exodus from Egypt supposedly took place, and last time we talked quite extensively about to what degree can the Hebrew Bible be used as a reliable source of information. The Exodus is a really good place to sort of look at this as an example of using the Hebrew Bible. Most people know about the Exodus and want to know what do we know about it archaeologically?

Well this is really a million dollar question. We have of course the description of the Exodus in the Hebrew Bible beginning with the plague that the Hebrew God, the Lord of Israel, sent to attack the Egyptians ending of course with the deaths of all of the firstborn and the relevant passage reads, "At midnight the Lord struck down all the firstborn in the land of Egypt, from the firstborn of Pharaoh who sat on his throne to the firstborn of the prisoner who was in the dungeon, and all the firstborn of the livestock." So of course not only are firstborn children killed, but event the firstborn of animals are killed by this plague. "Pharaoh arose in the night, he and all his officials and all the Egyptians; and there was a loud cry in Egypt, for there was not a house without someone dead."

Imagine the scenario; then he summoned Moses and Aaron, so the pharaoh summons Moses and Aaron in the night, and said, 'Rise up, go away from my people, both you and the Israelites! Go, worship the Lord, as you said. Take your flocks and your herds, as you said, and be gone. And bring a blessing on me too'!" So the pharaoh literally sends the Israelites out as a result of this final plague of the killing of the firstborn.

Then of course what happens is that the Israelites leave; there's the whole episode with the parting of the Red Sea, and the Israelites then spend the next 40 years wandering around in the desert before they actually enter Canaan, and it is during this time of wandering in the desert that they encamp at the foot of Mt. Sinai and receive the Torah from God. This event is described in quite a bit of detail in the Hebrew Bible, and it is a seminal formative point for the ancient Israelites. To what extent is this corroborated by archaeology?

The answer is that well really not at all, at least not to any degree that all scholars agree upon. The problem is that if there was an exodus from Egypt, and that's a question that I'll come back to, if there was an exodus from Egypt, this is the sort of event that would leave little if any traces in the archaeological record. What you have to imagine then are people sort of wondering around in a kind of nomadic or semi-nomadic fashion through the desert. They are not building cities as they go along; they're not building settlements; they're not leaving the kind of remains that really would be traceable in the archaeological record.

So archaeology actually is not a discipline that is well-equipped to answer the question of whether the Exodus took place, and if it took place does it correspond with the account described in the Hebrew Bible. In fact many scholars now believe that the Exodus, if it ever occurred, occurred not in the way that is described in the Bible, but as a much smaller event, that is perhaps as a small number of people leaving Egypt wandering perhaps to some extent in the desert eventually entering the land of Canaan and joining up in Canaan with other people who were already there or who had come from other places; and these groups then form into what become known as the Israelite tribes.

In other words, if there was an Exodus then most scholars believe that it occurred not in the way that it is described in the Hebrew Bible, but on a much smaller scale, on a much more modest scale, and in a way that did not leave really any remains that we can identify with certainty in the archaeological record. The news isn't all bad actually. We do have a very important piece of information about the early Israelites that comes from just about the time the Exodus would've taken place.

This is a stele that is a large standing stone called the Merneptah Stele, which comes from Egypt. It's called the Merneptah Stele because it's named after an Egyptian pharaoh, Merneptah. This is a kind of a stele that was often set up by rulers in antiquity, a kind of a stone that was often set up by rulers in antiquity to commemorate a victory. The front of the stone slab is carved in relief with figures depicting the pharaoh and gods and other figures, and then most of the face of the stone is carved with a lengthy inscription in which Merneptah describes his victories over various peoples.

Most of the victories described in the Merneptah Stele have nothing to do with ancient Israel. In fact most of the victories commemorated by this stele are about victories over the Libyans in North Africa. There is a line in the Merneptah Stele which refers to Merneptah's conquest and destruction of several towns in Canaan, including Gezer and Ashkelon, and then there is a reference to Israel and the way that this reference appears in the Egyptian hieroglyphic script is such that it is clear that Israel here is being referred to not as a town, not as a country, but as a people, specifically the relevant line says, "Israel is laid waste, his seed is not."

What's so important about this is that this is the earliest reference that we have to Israel, and specifically here Israel as a people, and it dates to just about the time that the Exodus supposedly occurred and this stele is from Egypt. In other words it suggests that there was a people who were identified as Israel at the very end of the late Bronze Age. This in no way corroborates the biblical story of the Exodus, it doesn't mean that there was an Exodus or there was not an Exodus, but it is important because it indicates already by the late Bronze Age, by the end of the late Bronze Age, the existence of a people named Israel and so that actually helps set the stage for the arrival of the Israelites in the land of Canaan.

The late Bronze Age then was a time of large kingdoms and empires around the Mediterranean, around the eastern Mediterranean, which were in contact with each other, which corresponded with each other, which traded with each other, sometimes went to war with each other, and in around 1200 B.C. this entire system collapsed. All of these kingdoms and empires simply dissolve, the Mycenean kingdoms in Greece, the Hittites, the new kingdom in Egypt, and also the Canaanite city-states.

What happens? We're not sure. It's a complex world and there are probably many different reasons for this collapse. So there's probably not one single thing that happened, but it is clear that one of the things that happens in about 1200 is that large numbers of people move around the eastern Mediterranean, whether these people were invaders who came from other areas and caused the destruction of these kingdoms and empires or whether at least some of them are refugees who are natives of these kingdoms, who are then displaced and start to wander around, probably actually some of both of that.

It is then in this period around 1200 that we have the arrival of the Dorians in Greece for example. It is precisely in this period that the Israelite tribes then enter Canaan and settle down. In about 1200 then the Israelite tribes enter Canaan and settle in the center of the country. In exactly the same time we also have other peoples in the area who either are there all along and somehow coalesce and acquire national identities, or like the Israelites, arrive from other places or maybe some of them arrive from other places and settle down.

We hear about these peoples from the Hebrew Bible, and these peoples include the Ammonites, the biblical Ammonites, who lived in the area of Ammon, that is the area around the modern city of Amman in Jordan, to the south of them the Moabites living in the biblical kingdom of Moab which is just to the south of the area of the Ammonites, to the south of the Moabites, that is at the southeastern end of the Dead Sea, the biblical kingdom of Edom with the inhabitants called the Edomites. What happens to the Canaanites when all of these peoples come in and the Israelites come in and settle in the country? What happens to the native Canaanite population?

Some of them probably continue to live in the country and get absorbed with the Israelite settlement, but some of those native Canaanites continue to live in the area to the north of Canaan, the area of modern Lebanon, that area then becomes known as Phoenicia, and the inhabitants become known as Phoencians, and we'll be talking more about the Phoenicians because they're very important in relation to the Israelites. Yet another people who enter the area of Canaan and settle down after about 1200 are the Philistines who settle the area of the southern coastal plane and who we also will be talking a lot more about.

First a little bit about these Phoenicians. Who are the Phoenicians? The Phoenicians were the descendents of the Canaanites, they were the Iron Age inhabitants of the area of modern Lebanon. Phoenicia was not a unified country. In other words, it consisted of a series of independent city-states, and because of the very mountainous interior, most of these city-states were located along the coast and faced outward to the Mediterranean Sea rather than inland, in other words the ancient Phoenicians were known among other things as traitors on the Mediterranean Sea.

Many of these ancient Phoenician cities are well known to us today. For example, Tyre, Sidon, Byblos, and Beirut, all of those are examples of ancient Phoenician city-states. In fact, the ancient Phoenicians did not call themselves Phoenicians. The word "Phoenician" actually comes from the Greeks; the Greeks called them Phoenicians lumping them all together. But they didn't call themselves that, they instead were residents or natives of the individual city-states. You would refer to an individual as being a native of the city-state of Tyre or Sidon or Beirut.

Notice that Phoenicia is just to the north of Canaan. Eventually this territory after 1200, this area of Canaan, is then settled by various peoples with the Israelites settling the interior of the country, not the coast but the interior. The Israelite tribes settled the interior of the country running in sort of a strip from Galilee through the center of the country and down into the northern Negev Desert.

This was very hostile territory. It was not the best part of the country. The reason why it wasn't the best part of the country is because it was hilly, mountainous, hard for agriculture, not really a very friendly and hospitable area, but that is the area where the Israelite tribes settled.

What do we know about the settlement of the Israelite tribes in Canaan? Again we go back to our biblical accounts. If you read the biblical accounts about the Israelite settlement, it sounds as though there was a series of wars between the Israelites and the Canaanites; that is, it sounds like from the biblical account it was not a peaceful settlement, but rather a settlement that was accompanied by a lot of conquest and destruction. Ahh the million dollar question again is: To what extent is the biblical account borne out by archaeological evidence or not?

Well the answer is that it's mixed. The picture is mixed. It's not unequivocal. There are places where the biblical account seems to be borne out by archaeological remains and yet there are other cases where it seems to be squarely contradicted by the archaeological remains. I want to show you just a couple of examples of these.

Let's start with perhaps the most famous example of a biblical town that supposedly is conquered by the Israelites, and that is Jericho. Everybody is familiar with the story of the Walls of Jericho. Let's take a look at what the passage in Joshua says. "So the people shouted, and the trumpets were blown. As soon as the people heard the sound of the trumpets, they raised a great shout, and the wall fell down flat, so that the people charged straight ahead into the city and captured it."

What do we have in terms of archaeological remains at Jericho? Excavations have been carried out at Jericho and indeed the Bronze Age Canaanite city of Jericho was fortified by a wall. That's no problem, right? Well, actually there is a problem here because archaeological excavations also indicate that that city wall at Jericho had fallen out of use, had been abandoned by the late Bronze Age. It turns out that by the late Bronze Age, by the time the Israelites arrive, Jericho was just a small town or a village that had no fortification wall at all.

If there is no fortification wall, it means there's no wall that could've come tumbling down. So this is a case where the archaeological evidence seems to squarely contradict the biblical account. We have other cases where the archaeological evidence actually seems to bear out the biblical account, for example, at the site of Hazor, that very large, very important Canaanite city in the very northern part of the country. Here we have a description of the Israelites coming and destroying Hazor.

> Joshua turned back at that time, and took Hazor, and struck its king down with the sword. Before that time Hazor was the head of all those kingdoms. And they put to the sword all who were in it, utterly destroying them; there was no one left who breathed, and he burned Hazor with fire. And all the towns of those kings, and all their kings, Joshua took, and struck them with the edge of the sword, utterly destroying them, as Moses the servant of the Lord had commanded. But Israel burned none of the towns that stood on mounds except Hazor, which Joshua did burn.

So here we have a very clear description of the Israelites coming in under Joshua and destroying Hazor and burning it with fire. Hazor has been excavated and there are remains at Hazor of a level where there is a clear destruction by fire. The excavators of Hazor believe that that level with the destruction by fire is, in fact, the level of the Israelite destruction that's described in the Hebrew Bible.

What's the problem? Not everybody agrees, because we're in a period that is prehistoric, a period when our dating of archaeological remains is not precise enough to allow for the fact that well it could be that that level that is identified with the level of the Israelite destruction at Hazor, could be that that level in fact should be associated with the Israelite destruction and dates to the right period, but it also could be that well our dates need to wiggle a bit and it could be a little earlier; it could be a little later. So there's a problem of dating first of all.

There's an even more important problem because even if the level at Hazor that's been identified by the excavators as being the level associated with the Israelite destruction, even if it's the right time period, archaeology alone cannot tell us who destroyed that level. It cannot tell us who set that fire. Different peoples could have set that fire, there could've been internal fighting. There could've been fighting between various city-states. It didn't have to be the Israelites who caused that fire, that destruction. It could even be an accidental internal fire or it could be an earthquake event that overturned oil lamps and caused a fire.

In other words, destruction like that can be caused by any one of a number of factors. The only way to identify that destruction with the Israelites is to rely on the biblical account, and there are scholars who say well it's a little bit early here to be relying on the biblical account. So the most we can say is well there appears to be a destruction at Hazor that may correspond with what's described in the biblical account, but maybe not.

This actually brings up the whole question of the nature of the Israelite settlement in Canaan because if you read the biblical account, it sounds like it was violent and accompanied by lots of destruction, but many archaeologists now think that that's not the case. Many archaeologists now think that, in fact, the Israelite settlement was a much more peaceful event, that there were various peoples who came in, infiltrated, settled down and mingled with natives who were already in the country and that this then forms the basis of what later become known as the Israelite tribes.

If we look at the area of the Israelite settlement and, in fact, we have archaeological remains in the central hill country of houses and villages associated with presumably these early Israelites, whoever they are, whether they're some natives and some people who come in from outside, we do have villages that we can describe as early Israelite, and these houses and villages are characterized by their simplicity, by a relatively low standard of living, by the fact that we don't have a well-developed hierarchy here, that is that we don't seem to have people who are much wealthier and people who are much poorer, but rather everybody is living at the same kind of socioeconomic level. In other words, in fact, it actually does somewhat correspond with what we read in the Bible as the period of the Judges. There's no king yet. There's no real elite yet. It's just these settlers who are living in simple villages in this very harsh environment.

And so we have remains of their houses scattered around houses which reflect a kind of a simple country living. Most of the economy is based on cattle rearing, sheep and goats, so livestock rearing, agriculture. Really that's about the basis of the economy. And we also have the kind of pottery that these people were using in these villages and it goes along with everything else. It's a very simple kind of pottery, very little in the way of imports, very little in the way of fine expensive kind of china kinds of pottery, a lot of storage jars for storing agricultural produce, cooking pots for doing your cooking.

The Israelites actually got sort of the short end of the stick in the settlement in the sense that they settled in the part of the country that is the harshest, the most forbidding, and in many ways the least fertile. The Philistines got the better part of the country. They settled in the southern coastal plane, and that area along the coast is not nearly as harsh as those mountains inland.

What do we know about the Philistines? Apparently they were one of a number of peoples called the Sea Peoples who originally came from somewhere in the area of the Aegean; that is somewhere in the area of Greece and the Greek islands. They originally arrived in Egypt and tried to enter Egypt but were repulsed, were repelled by the Egyptian pharaoh and were then settled along the southern coastal plane of Palestine.

The Philistines then are just the most famous of these Sea Peoples, and they then establish a kingdom in the area of the southern coastal plane called

Philistia including a series of five major cities, Philistine civilization in contrast to Israelite civilization was an urban culture and they established a kingdom with major cities including Gaza, Ashkelon, and Ashdod. Notice that the Philistines settled in an area that is directly adjacent to the area of the Israelite settlement and so it is not a coincidence, it is not surprising then, that the Philistines and the Israelites soon came into contact and conflict with each other.

In fact, the Hebrew Bible is filled with stories about wars and battles between the Philistines and the Israelites. In one of these for example, the Philistines actually take the Ark of the Covenant.

> Now it happened in those days, that the Philistines mustered against Israel for war; and Israel went out to meet the Philistines in battle and encamped at Ebenezer; while the Philistines encamped at Aphek. ... Now the Philistines had captured the ark of God, and taken it from Ebenezer to Ashdod; then the Philistines took the ark of God and brought it into the house of Dagon and placed it beside Dagon.

Notice by the way according to the biblical account the patron God, the patron deity of the Philistines is named Dagon and therefore the temple of Dagon is called the house of Dagon.

Perhaps one of the most famous episodes related to the Philistines is the story of how Samson brings down the temple of Dagon with his own bare hands. Specifically the Hebrew Bible describes Samson in a temple dedicated to Dagon at Gaza and the way Samson brings down the temple is by taking his arms between two pillars that supported the roof of the temple and pushing them out so that the entire roof and therefore the temple collapsed.

Well we don't have archaeological remains of a Philistine temple at Gaza, not at least that have been discovered so far. But further north along the coast at an archaeological site called Tell Qasile excavations brought to life the remains of a Philistine temple; and very interesting, in the center of this temple were two pillars, remains of two pillars that are approximately seven feet apart. So if we want to visualize the kind of temple that Samson brought down in the biblical story, this Philistine temple at Tell Qasile provides a good illustration of that.

The wars between the Israelites and the Philistines continued for several hundred years. In fact, eventually the Israelite tribes united under the role of a monarch, a king named Saul, and the fighting between the Israelites and the Philistines continued right through the reign of Saul. So for example, in the first book of Samuel we read, "There was hard fighting against the Philistines in the days of Saul." We also read about David and Goliath, who was the giant champion of the Philistines fighting David the Israelite with his sling and David's victory over Goliath.

Finally we read about the death of Saul and his sons in an important and decisive battle at the foot of Mount Gilboa where the biblical account says, "The Philistines fought against Israel; and the men of Israel fled before the Philistines, and fell slain on Mount Gilboa. Then Saul died, and his three sons, and his armor-bearer, and all his men, on the same day before." In other words Saul loses his life in a battle against the Philistines and it is this event then which sets the stage for David to become the next kind of the Israelites, and this then sets the stage for the creation of a united kingdom under the rule of David and his son Solomon, which we will be talking about next.

Jerusalem—An Introduction to the City
Lecture 3

Why did David make Jerusalem the capital of his kingdom? A couple of good reasons: First of all, Jerusalem was located in the center of the country, so geographically speaking, it's a good point to put your capital. But there is another reason: because Jerusalem ... did not belong to any one of the 12 tribes. In other words, Jerusalem was a politically neutral city.

In our last lecture, we ended by noting that the death of Saul set the stage for **David** to become king, followed by his son **Solomon**. Perhaps the most famous events in their reigns are David's bringing of the Ark of the Covenant to Jerusalem, his capital, and Solomon's building of the First Temple there.

Because Jerusalem is central to this course, we should understand how the city is laid out. The original settlement in Jerusalem was on a small, low-

King David chose Jerusalem as his captial for its political neutrality and its geographic centrality.

lying hill and was known as the **City of David**. This hill lies outside the Old City (which dates from Ottoman times) and is dwarfed by both the Old City and the modern city. However, the only perennial source of fresh water in Jerusalem, the Gihon Spring, comes out of the ground at the foot of the eastern slope of this little hill. Furthermore, the site is protected by natural valleys on two of its three sides.

Solomon expanded the city northward to include the area of the Temple Mount, which dominated the biblical City of David and became the ancient acropolis of Jerusalem, where the most important political and religious institutions were built. Later, the city spread westward onto the Western Hill, protected by valleys on three sides.

Having reviewed the topography of Jerusalem, let's return to its history during the time of David and Solomon. David made Jerusalem the capital of his kingdom for two likely reasons: its central location and the fact that it had never been controlled by any of the Israelite tribes but was politically neutral. Into this City of David he brought the Ark of the Covenant. His son Solomon is most famous for building the First Temple on the Temple Mount north of the city. After Solomon died, in about 930 B.C., a quarrel broke out over the succession to the throne, and the kingdom split into a northern half, Israel, with its capital at Samaria, and a southern half, Judah, with its capital at Jerusalem. Each of these kingdoms had its own independent political history.

> **Jerusalem survived the Assyrian siege but was later taken by the Babylonians, the next great power, based in southern Mesopotamia.**

Meanwhile, to the east, a great empire arose, **Assyria**, based in northern **Mesopotamia**. Assyria expanded westward toward the Mediterranean coast and began launching invasions into the kingdom of Israel. In the year 722 B.C., the Assyrians conquered the northern kingdom of Israel, and 20 years later, they invaded the kingdom of Judah, destroying many of the major Judean cities and besieging Jerusalem itself.

Jerusalem survived the Assyrian siege but was later taken by the Babylonians, the next great power, based in southern Mesopotamia. In 586 B.C., the Babylonians conquered the city, burned the temple, and forced the inhabitants of Judah into exile. This historical review of Jerusalem down to its destruction by the Babylonians is based largely on biblical accounts. In the next lecture, we will compare the archaeological remains in Jerusalem that date to this period with the descriptions in the Hebrew Bible. ■

Names to Know

David (fl. 10th century B.C.): The eighth and youngest son of Jesse, from the tribe of Judah, David succeeded Saul as king of Israel and ruled the United Kingdom for 40 years, from c. 1010 to 970 B.C. He conquered Jerusalem and made it the capital of his kingdom. David also brought the Ark of the Covenant to Jerusalem. He was succeeded to the throne by his son Solomon.

Solomon (r. c. 970–930 B.C.): Son of David and successor to the throne of the United Kingdom. Solomon is renowned for his wisdom; his many wives; his political and commercial alliances with Hiram, king of Tyre, and with the queen of Sheba; and for having established the First Temple on Jerusalem's Temple Mount.

Important Terms

Assyria: Ancient empire based in the northern part of Mesopotamia (modern Iraq).

Babylonia: Ancient empire based in the southern part of Mesopotamia (modern Iraq).

City of David: Eastern Hill; Lower City.

Mesopotamia: In Greek, literally means "the land between the rivers," referring to the Tigris and Euphrates rivers; a territory that corresponds roughly with modern Iraq.

Questions to Consider

1. What combination of natural features attracted settlement in Jerusalem 5,000 years ago?

2. Why was Jerusalem a good choice to be the capital of David's kingdom?

Jerusalem—An Introduction to the City
Lecture 3—Transcript

In our last lecture, we ended by talking about the death of Saul, which sets the stage for David to become king establishing a united kingdom that he ruled and that was succeeded by his son Solomon. Perhaps the most famous event in the time of David and Solomon is David bringing the Ark of the Covenant to Jerusalem which he made the capital of the Israelite kingdom, and later Solomon building the First Temple on the Temple Mount in Jerusalem.

Jerusalem is going to be a central city throughout this course and therefore in order to begin talking about Jerusalem we first have to understand how the city is laid out. What is the topography of the city of Jerusalem? In fact why is there a city in this particular spot? When you think about it, why do people settle in particular places, trade roots, strategic locations, whatever, so why has there been a settlement at the spot where Jerusalem is located continuously for over 5,000 years? What is it that has drawn people to this particular spot?

If we look at the location of Jerusalem we see that it's located smack dab in the center of the country on top of this hilly mountain, or ridge, which runs through the country like a backbone from north to south. This is the Judean Mountains or the Judean hills, and all throughout antiquity and even up until today there has been a road going along the top of this mountain ridge. It's the same road that goes today from the area of Hebron on the south, then to Bethlehem, then to Jerusalem, then north to Ramallah, Annapolis.

Of course always the major north-south road through Palestine has been along the coast which is the easiest way to go. But this was a secondary route through the center of the country and so Jerusalem lies on that road. The most important reason for there having been a settlement in Jerusalem throughout the ages is because of water.

If we look at a map of Jerusalem we see that the city is located on a series of hills that are separated by valleys. The earliest settlement in Jerusalem lies on a small, low-lying hill that's called the City of David. Most people who go to Jerusalem today and see the modern city see that inside the center of the modern city is an area surrounded by an old wall and this is called the Old City of Jerusalem.

Most people who go to Jerusalem today are under the mistaken impression that the area of the old city is the ancient city of Jerusalem, and that's actually incorrect. Those walls of the old city as you see them today are relatively recent in Jerusalem's history. They go back to the Ottoman Turkish period, the 16th century A.D., and the area enclosed by those Ottoman city walls does not necessarily correspond with the ancient City of Jerusalem. In fact, the earliest settlement in Jerusalem, the original settlement in Jerusalem lies on this little hill, the City of David, which today is totally outside the walls of the old city. It comes out like a little spur to the south of the Temple Mount.

This is where over 5,000 years ago people first settled in the area of Jerusalem. The question is why did the first people who arrived in Jerusalem settle on this small, relatively low-lying hill? The hill is only about 11 acres in size and in fact it's much lower in elevation than the other hills in the area. Why didn't people choose to settle on one of the bigger, taller hills? You would think strategically that's what they would've done, after all.

Well in fact it all is about water. It all has to do with sources of water here in the Middle East, because the only perennial source of fresh water in Jerusalem is a spring called the Gihon Spring, which comes out of the ground at the foot of the eastern slope of this little hill of the City of David. In order to be as close as possible to the source of water, over 5,000 years ago people chose to settle on this little hill. Not only is the City of David convenient because it's located next to the water supply, but also it was protected by natural valleys on two of its three sides. It had natural protection of fortifications on two of its three sides.

On the east, the City of David is protected by a very deep valley called the Kidron Valley, which separates it and the Temple Mount to the north from a mountain ridge on the other side of the Kidron Valley, to the east of the Kidron Valley, that is called the Mount of Olives. On the west, the City of David was protected by a valley called the Tyropoeon Valley. Tyropoeon is actually an ancient Greek word meaning the Valley of the Cheesemakers.

The Tyropoeon Valley is sometimes also called the Central Valley because today it runs through the center of the Old City of Jerusalem starting on the north in the area of the modern Damascus gate coming down along the western side of the Temple Mount, the western side of the City of David, and joining up with the southern tip with the Kidron Valley. The City of David was protected on two of its three sides by these valleys.

If you look at the configuration of bedrock in the area of the City of David you will notice that the bedrock slopes down as you go south, but rises up as you go north. From the City of David as you go north you get into the area of the Temple Mount. When the very first people came and settled in Jerusalem thousands of years ago, they settled on that little hill of the City of David. That is the city that David took from the Jebusites and that's when it becomes known as the City of David.

After David died his son Solomon expanded the city to the north to include the area of the Temple Mount, which is higher in elevation than the City of David and so is a natural high point physically dominating the biblical City of David, and so the Temple Mount literally became the ancient acropolis of Jerusalem, a natural highpoint where the most important political and religious institutions were built. Because the City of David is so small in size it couldn't accommodate a large population.

When the city grew in antiquity where did the population spread? Never did the population spread east across the Kidron Valley to the slopes of the Mount of Olives. The Mount of Olives has always been outside the walls of the city and therefore from the very earliest periods, the Mount of Olives served as the necropolis, the cemetery, the burial grounds, for the population of Jerusalem. Instead in antiquity when the population grew it went westwards across the Tyropoeon Valley and on to the next hill over.

The next hill over to the west of the Tyropoeon Valley is a large and relatively high in elevation hill which we call the Western Hill to distinguish it then from the City of David, which becomes known as the Eastern Hill. Sometimes we call the Western Hill also the Upper City because it's high in elevation, and the City of David then becomes known as the Lower City. The Western Hill also is protected by valleys on three of its four sides.

On the east it's protected by the Tyropoeon Valley which separates it from the City of David; on the west it's protected by a valley which starts at its northwest corner, the area today where the Damascus Gate and David's Citadel are located. This valley then wraps around the Western Hill from the west and around the south and joins up at the southern tip with the Kidron Valley and the Tyropoeon Valley. This valley which literally encircles the Western Hill is called the Ben-Hinnom Valley and the Ben-Hinnom valley is a valley which is known from the Hebrew Bible.

In fact a passage in Jeremiah refers to the Ben-Hinnom Valley in a very negative way,

"For the children of Judah have done what is evil in my sight," is the oracle of the Lord, "They have set up their detestable things in the house which bears my name to defile it, and have built the high place of Tophet in the valley of Ben-Hinnom to burn their sons and daughters in the fire."

In other words in this passage Jeremiah is condemning the practice of child sacrifice by the Israelites in the valley of Ben-Hinnom, this very valley that encircles the Western Hill.

The northern end of the Western Hill is determined by a valley which runs directly east across to the Temple Mount and which is called the Transverse Valley. This is not a deep valley like the other valleys and in fact the northern side of the city of Jerusalem was always its weak side in antiquity. Almost always in antiquity when the city was attacked it was attacked from the direction of the north because unlike the other sides, the north side of the city was not protected by deep natural valleys.

If you look at the area that we just talked about, which is really the core of the ancient city of Jerusalem, the City of David, the Temple Mount, and the Western Hill, if you look at this area you will see that it overlaps with the area that is today enclosed within the walls of the Old City, but it's not a complete overlap, and that the Old City today represents a shift to the north from the ancient city with the area of the City of David, today lying outside the walls of the city and also the southern tip of the Western Hill, which today is called Mount Zion, lying outside the walls of the Old City.

This shift to the north we will see later in the course occurred in the Roman period in the 2nd century A.D. when Jerusalem was rebuilt by the Roman Emperor Hadrian.

The core of the ancient city of Jerusalem lies somewhat to the south of the area that is today enclosed within the walls of the Old City and only partly overlaps with that. All of this has been somewhat abstract so let's now talk a little bit more and look a little bit more at what all of these features look like.

The Gihon Spring still has water coming out of it today. In fact it's a very interesting kind of a spring. The word Gihon comes from the Hebrew word "gichah" which means to gush because it's a kind of a caustic spring where the water gushes forth and abates, gushes forth and abates. So that water still comes out of the ground today.

If we look at an aerial map of Jerusalem we can very clearly see the various topographic features. We can see the layout of the Old City today, which is roughly enclosed by kind of a square. Marking the eastern edge of the city is a mountain ridge which includes the Mount of Olives. The northern end of that mountain ridge is today called Mount Scopus.

The area of the Temple Mount platform is also clearly visible. It is a gigantic paved esplanade surrounded by walls with the Dome of the Rock, which has a gold dome sitting in the middle of it, a natural high point probably where the two ancient temples used to be located, and to the south of it at the southern end of the Temple Mount a silver-domed structure which is the Al-Aqsa Mosque. Here's a wonderful picture showing the City of David which shows so clearly what a small and low-lying hill this is shown very clearly how the Temple Mount physically dominates the City of David and therefore was the acropolis of the ancient city of Jerusalem and which clearly show the Kidron Valley, very deep valley on the right-hand side, that is on the eastern side separating the City of David and the Temple Mount from the Mount of Olives.

On the western side of the city of David a valley not so clearly visible anymore, largely filled in by debris, but with more or less a line of a modern road following it, which is the line of the Tyropoeon Valley or that central valley. Today if we stand on top of the Mount of Olives we get a very good view over the city looking from east to west. Immediately below us covering the slopes of the Mount of Olives are graves.

This is a cemetery where again the practice of Jewish burial in Jerusalem on the slopes of the Mount of Olives goes back literally from millennia so we can see this cemetery still covering the slopes of the Mount of Olives today, this area having always been outside the walls of the city. The slope then goes down very deep to this valley, the Kidron Valley and on the other side of the Kidron Valley we see the area of the Temple Mount and then sloping off to the left of that is the beginning of the slope down for the area of the City of David.

In fact, the City of David is so small and so low-lying that it's almost not visible even from the top of the Mount of Olives. It's sort of swallowed up by the rest of the features and behind the City of David you can then see the area of the Western Hill, which is again much higher in elevation and also a larger area.

Another aerial view of the Old City looking from west to east immediately at the bottom is the area of the Jaffa Gate today. Next to it is the citadel, David's Citadel, which we will be talking about. This is the point where the Ben-Hinnom valley starts, and going straight east across to the Temple Mount from the Jaffa Gate that would be the line of the Transverse Valley, that relatively small valley that marks the northern end of the Western Hill. Finally at the upper end, very visible, is this ridge, this mountain ridge of the Mount of Olives and Mount Scopus which marks the eastern end of the city on the other side of the Kidron Valley.

The modern Old City of Jerusalem transposed upon these geographic features shows clearly how the City of David and Mount Zion lie today outside the walls of the Old City. Within the area of the Old City today there are different quarters, which is a late development in the history of the city, but basically the area of the northwest part of the Old City is the Christian quarter; northwest, because that is the area around the Church of the Holy Sepulcher, which we will be talking about quite a bit later in the course.

The northeast part of the city is the Muslim quarter. The southwest part of the city is the Armenian quarter, and the southeast part of the city across from the area of the Wailing Wall or Western Wall is today's Jewish quarter.

Now that we've sort of reviewed the topography of the city of Jerusalem let's talk about the history of Jerusalem during the time of David and Solomon and the other kings of Judah. Remembering now what happened with the Israelite settlement, the Israelite tribes enter the country in about 1200 B.C., settle the interior hill country, eventually form together into one entity and choose a king, Saul, to rule over them. Saul is then killed in battle against the Philistines.

After Saul's death he was succeeded to the throne by David. David then becomes king and one of the things that David does when he becomes king is to capture the city of Jerusalem from the Jebusites. One of the peculiarities of the early Israelite settlement is that although the Israelites settle the interior hill country and although Jerusalem was located in the center of that area, Jerusalem was not taken by the Israelite tribes. In fact Jerusalem remained a foreign enclave in the heart of the Israelite settlement for approximately 200 years until the time of David.

According to the Hebrew Bible, the reason for this is that Jebusite Jerusalem was so strongly fortified that the Israelites were not able to take the city until the time of David. The Bible then describes the conquest of Jerusalem by David. David takes Jerusalem from the Jebusites and makes it the capital of his kingdom, very interesting choice by the way. Why did David make Jerusalem the capital of his kingdom? A couple of good reasons; first of all Jerusalem was located in the center of the country, so geographically speaking it's a good point to put your capital.

But there is another reason; because Jerusalem since it had not originally been taken by any one of the 12 tribes, therefore did not belong to any one of the 12 tribes. In other words, Jerusalem was a politically neutral city. It's sort of the same idea as today that Washington D.C. doesn't belong to any one of the 50 states, so with Jerusalem. So David then makes Jerusalem the capital of his kingdom.

The Hebrew Bible says, "And David dwelt in the stronghold [of Jerusalem] and called it the City of David." So obviously before the time of David the city was not called the City of David. Once David takes it, it becomes known as the City of David and since Jebusite Jerusalem consisted of that little hill to the south of the Temple Mount, that is the hill that is called the City of David. That was the city of Jerusalem in the time of the Jebusites and in the time of David. According to the Hebrew Bible David brings the Ark of the Covenant to Jerusalem and I quote from 2 Samuel, "David went and brought the ark of God with joy from the house of Obed-Edom to the City of Jerusalem."

After David died he was succeeded to the throne by his son Solomon. Solomon is famous for many different things. One thing that Solomon is known for is having been a lover of many women. He's known for having had many wives, and the relevant passage in the Hebrew Bible says, "Now King Solomon was a lover of women; and he married many foreign wives—Moabites, Ammonites, Edomites, Sidonians, and Hittites." Notice a very interesting thing here. Maybe Solomon really was a lover of women, but when you look at the foreign wives who we had, you see that there is a lot more going on here.

These were strategic political alliances. The women who Solomon married literally are from all of the peoples who neighbor on, who surround the area of the Israelite kingdom. Moabites, Ammonites, Edomites, those are all those people in the area of modern Jordan to the eastern side of the Jordan River and the Dead Sea and Sidonians. Who are the Sidonians, the people of Sidon, the Phoenicians just to the north and the Hittites are the people of course in Asia Minor. Obviously these marriages were strategic for political purposes, so Solomon was basically forming political alliances through marriage, something of course that was very common in antiquity.

In addition to his many wives Solomon of course is also known for having built the First temple on the Temple Mount in Jerusalem as 1 Kings says, "In the fourth year of Solomon's reign over Israel … he built the house of the Lord." Notice the temple is a house. In antiquity, a temple was a house of a deity. We talked about the House of Dagon, the Temple of the Philistines.

Here we have the House of the Lord, the God of Israel, and this is the temple that Solomon builds on the Temple Mount in Jerusalem.

Together, the kingdom of David and Solomon is known as the United Kingdom or the United Monarchy, because all of the 12 tribes were united under the rule of David and Solomon. When Solomon died, though, in about roughly 930 B.C. the United Monarchy comes to an end because the kingdom splits. There's a quarrel over the succession to the throne and this United Kingdom splits into two halves. The northern half now becomes known as the kingdom of Israel and it has as its capital a city eventually at a place called Samaria, which is in the heart of this northern kingdom of Israel. The southern kingdom becomes known as the kingdom of Judah with its capital at Jerusalem.

Each of these kingdoms then has its own series of kings and its own independent political history despite the fact that the inhabitants of both kingdoms continue to worship the God of Israel in his temple on the Temple Mount in Jerusalem. The kingdom splits into two parts after the death of Solomon and you have these two kingdoms, the northern kingdom of Israel and the southern kingdom of Judah. While all of this is going on though something happens farther to the east that's going to impact both of these kingdoms.

What happens is that in the 9th and 8th centuries B.C. a great power was growing to the east. This power was the kingdom or empire of Assyria; that is a territory that is located in the northern half of what is today Iraq, the northern part of ancient Mesopotamia. In the 9th and 8th centuries B.C. Assyria became the dominant power in the ancient Near East. As the Assyrian became stronger and stronger they began to expand their control over more and more areas eventually moving westwards towards the Mediterranean coast and launching a series of invasions into the kingdom of Israel.

In the year 722 B.C., the Assyrians conquered the northern kingdom of Israel and 20 years later they launched an invasion of the kingdom of Judah. The Hebrew Bible describes the Assyrian attack on Judah and specifically on the city of Jerusalem.

The king of Judah in 701 B.C. when the Syrians invaded was Hezekiah, and the Hebrew Bible describes the Assyrians coming and ravaging the Judean countryside destroying many of the major Judean cities, the cities of Judah, and then besieging the city of Jerusalem itself. Here is what the biblical account says,

> In the fourteenth year of King Hezekiah, King Sennacherib of Assyria came up against all the fortified cities of Judah and captured them. King Hezekiah of Judah sent to the king of Assyria at Lachish, saying, "I have done wrong; withdraw from me; whatever you impose on me I will bear." ... Then the king of Assyria sent the commander-in-chief and the chief of the eunuchs and the field marshal from Lachish with a large army against King Hezekiah at Jerusalem.

Notice in this passage that the Assyrians are encamped at Lachish. Lachish was one of the major cities in Judah outside of Jerusalem, and we have very, very interesting evidence archaeologically and also documentary of the Assyrian siege and destruction of this major city of Lachish. We have an aerial view of Lachish, but most interesting on one side of this very large site are remains of an Assyrian siege ramp, a ramp that the Assyrians built so that they could break through the fortification wall of the city.

Furthermore the Assyrian king then decorated his palace with carved stone reliefs showing the fall of the city at the end of the siege. Those reliefs now are on display in the British museum in London, and those reliefs clearly show the Assyrian siege machines and in particular the battering ram coming up and battering against the city wall and the various darts and arrows and other things that are being shot back and forth and we have very clear remains of the Assyrian siege ramp at the site that remain until today.

One thing that happens in 701 B.C. is that the Assyrians then come, ravage the Judean countryside, destroy the city of Lachish, and then besiege the city of Jerusalem, the capital of Judah. This Assyrian siege of Jerusalem is also described in the Hebrew Bible as follows, "Therefore thus says the Lord concerning the king of Assyria: He shall not come into this city, shoot an arrow there, come before it with a shield, or cast up a siege ramp against it.

By the way that he came, by the same he shall return; he shall not come into this city, says the Lord. For I will defend this city to save it, for my own sake and for the sake of my servant David."

So very interesting, according to the biblical account, the God of Israel then says I am going to protect the city of Jerusalem from the Assyrians; they will not be able to take this city. "That very night the angel of the Lord set out and struck down one hundred eighty-five thousand in the camp of the Assyrians; when morning dawned, they were all dead bodies. Then King Sennacherib of Assyria left, went home, and lived at Nineveh."

According to the biblical account, the Assyrians were not able to take the city of Jerusalem during the siege because of a plague that broke out and killed many of the soldiers in their camp. We actually have Assyrian documents which present a slightly different story, which suggests that the Assyrian king was called back to Assyria because of internal problems, because of some sort of internal rebellions or unrest. Either way Jerusalem survived the Assyrian siege and continued to exist with the kingdom of Judah continuing to exist, albeit weakened, after the Assyrian invasion in 701.

The Assyrian empire itself eventually weakened and collapsed, and in fact, in the year 612 B.C. the Assyrians were replaced as the dominant power in the ancient Near East by the Babylonians. The Babylonians were based in the southern part of what is today Iraq; that is the southern part of Mesopotamia. When the Babylonians then become the dominant power in the ancient Near East they begin to launch a series of invasions into the kingdom of Judah.

In 586 B.C. the Babylonians conquered Jerusalem and destroyed the temple on the Temple Mount. So it is described in the 2 book of Kings.

> In the fifth month, on the seventh day of the month—this was in the nineteenth year of King Nebuchadnezzar, king of Babylon—Nebuzaradan, the commander of the guard, a servant of the king of Babylon, came to Jerusalem and burned the house of the Lord [so notice the temple], and the king's house [the palace], and all the houses of Jerusalem.

So 586 B.C. the Babylonians conquer Jerusalem, burn the palace, burn down the temple, burn the houses in the city, and what do they do, they then force the inhabitants of Judah to go into exile and Babylonia beginning a period in Jewish history that we refer to as the period of the Babylonian exile.

What we have done here is to review the history of Jerusalem based largely on the biblical accounts beginning with David and Solomon and going down to its destruction by the Babylonians in 586 B.C. This now sets the stage for us to look at the archaeological remains that we have in Jerusalem that date to this period and compare the archaeological remains that we have with the descriptions in the Hebrew Bible.

The Jerusalem of David and Solomon
Lecture 4

In 1993 at Tel Dan, in the very northern part of the country, excavators found part of a stele, a big inscribed stone, which actually mentions the House of David and dates to the middle of the 9th century B.C.

In this lecture, we will look at the archaeology of Jerusalem in the biblical period, focusing especially on the time from David and Solomon to 586 B.C. When we talk about biblical Jerusalem, people often ask about the remains of Solomon's Temple—the First Temple—which originally stood on top of the Temple Mount. Unfortunately, we don't have any archaeological remains at all of this building, though we have descriptions of it in the Hebrew Bible.

We do, however, have archaeological remains in the City of David that go back to the time of David and Solomon and even earlier. Those remains are concentrated on that little spur to the south of the Temple Mount that was the original Jebusite city of Jerusalem. There have been excavations during the last century focusing on the northern part of this site, which was higher in elevation than the rest of the City of David. Here, a massive step-stone **glacis** (slope or incline) has been discovered, which would have supported some large structure further up the steep slope. Recently, remains of a monumental building have been found above the glacis. Probably this structure was part of the original acropolis of the city before Solomon extended the city to the north to include the Temple Mount.

Excavations have also revealed in the City of David the remains of Israelite houses dating to as early as the 8th and 7th centuries B.C.

Excavations have also revealed in the City of David the remains of Israelite houses dating to as early as the 8th and 7th centuries B.C. In some of these houses have been found clay figurines that almost always depict a woman naked to the waist and cupping her breasts under her hands. Thus, we have some physical evidence for the very kinds of pagan practices that the prophets warned the

Archaeological digs around the Temple Mount, where the Dome of the Rock stands today, reveal artifacts dating to the reigns of David and Solomon.

Israelites about. And we know these houses could have been Israelite because in at least one of them was found more than 50 **bullae** with Hebrew names written on them. Bullae are clay seals for scrolled documents.

At least one bulla seems to refer clearly to a person mentioned in the Hebrew Bible, Gemaryahu, son of Shaphan. This name is unusual, and a passage in Jeremiah refers to a scribe with this very name. Further, a scribe is the sort of person we would expect to use a personal seal on documents. This Gemaryahu was active in the court of the king of Judah roughly around 600 B.C., and the excavated house was destroyed in 586 B.C., so the dates fits very nicely together. We can say, therefore, with about as much certainty as possible, that this seal was affixed by the same figure who is mentioned in the book of Jeremiah.

We have talked in this lecture about Jerusalem in the biblical period, focusing especially on the remains in the City of David. In our next lecture, we'll look at the water systems that supplied the biblical city of Jerusalem. ■

Important Terms

bullae: A clay sealing.

glacis: In general, a plastered mound of earth piled around a town, with a fortification wall on top; a rampart.

Questions to Consider

1. What does archaeology tell us about Davidic and Solomonic Jerusalem—and, by way of extension, about David and Solomon?

2. What do the finds from houses of the 8th–7th centuries B.C. in the City of David tell us about the Israelite population of Jerusalem?

The Jerusalem of David and Solomon
Lecture 4—Transcript

In our last lecture, we surveyed the history of biblical Jerusalem focusing especially on the period from the reigns of David and Solomon and ending with the Babylonian destruction in 586 B.C. This sets the stage for looking at the archaeology of Jerusalem in the biblical period, focusing especially on this very same time from David and Solomon to 586 B.C.

What I'd like to do in our first lecture on biblical Jerusalem is look at the archaeological remains of the settlement in the city and then in the next lecture look at the water systems that supplied biblical Jerusalem. The first thing that people want to know when we talk about biblical Jerusalem is what remains do we have of Solomon's Temple, the First Temple, which originally stood on top of the Temple Mount. Unfortunately we don't have any archaeological remains at all of this building.

We do however have literary references to Solomon's Temple, specifically descriptions in the Hebrew Bible, and we can also get a sense of what the temple looked like or might've looked like by comparing it with contemporary ancient temples, something that we will be doing in some of our lectures. When we look at the biblical city of Jerusalem we see the Temple Mount physically dominating the City of David and we have to imagine Solomon's Temple originally sitting on top of that high place overlooking the city and next to it and just a little to the south of it originally his palace.

So what do we have in the way of literary sources? We have the biblical account. Although we have quite a detailed description in the Hebrew Bible, it is nevertheless difficult for us to put together the elements as they would've originally existed. One of the interesting things about Solomon's Temple is who it was constructed by.

The Hebrew Bible actually tells us that Solomon's Temple was built using workmen from Phoenicia. Specifically the biblical passage reads, "Now King Hiram of Tyre sent his servants to Solomon, when he heard that they had anointed him king in place of his father; for Hiram had always been a friend of David." One of the interesting things parenthetically to note about this passage is that what we have here is a Phoenician king ruling over the city of Tyre. Remember that Phoenicia was just to the north of the Israelite kingdom and that Solomon. in fact. had intermarried with princesses of the neighboring kingdoms including Phoenician princesses in order to form political alliances.

So the biblical passage continues, "Solomon sent word to Hiram, saying, ... 'I intend to build a house for the name of the Lord my God. ... Therefore command that cedars from the Lebanon be cut for me ... for you know that there is no one among us who knows how to cut timber like the Sidonians.'" Well this is again very interesting for the following reason. First of all not only is Solomon forming an alliance with the Phoenician king, but also importing raw materials, cedars of Lebanon, which of course were desirable because they were the longest pieces of wood in the area that you could obtain and also the expertise to cut and shape those wooden timbers by bringing workmen from Phoenicia as well.

It's clear that Solomon's Temple, even though we don't have physical remains of it, would've incorporated both Phoenician materials and also some Phoenician elements, for example, in the style of architecture and in the decoration. If we can't say much archaeologically about the remains of Solomon's Temple, the situation is actually different when it comes to the biblical city of Jerusalem and specifically the City of David because we do have archaeological remains in the City of David that go back to the time of David and Solomon and even earlier.

Those remains are concentrated on that little spur to the south of the Temple Mount, which was the original Jebusite city of Jerusalem. There have been some excavations conducted around the area of the City of David over the course of let's say a century or so. Most of those excavations however have focused on the northern part of the City of David; that is the area just to the south of the Temple Mount. Remember what the configuration of bedrock is in this area; that the bedrock rises up as you go north and slopes down as you go south to the southern tip of the City of David.

In other words, excavations in the City of David have focused not only at the northern end of the area of this hill, but at the end that was physically higher in elevation than the rest of the City of David. The reason this is important is because likely this is the same area where the original acropolis of the city was located before Solomon extended the city to the north to include the Temple Mount. This is something we will be returning to in a little while.

The area that has been so intensively investigated is located specifically on the northeastern side of the city, the area around the Gihon Spring and the area above the Gihon Spring; that is the slope of the hill going up to the crest above the Gihon Spring. This area has been explored by various archaeological expeditions over the course of a number of decades. In fact, the first archaeologist to come and investigate this area at the crest of the hill on the northern side was a British archaeologist named Robert Macalister who came here in the 1920s.

In the 1960s, another archaeologist, British archaeologist named Kathleen Kenyon, conducted excavations here as well. In the 1970s, an Israeli archaeologist named Yigal Shiloh investigated this very same area.

What did Robert Macalister find back in the 1920s, the very first archaeologist who excavated at the crest of the northern end of the City of David? Robert Macalister came to the City of David looking for the Jebusite fortifications. Macalister literally came to the City of David with a spade in one hand and with the Bible in the other hand. He knew from reading the biblical account that the City of David under the Jebusites was strongly fortified, so strongly fortified that the Israelites were not able to take the city until the time of David.

Macalister, knowing that there were Jebusite fortifications, came and looked for those Jebusite fortifications. He started to dig on top of the crest of the hill or very close to the top of the crest of the hill and almost immediately came down on the remains of a city wall, a fortification wall with two towers. On the basis of no good archaeological evidence really, Macalister automatically assumed that this must be the Jebusite fortification wall, and so he dated it to the Jebusite period, the biblical period.

In the 1960s, Kathleen Kenyon came to the same area and conducted excavations just underneath the wall that Macalister found. While excavating the wall she found that it dates not to the Jebusite period, that is not to the biblical period, but instead much later. It dates to the Second Temple period. It dates to after 586 B.C.

Kathleen Kenyon then re-dated the wall. Not only did she re-date the wall though, but she found that the wall sits on top of a massive step-stone structure which archaeologists sometimes describe as a glacis. It looked to Kathleen Kenyon as though this step-stone structure or glacis had been built to buttress the city wall above and so she dated the glacis also to the Second Temple period to after 586 B.C.

In the 1970s another archaeologist, Yigal Shiloh, an Israeli, came and continued to investigate this area. As Yigal Shiloh pulled down the slope of the hill he exposed more of this massive step-stone structure, more of this glacis, and he found sitting on top of the lower part of the glacis ancient Israelite houses dating to the 8th and 7th centuries B.C. If the houses sitting on top of the glacis date to the 8th and 7th centuries B.C. then the glacis itself must be earlier than that, which means that Kathleen Kenyon was wrong.

How does this all work out? At the very top we can see, very close to the crest of the hill, the original wall with the towers that Macalister found, which he dated to the Jebusite period, but in fact dates to the Second Temple period. Then below that we can see this massive step-stone structure, or glacis, and down below sitting on top of the glacis we can see Israelite houses that Yigal Shiloh found.

How do we put this all together then? What is the correct sequence of remains in this excavated area, an area by the way which in Yigal Shiloh's excavations was called Area G? The step-stone glacis must be the earliest thing that existed here. What is the date of this massive step-stone glacis? Apparently it's either Jebusite or Davidic; that is from the time of King David.

The Israelite houses which sit on top of the glacis then were built a few centuries later in the 8th and 7th centuries B.C. All of this was wiped out, destroyed, when the Babylonians destroyed Jerusalem in the year 586 B.C. Then after 586 B.C. when the city was rebuilt, the fortification wall and towers were built at the crest of the hill without any direct connection with the glacis or the early Israelite houses. That then is the correct sequence.

I it still leaves one big problem unsolved. If the glacis was not built in order to buttress that wall at the top that Macalister found and thought was Jebusite, but is much later, then what was it built to buttress? It's clear that it was built to buttress something. It is a massive structure and it must've been built as a buttress because it strengthens and supports the very steep slope of the hill. So what originally stood above it?

Remember the configuration of bedrock here in this area in the City of David. The bedrock rises up as you go north and drops off as you go south; where the natural high point here in the City of David what would've been the area of the original acropolis of the city before Solomon expanded the city to the north to include the Temple Mount. In other words we should expect that the original royal citadel of the City of David was located in this area.

You may have actually caught some of this in recent news reports because excavations in the City of David are still ongoing. These ongoing excavations have brought to light ancient remains in the area above the glacis, remains of a large and monumental building which the excavator Eilat Mazar claims is the palace of King David. This identification has been the subject of lot of controversy because the dating evidence for the building is not secure, it's not that good. It's not clear that the date of this building really is from the time of David or could it be that some or all of the building is later than the time of David.

Archeologists have been going back and forth on this. But whether or not this is in fact the palace of David, we can actually assume that the area where this monumental building is located was the original acropolis of the biblical city of Jerusalem before the time of Solomon.

In his excavations in the 1970s, Yigal Shiloh found the remains of early Israelite houses dating to the 8th and 7th centuries B.C. sitting on top of the lower part of the glacis. By the 8th and 7th centuries B.C. the acropolis, of course, had moved further to the north and so houses were built then on the lower part of the glacis. Shiloh excavated a series of these early Israelite houses which are very interesting because they're very typical examples of Israelite houses, typical of Israelite houses not only in the area of Jerusalem but actually all throughout the country.

The best preserved example of one of these houses is a house that Yigal Shiloh called the House of Ahiel because inside this house he found an inscribe potsherd with the name Ahiel, a Hebrew name, on it. Whether or not this house really belonged to somebody named Ahiel or somebody named Ahiel lived there we don't know. But anyway that's what we call it now.

The house has been partially reconstructed and what we can see is a house that consists of three long, narrow, side by side rooms in the front and one room running along the back along its width. Furthermore outside the main entrance to the house and in front of the house we can see a stone staircase or part of a stone staircase that originally led up to a second story level. This very typical kind of Israelite house is the kind of a house that archaeologists call a four-room house because the ground floor of the building had four rooms, three long, narrow, side by side rooms in the front and one room running along the width of the back. But originally actually there were more than four rooms because there was a second story level.

In the City of David Yigal Shiloh found remains of very typical Israelite houses. Inside these Israelite houses Shiloh found something surprising. Pillar figurines, a kind of figurine that is kind of schematic, made out of clay, fairly small, and which almost always depicts a woman naked to the waist and cupping her breasts under her hands. Well it's kind of surprising actually to see figurines like this coming from an Israelite context. What's so interesting about it of course is that this is the very same kind of practice, the adoption of sort of pagan practices that the biblical prophets warned the Israelites about.

For example Isaiah, "Whoever, then, fashions a god or casts an image that is good for nothing, all who hold it will be put to shame, since the workmen are all human beings." How do we then explain the discovery of these sorts of figurines in an Israelite context and not only in Israelite context, but in Jerusalem within viewing distance of the temple on the Temple Mount? Obviously the prophets would not have been cautioning the Israelites against adopting these sorts of practices unless some people were actually doing that. So we see here some physical evidence for the very kinds of practices that the prophets warned the Israelites about.

You may be wondering well gee are these really Israelite houses? But we do have evidence that they are, because in one of the houses that Yigal Shiloh excavated he found a cache of over 50 bullae. What are bullae? Bullae are little lumps of clay that were used as sealings. Let me explain this. In antiquity when you had a document and you wanted to seal it, what did you do? They didn't have envelopes back then so you didn't have the option of folding up your letter, putting it in an envelope and licking the envelope shut in order to seal it.

What you had back then of course were scrolls. How do you seal a scroll? You roll it up; you take a piece of string, wrap it around it, and then take a lump of raw clay and put it over the string. A lot of times then what you would do is take your personal seal; that is a piece of jewelry that you would wear around your wrist or as a ring or maybe around your neck, which had either your name or your personal symbol on it, and you would impress it into that lump of raw clay. Whoever wanted to open the document then had to peel that lump of raw clay off of the string, thereby breaking the seal.

That's what a bulla is. In one of these houses in the City of David, in Area G, Yigal Shiloh found over 50 bullae. The fact that he found over 50 bullae in this house indicates that once upon a time there was an archive of documents in this house. Let's think about this for a minute. Why did Shiloh find bullae, but why did he not find documents? Very simple! Because in 586 B.C. all of these houses were destroyed by the Babylonians, set on fire and burned down. The fire that destroyed these houses burned the documents, but also fired the little lumps of raw clay and preserved them, because ordinarily lumps of raw clay would not be preserved after thousands of years, they would've turned back into mud. But the fire that burned the houses fired the little lumps of clay and preserved them.

If we look at these little clay sealings then, these bullae that Yigal Shiloh found in the house, they indicate that there was once an archive of documents stored in this house. They're also interesting for another reason, because these bullae are inscribed with names in biblical Hebrew that presumably indicate the name of the owner, that is the person who made the impression into the lump of raw clay. These inscriptions in biblical Hebrew are extremely important for telling us about the population of Jerusalem in the 8th and 7th centuries B.C.

One of the first things of course that we want to find out is, is there anybody mentioned, named, on these bullae who we can match with a figure mentioned in the Hebrew Bible? The problem here is that most people in biblical Jerusalem had the same names; that is the same small pool of names was used over and over again for the majority of the population. In most cases the names are so generic that we cannot say with certainty that the person whose name appears on the sealing is the same as a person mentioned in the Hebrew Bible.

For example, I don't know Joe Cohen, but actually it's not Joe Cohen, that's not the formula, because the typical formula of these biblical names is Joe son of Samuel let's say. So the typical formula is so and so son of or daughter of so and so and this is where the problem is that people didn't have last names. You were simply known as so and so the son of or daughter of so and so. So the problem is that the names on these sealings tend to be from the same small pool of names of fathers and sons that sort of repeat and they're very generic.

In most of the cases we cannot say for sure whether the person whose name appears on the bulla is the same person mentioned in a given passage in the Hebrew Bible. That's the case for the most part. But there is at least one bulla that Yigal Shiloh found that we can say almost for a certainty is the same person mentioned in the biblical account. It is inscribed Gemaryahu son of Shaphan. That is not a typical name; it's an unusual name.

Very interesting we have in Jeremiah a reference to somebody who has this very same name, and here is the passage. It reads, "Baruch in the hearing of all the people read from the book the words of Jeremiah in the house of the Lord, from the chamber of Gemaryah the son of Shaphan, the scribe." Notice several interesting things about this. First of all Gemaryah in this passage is described as a scribe, the very sort of person you would expect to be using a personal seal to seal documents.

This Gemaryah, the scribe, who is mentioned in this passage in Jeremiah was active in the court of the King of Judah roughly around 600 B.C. These houses are destroyed in 586 B.C. so the timing fits as well. It all fits very nicely together and therefore we can say, well with about as much certainty as we can get, that this sealing was sealed by the same figure who is mentioned in the book of Jeremiah.

These sealings are inscribed not just with biblical Hebrew names, but the writing on them is in biblical Hebrew script. If you have ever studied Hebrew and you look however at the sealing, you will see that you can't read it, you can't make out the letters even if you know Hebrew today. The reason is that the Hebrew alphabet that is used on these sealings is the ancient biblical Hebrew alphabet, which is different from the Hebrew alphabet that is used today.

Let me explain this. First of all we have to distinguish between language and script, so the script is the alphabet and the language is the language. You can write the same language in different scripts. In fact, a modern analogy is that this happened in Turkey in the 20th century when Ataturk changed the alphabet that was used to write the Turkish language. Up until then the Arabic alphabet had been used, and now the Latin alphabet is used. So you can write the same language in different scripts or in different alphabets. This is what happened in the case of Hebrew.

Originally Hebrew was written using a script that is called the Paleo-Hebrew or the ancient Hebrew or the Biblical Hebrew script and later a different script, a different alphabet, was adopted and that's the alphabet that's used today. How does this all sort of play out? What is this Biblical Hebrew script or Biblical Hebrew alphabet that we see for example on the sealings that were found in the City of David?

This Biblical Hebrew script or alphabet is not an alphabet that was invented by the Israelites. It's actually an alphabet that they adopted from the Canaanites. Before the Israelites arrived in Canaan, the Canaanites had started to write, and in fact the Canaanites had invented a very interesting alphabet. What the Canaanites did was to modify some of the symbols that were used in Egyptian hieroglyphs and turned them into their own alphabet and they made some very significant changes when they did this.

In Egyptian hieroglyphs what you have is a system basically where each symbol represents an entire word. The great stroke of genius of the Canaanites was to take some of those symbols and adopt them into their alphabet, and instead of having each symbol represent an entire word each symbol instead represents a single syllable. Why is this a great innovation?

If you have an alphabetic system where every symbol depicts an entire word, you're going to need lots and lots of symbols for every different word. But if you have a system where each symbol instead is only one syllable, then you only need a small number of symbols because you can combine those symbols together in order to form words. In other words, what we do in our alphabet today. This was the Canaanite innovation. When the Israelite tribes come in and settle down and eventually start to write, what they do is to adopt the Canaanite alphabet; they make a few minor modifications, but they basically adopt that alphabet, and by the way, the Israelites weren't the only ones who did. All of the neighboring peoples in the areas, the Moabites, the Edomites, the Ammonites, they all adopted this alphabet for writing their own languages.

All of these languages were actually related. They're all part of the same language family. They're all Semitic languages. They're all related but different just in the way, let's say, French and Spanish and Italian are related but different languages. So all of these languages that were spoken by the Israelites and their neighbors including the Phoenicians, who of course are Canaanites in the Iron Age, these are all related languages and they're all basically using some form of what had originally been the Canaanite alphabet to write their languages.

Biblical Hebrew is basically a form of Canaanite script, the Biblical Hebrew alphabet is a form of the Canaanite script and is therefore closely related to the alphabet that was used by the Phoenicians just to the north. This script, the Biblical Hebrew script or alphabet, was used until 586 B.C. After 586

B.C., after the time of the Babylonian conquest, the Israelites stopped using the Biblical Hebrew script and instead adopted a different script which is related but different, called the Aramaic script.

That is the script that, that is the alphabet that is used to write Hebrew up until today. Modern Hebrew, even though the language is Hebrew, is written using the Aramaic alphabet or the Aramaic script. This isn't the end of the story. It's even more interesting because our alphabet today actually originally derives from the Phoenician alphabet; that is from the Canaanite alphabet, because remember that basically the Phoenicians are Canaanites. They're the continuation of the Canaanites in the area of Lebanon after 1200 during the Iron Age.

The Phoenicians were writing in an alphabet that was derived from the original Canaanite alphabet. How does that affect us? How do we get that to where we are today? During the Iron Age there was no writing in Greece. Before the Iron Age, in the Bronze Age, there had been writing in Greece, but after 1200 there is no writing in Greece for several centuries. Greece enters a Dark Age after 1200 as a result of the collapse of the Mycenaean kingdoms. For several hundred years there was no writing at all in Greece.

In the course of contacts with the Greeks the Phoenicians apparently made the Greeks aware of their alphabet; that is through trade, the Greeks became familiar with the Phoenician alphabet, and in the 8th century B.C. adopted that alphabet.

When the Greeks adopted the Phoenician alphabet they made some very important changes. In Semitic languages you don't write vowels, only consonants, so there are no letters in the Phoenician alphabet that are the value of a vowel. One of the changes that the Greeks made was to turn some of the Phoenician consonants into. The best example of this is the first letter of the alphabet. The first letter of the alphabet in Phoenician and also in Hebrew is aleph, which is a silent letter, it's a consonant, has no value in its own in terms of being pronounced.

The Greeks took this letter which was useless for their purposes, they didn't need it, and they turned it on its side into the form of a letter A and gave it the value of a vowel and called it alpha. The second letter of the Greek alphabet, beta, comes from the Semitic bet and so on.

Eventually the Romans picked up the alphabet by way of the Greeks, and so the Latin alphabet that we use today is ultimately derived from the Greek alphabet, which originally goes back to the Phoenician alphabet and to the Canaanites.

Examples of very early Israelite inscriptions are extremely rare. Apparently there's not a lot of writing among the Israelites before let's say the 10th, 9th centuries B.C. When we find inscriptions that date to this period they get a lot of publicity. In the summer of 2005 for example an early Hebrew abecedary that dates to the 10th century B.C. was found in excavations at a site called Tel Zayit in Israel. An abecedary means somebody was practicing writing the alphabet.

One of the most famous examples of one of these early inscriptions is an inscription that was found in 1993 at Tel Dan in the very northern part of the country where part of a stele, a big inscribed stone, was found that actually mentions the House of David and which dates to the middle of the 9th century B.C. This is extremely important because this actually suggests that by the middle of the 9th century B.C. there was an established dynasty that was referred to as the House of David tracing the ancestry back to the original founder of this dynasty and presumably kingdom, a man named David which of course then corresponds with what we know about David in the biblical accounts.

We have talked here about Jerusalem in the biblical period and we have focused especially on the remains in the City of David with the settlement in the City of David. What I'd like to do when we turn to our next lecture is take a look at the water systems that supplied the biblical city of Jerusalem.

Biblical Jerusalem's Ancient Water Systems
Lecture 5

> One of the most exciting things about archaeology in Jerusalem is that ongoing discoveries are constantly causing us to revise our understanding of what the original city looked like.

In this lecture, we will talk about the water systems that supplied the City of David. The main water supply was the Gihon Spring, which comes out of the ground at the eastern foot of the hill of the City of David. Unfortunately, because this spring is located at the foot of the hill inside a valley, putting a fortification wall around it wouldn't work because people on the Mount of Olives, which is higher, could shoot over the wall. Thus, the **Jebusites** placed their fortification wall halfway up the slope of the hill. This leaves the water supply outside the walls, a serious problem during times of siege.

During the Bronze and Iron Ages, three different water systems were built in order to cope with this problem: **Warren's Shaft** (named for the explorer who discovered it), the Siloam Channel, and Hezekiah's Tunnel. Warren's Shaft, which seems to date from Jebusite times, led to a gigantic rock-cut pool surrounded by massive towers. The description in the Hebrew Bible of David's conquest of Jerusalem may refer to this water system: The account indicates that David's men climbed up through the *tsinnor* to take the city. In modern Hebrew, the word *tsinnor* means a pipe, such as a water pipe, but in the Hebrew Bible, it's not clear what this term means.

> **Warren's Shaft, which seems to date from Jebusite times, led to a gigantic rock-cut pool surrounded by massive towers.**

The second water system is the Siloam Channel. The Siloam Channel was meant to provide a place for water to go when the massive pool associated with Warren's Shaft was full. It channeled the excess water through the base of the **Kidron Valley**, where water could flow out and irrigate plots of land. Another large pool for storing excess water was located at the very southern tip of the City of

David. Because this second system worked together with the first, it also was probably Jebusite.

The most famous and latest of the three water systems is Hezekiah's Tunnel, built by this king of Judah in preparation for the Assyrian invasion and siege of Jerusalem. The Hebrew Bible tells us that Hezekiah wished to prevent the Assyrians from having access to the water from the spring that was flowing through the Siloam Channel; thus, a new tunnel was built, one that was completely underground and led to a pool inside the city walls. (Hezekiah also built a new fortification wall, more than 20 feet thick, to surround the Western Hill, where people were living by his time.)

Hezekiah's Tunnel winds its way in a very irregular, snaky manner for 500 meters underneath the City of David. What is so amazing is that the gradient, the slope, of the bottom of this water tunnel, is only 0.6 percent—a difference of only 30 cm from beginning to end. Furthermore, the tunnel was cut by two teams of men, one starting at the Gihon Spring and the other at the outlet end; both of those teams cut through solid bedrock underneath the City of David and somehow met in the middle.

In the next lecture, we will look at the history and archaeology of the northern kingdom of Israel. ■

Important Terms

Jebusites: The original (Bronze Age) population of Jerusalem.

Kidron Valley: Separates the Mount of Olives from the Temple Mount and the City of David.

tsinnor: Biblical Hebrew word perhaps referring to the Warren's Shaft system in the City of David.

Warren's Shaft (along with the Siloam Channel and Hezekiah's Tunnel): Ancient water systems of Jerusalem.

Questions to Consider

1. How did Jerusalem's ancient inhabitants deal with the critical problem of water supply and access?

2. How does archaeology complement or supplement our knowledge of Jerusalem in the time of Hezekiah, as reported in the biblical account?

Biblical Jerusalem's Ancient Water Systems
Lecture 5—Transcript

In our last lecture, we talked about the biblical city of Jerusalem, focusing on the archaeological remains of the settlement in the City of David. What I'd like to do now is continue talking about the archaeology of the City of David focusing especially on the water systems which supplied the inhabitants of the city.

The main water supply in biblical Jerusalem was the Gihon Spring, which comes out of the ground at the eastern foot of the City of David just below the area where Area g with the glacis and the Israelite houses that Yigal Shiloh found are located. The problem is access to the water supply in the Gihon Spring. All of our discussion is going to focus on the water in the Gihon Spring.

What is the problem with the access to the water supply? This is actually connected with the location of the city wall, the fortification wall of the City of David. If we were to take a section looking through the City of David from south to north it would look something like this, a ridge with the Kidron Valley on the east and the Tyropoeon Valley on the west and cresting at the top of the hill.

The Gihon Spring comes out of the ground at the foot of the eastern slope of the City of David, so here is the problem. If you are building a fortification wall around the settlement on this little hill, where are you going to put that line of wall relative to the water in the spring? Ideally what you would want to do is include the spring inside the fortification wall. The problem is since the spring is located at the foot of the hill inside a valley, putting your fortification wall around the spring isn't really going to work well because what it's going to do is leave you vulnerable to attack. People sitting a little bit up on the slope of the Mount of Olives across from you for example are going to be able to shoot easily over that line of fortification wall.

Therefore, the line of the fortification wall should be further up the slope. Macalister, as we saw, thought that he found the line of the fortification wall all the way at the crest of the hill, but that wasn't the original fortification wall of the Jebusite city. In fact, the fortification wall of the Jebusite city, the original City of David, was found originally in excavations by Kathleen Kenyon and later more of it in excavations by Yigal Shiloh in the 1970s halfway down the slope of the hill. This actually makes very good sense because strategically then the wall was located enough above the valley floor so that people outside the wall can't easily shoot over it.

Yet you are leaving enough space for settlement inside the line of that city wall because that already is a very small hill. The farther up the hill you put the wall the smaller area you have within the space of that wall. But this still leaves a problem. The problem is your water supply is outside the line of the city wall.

In times of peace that's not a problem. You simply go out a gate in the wall and down to the spring and collect your water and go back into the city. The problem is in times of war, in times of siege. Because in times of siege you will then have to go outside the fortification wall to get water exposing yourself then to danger, to being killed by the enemy. So in biblical Jerusalem then there was a major problem, a major concern with protecting the access to the water supply in times of siege.

Over the course of the biblical period, that is over the course of the Bronze Age and the Iron Age, three different water systems were built in order to cope with this problem. These three systems are called as follows: the first and earliest system is called Warren's Shaft named after the early explorer who discovered it; the next system is called the Siloam Channel; and the third and latest of the three systems is called Hezekiah's Tunnel. We are going to start by talking about Warren Shaft, then the Siloam Channel, and then Hezekiah's Tunnel.

Let's begin first with Warren's Shaft. Warren's Shaft is named after Charles Warren, the explorer who discovered it. When we look at a cross-section of Warren's Shaft, what we see are a series of underground tunnels that go underneath the city wall which is located about halfway up the slope of the hill. The idea of Warren's Shaft was to provide access to the water in the spring without going outside the walls of the city, and therefore we have this intricate series of underground tunnels.

One of the most exciting things about archaeology and especially working in Jerusalem is the fact that ongoing discoveries are constantly causing us to revise our understanding of what the original city looked like. This is the case with Warren's Shaft because for a very long time, from the time of Warren's original discovery until very recently, we thought that Warren's Shaft operated in the following way.

We thought that you entered the shaft partway up the slope inside the wall of the city through an underground tunnel which led you down into a stepped passage and then to a horizontal tunnel. When you reached the end of that horizontal tunnel, there was a tall vertical shaft that went straight down to yet another horizontal tunnel that would've brought water from the spring to the base of the vertical shaft. The idea being that you would've walked through the horizontal tunnel to the top of the vertical shaft, reached some sort of wooden platform there, and then be able to drop down your bucket down that vertical shaft to the water that flowed to the base of it, and pull the water up and draw the water and go back into the city.

In other words, for a long time we thought that's how Warren's Shaft worked. But excavations ongoing in Jerusalem in the last 10 to 15 years have literally revolutionized our understanding of the way this water system originally worked.

What we are looking at here is a plan that shows the old way we thought Warren's Shaft used to work.

That vertical shaft that used to be thought to be such an integral part of Warren's Shaft system is now known not to be part of the system at all. It apparently is a natural shaft in the bedrock that was eaten away by the water at some point that has nothing to do with the water system at all. So how did Warren's Shaft originally work? How did this system originally work?

Originally you entered Warren's Shaft in the same way as we thought before. That is you came in through the tunnel within the wall of the city, partway up the slope of the hill through a sort of a stepped tunnel that led down to that horizontal tunnel or passage. Instead of then reaching the top of that vertical shaft, which is not part of the water system at all, you continued along and reached the edge of a gigantic rock cut pool.

This gigantic rock cut pool stored water from the Gihon Spring, and when you reached the edge of that pool you would then drop down your bucket from some sort of a platform, fill it up, and then go back in through the wall of the city. The ongoing excavations have brought to light not just this gigantic rock cut pool, but also a series of massive towers that protected the pool and also enclosed the spring. The size of the pool and the size of the towers is hard to describe.

We are looking at a picture of a small corner of this rock cut pool. This water system then is a massive water system, much bigger and more monumental then we ever suspected. So that is how the system worked. We know now how the water system worked.

Next question is: What is the date of this water system? One possibility is that it dates to the time of David and Solomon. Yigal Shiloh, who conducted excavations in the City of David, thought that the system must date to the time of David and Solomon on the basis of parallels with water systems at other Israelite sites. I think that most scholars probably agree that this system dates to the middle Bronze Age; that is to about 1800 B.C., which means that it was part of the Jebusite system of Jerusalem. So this was a water system that was functioning under the Jebusites and which then continued to function after David comes in with the Israelites and they take over the city and settle in it.

In addition there is a controversy about the identification of this water system relative to a passage or an episode that's described in the Hebrew Bible and specifically that is the conquest of Jerusalem by David. Remember that it was David who took Jerusalem from the Jebusites. Before the time of David, the Israelites had not been able to take Jerusalem because, according to the biblical account, it was such a strongly fortified city.

So the biblical account describes David's conquest of Jebusite Jerusalem, and the passage is very interesting because it might actually include a reference to this water system. "And the king and his men went to Jerusalem against the Jebusites, the inhabitants of the land, who said to David, 'You will not come in here, but the blind and the lame will ward you off',—thinking, 'David cannot come in here.' " So in other words the Jebusites are mocking David and his army; our city is so strongly fortified that even blind men and lame men can keep you from conquering it.

> Nevertheless David took the stronghold of Zion, that is, the City of David. And David said on that day, "Whoever would smite the Jebusites, let him get up the [and now we get a Hebrew word] tsinnor to attack the lame and the blind, who are hated by David's soul." ... And David dwelt in the stronghold and called it the City of David.

In another passage we are told that it was David's general Joab son of Sirah who managed to climb up through this tsinnor.

In other words the biblical account suggests that David's army was able to take Jerusalem by climbing up through something called a tsinnor. The problem is what is a tsinnor? This is the only place in the Hebrew Bible where this word occurs. In modern Hebrew the word "tsinnor" means a pipe like a water pipe. But in the Hebrew Bible it's not clear what this term means. Some scholars have suggested that maybe tsinnor is Warren's Shaft system and that maybe what happened is that the Israelites were able to take the city by climbing up through this water system, entering the city and then opening the gates to the Israelite army.

If this is the case, then the tsinnor that is referred to in this passage is Warren's Shaft system. Remember, by the way, that the system apparently was built in the time of the Jebusites, so it actually would've already existed and been functioning when David took the city.

The second water system is the Siloam Channel. The Siloam Channel is very different from Warren's Shaft. It is a channel that starts again at the Gihon Spring and runs outside the wall of the city at the foot of the Kidron Valley to a big pool at the southern tip of the City of David. Here's the question: Why do you need a second water system; that is why is the Siloam Channel necessary?

The Gihon Spring is a kind of a spring that gushes and abates, water gushes and abates. What happens is that the water gushes and as it starts to flow, some of it was stored in that gigantic rock cut pool that has recently been discovered. But what happens when that pool is full and the spring continues to gush forth; that is, what do you do with the excess water from the spring? You must provide an outlet for the excess water. That's exactly what the Siloam Channel was.

The Siloam Channel was the access for the excess water from the Gihon Spring. When that gigantic pool, rock cut pool, next to the Gihon Spring was filled up, the extra water then was channeled into the Siloam Channel through the base of the Kidron Valley where there were openings in the channels so that water could flow out and irrigate plots of land in the valley. Then finally at the very southern tip of the City of David there was another very large pool for storing all of that excess water, and that pool is called the Siloam Pool or Pool of Siloam, and we will come back and talk about that as well.

The remains of the Siloam Channel are known and can actually be seen today running along the eastern foot of the City of David through the Kidron Valley, and in some places you can see it cut into bedrock with massive stone slabs still covering the top of the channel. There's a question then: What is the date of the Siloam Channel? Actually the date of the Siloam Channel must be the same as the date of Warren's Shaft because the two worked together. Because the whole idea, the whole point of the Siloam Channel is to carry off the excess water from the Gihon Spring; so whatever the date is of Warren's Shaft must also be the date of the Siloam Channel.

If Warren's Shaft is from the time of David and Solomon, then so is the Siloam Channel. But again most likely Warren's Shaft is from the middle Bronze Age, and therefore the Siloam Channel should also be dated to the middle Bronze Age.

The most famous and latest of these three water systems is Hezekiah's Tunnel. This tunnel was made in the time of King Hezekiah. Hezekiah was the King of Judah at the end of the 8th century B.C. In preparation for the Assyrian invasion and siege of Jerusalem in 701, Hezekiah built this water system. The water system still functions today, still has water flowing through it, and in fact visitors to Jerusalem often walk through Hezekiah's Tunnel as part of their visit.

The tunnel is very interesting because it winds its way in a very irregular, snaky manner underneath the City of David beginning at the Gihon Spring, on the northeast side of the City of David, and ending on the southwest side of the City of David, all of it cut through solid bedrock underground. In fact the tunnel winds for a distance of about 500 meters, although the distance between the beginning point and the end point are only 300 meters, a meter is about a yard. So the crow flies, as the crow flies, it's only about 300 meters from beginning to end, but the actual length because it winds around so much is over 500 meters.

What is so amazing is that the gradient, the slope, of the bottom of the tunnel, this water tunnel, the gradient is only 0.6 percent from beginning to end. That's a difference of only 30 cm from the beginning till the end. This is really an engineering feat.

Today you can walk through Hezekiah's Tunnel, and when you do you're walking through with the water usually up to about the level of your hips. One of the interesting things as you walk through the tunnel is that you can see how it was made, and we actually know and we're going to see that the tunnel was cut by two teams of men; one team starting at the Gihon Spring and the other team starting at the outlet end, and both of those teams cut through solid bedrock underneath the City of David winding their way around and somehow met joined up in the middle.

How they met, how they joined up, we don't know. Some scholars have suggested that maybe they were following a natural crack in the bedrock through which water was already flowing. I actually don't believe that, and the reason is as you walk through Hezekiah's Tunnel today you can see places where there are false starts, cuttings in the bedrock where they started to go off in a different direction. If they were following already an existing crack with water flowing in it, then why would you have false starts.

So we really don't know exactly how these two teams of men managed to wind their way cutting through solid bedrock and meet up somehow in the middle. It's an engineering feat that we actually don't understand. One of the interesting things too, as you walk through the tunnel, is that you notice that the ceiling is higher in some points, lower in some points, sometimes it's so low that you have to stoop a bit as you walk through it. Sometimes it gets very high and yet the gradient of the floor is that very, very gentle gradient. They managed to keep that floor level a very gentle gradient from beginning to end.

One of the questions about Hezekiah's Tunnel is: Why did he make this new water system? When Hezekiah became King on the eve of the Assyrian invasion, there already were two perfectly good functioning water systems in Jerusalem; Warren's Shaft and the Siloam Channel were still working. So why did Hezekiah make a new water system when the other two were still functioning perfectly well?

The Hebrew Bible actually tells us why. Let us now see what the Hebrew Bible says and try and understand it.

> When Hezekiah saw that Sennacherib [that's the Assyrian king] intended to attack Jerusalem, he planned with his civil and military officers to stop up the water of the springs outside the city; and they helped him. They gathered together a large number of people and stopped up the springs and the stream which flowed through the land. "Why should the kings of Assyria come here and find much water?" they asked. ... Hezekiah closed the upper outlet of the waters of Gihon and directed them down to the west side of the City of David.

This passage explains exactly the problem. The problem was not that the two water systems weren't working. The problem was the Siloam Channel. The Siloam Channel was a non-defensive system located outside the walls of the city. When the Assyrians came and besieged the city then, they would've had access to water from the spring, the water from the spring that was flowing through the Siloam Channel. Hezekiah didn't want the Assyrians to have access to that water, so they stopped up the Siloam Channel. But if you stop up the Siloam Channel, you still have the problem that you have to provide an outlet for the excess water from the spring.

So they built a new tunnel, one that was completely underground, and one that led to a pool that was inside the walls of the city so that when the Assyrians came and besieged the city, they would not have access to the water from the spring. The story actually continues, because in 1880 a little Arab boy from the local village was playing at the outlet end of Hezekiah's Tunnel; that is the end where the tunnel ends up with a pool which is today called the Pool of Siloam. There's still a pool there. It's a different Pool of Siloam than the original one, than the one that was at the outlet of the Siloam Channel, but there's a pool now at the end of Hezekiah's Tunnel called the Pool of Siloam.

A little Arab villager was playing, a little boy was playing in the outlet in there, in the area of the Pool of Siloam, and just inside looked up and saw an inscription on the wall. That inscription then was removed and eventually was taken to Istanbul, because in 1880 Palestine was part of the Ottoman Empire. This inscription was taken to Istanbul, the capital of the Ottoman Empire, and was put on display in the archaeological museum in Istanbul where it remains on display until today.

This inscription is an inscription that dates to the time of Hezekiah, to the late 8th century B.C. It is written in Biblical Hebrew script and Biblical Hebrew language and it describes the completion of Hezekiah's Tunnel and here is what it says.

> This is the story of the boring through. While [the tunnelers lifted] the pick-axe each toward his fellow and while 3 cubits [remained yet] to be bored [through, there was heard] the voice of a man calling his fellow—for there was a split [or overlap] in the rock on the right hand and on [the left hand].

In other words this is describing that moment when the two teams of men are so close together that they can hear each other's voices through the bedrock, but they haven't yet actually reached each other.

"When the tunnel was driven through, the tunnelers hewed the rock, each man against his fellow, pick-axe against pick-axe. And the water flowed from the spring toward the reservoir for 1,200 cubits. The height of the rock above the head of the tunnelers was a 100 cubits." So this is a very important and very interesting inscription that dedicates the completion of this monumental water tunnel.

Ongoing excavations in the area of the City of David are bringing to light another part of ancient Jerusalem's water system, because the outlet today of Hezekiah's Tunnel is called the Pool of Siloam. But that pool as you see it today, and which many visitors to Jerusalem see and visit, dates to the Byzantine period, that is to the 5th and 6th centuries A.D. It's centuries later than the time of Hezekiah.

What did the original Pool of Siloam look like? Excavations in the area of the City of David for the last, let's say, five to ten years have been bringing to light a monumental pool that is an earlier version of the Pool of Siloam, not from the Byzantine period, but from the late Second Temple period. Specifically what we have here is a gigantic pool, much larger than the Byzantine pool is, that is surrounded by rows of steps. The rows of steps by the way indicate that this was not just a pool used for storing water, for drinking, and for general purposes, but that this pool was also used as a Jewish ritual bath, something that we will be discussing later in this course.

What's so exciting about this is that this Pool of Siloam that is now coming to light, which is so big and which has steps going all around it, is a pool that dates to the time of Jesus. In other words, this pool that is coming to light is the Pool of Siloam that existed when Jesus was in Jerusalem. This is so important because of course we have a passage in the fourth gospel John that talks about Jesus performing a miraculous healing at the Pool of Siloam.

And it says,

> And he [Jesus] passed along and he saw a man who had been blind from his birth. ... And as he said this, he spat on the ground and made clay with the saliva, and he put the clay on the man's eyes, and said to him, "Go and wash in the Pool of Siloam"—a name

which means One who has been sent in Hebrew Shiloah. So he went and washed them, and went home able to see.

So if we want to imagine the setting for this story as told in John, then we should imagine this gigantic Pool of Siloam that is now being brought to light in archaeological excavations in the City of David.

In advance of the Assyrian attack and siege of Jerusalem, Hezekiah not only built a new water system, but he also built a new fortification wall, not a new fortification wall around the City of David, which had perfectly good existing fortification walls, but a different fortification wall to surround the western hill, because by the time of Hezekiah people were now living on the western hill. Originally when David takes Jerusalem, the city consists only of the City of David and then Solomon expands the city to the Temple Mount.

By the time of Hezekiah, by the late 8th century B.C., people were now living on top of the western hill and that part of Jerusalem was not fortified. Remains of this fortification wall were brought to light in excavations in Jerusalem in the 1970s, and this wall is so thick, over 20 feet thick, that the excavator called it The Broad Wall.

One of the most interesting things about talking about biblical Jerusalem is talking about the modern exploration of the city of Jerusalem. We are greatly indebted to 19th century explorers who went through the city under very difficult conditions and mapped and explored it and documented remains that in many cases are no longer preserved. One of these early explorers was a British explorer named Captain Charles Warren. We've already talked about Warren in relation to Warren's Shaft.

In addition to documenting, to finding and documenting Warren's Shaft, Warren also surveyed Hezekiah's Tunnel in the year 1867. What he did is to go through the tunnel and make a plan of it, documenting it completely, and he took in an assistant and they went through this tunnel. Today when you walk through Hezekiah's Tunnel, it's actually a very easy and kind of fun thing to do. It takes about a half an hour to walk through it now, and you take your flashlight and you walk through and no problem at all. But in 1867, walking through Hezekiah's Tunnel was not nearly so easy.

Charles Warren has left us a description of his exploration of Hezekiah's Tunnel, and I would like to read it with you because it is actually funny for some of the wrong reasons. I'm sure it wasn't funny to him. But reading it today, not only shows how difficult this exploration was, but also shows how determined Warren was to complete his scientific investigation of this water system.

> In the month of December 1867, I [that's Charles Warren] made a thorough examination and survey of the passage leading from the Virgin's Fount [that's the Gihon Spring] to Siloam [i.e. the Pool of Siloam]. We entered from the Siloam end, so as to have as much clean work as possible. [In other words they started from the end of the Pool of Siloam, the outlet, the reason being that the ceiling there is higher than at the beginning end.] For the first 350 feet it was plain sailing. ... At 450 feet the height of the passage was reduced to 3 feet 9 inches. ... At 600 feet it is only 2 feet 6 inches high. ...
>
> Our difficulties now commenced. Sergeant Birtles [who was the assistant] with a Fellah [a local villager] went ahead, measuring with tape, while I followed with compass and field book. The bottom is a soft silt, with a calcerous crust at the top, strong enough to bear human weight, except in a few places, where it let us down with a flop. ... We were now crawling on all fours, and thought we were getting on very pleasantly, the water being only 4 inches deep, and we were not yet wet higher than our hips. Presently bits of cabbage-stalks came floating by, and we suddenly awoke to the fact that the waters were rising. ...
>
> The rising of the waters had not been anticipated, as they had risen only two hours previous to our entrance. At 850 feet the height of the channel was reduced to 1 foot 10 inches, and here our troubles began. The water was running with great violence, 1 foot in height, and we, crawling full length, were up to our necks in it. I was particularly embarrassed: one hand necessarily wet and dirty, the

other holding a pencil, compass, and field-book; the candle for the most part in my mouth. Another 50 feet brought us to a place where we had regularly to run the gauntlet of the waters. [They had to go completely under water.] The passage being only 1 foot 4 inches high, we had just 4 inches breathing space, and had some difficulty in twisting our necks around properly. When observing, my mouth was underwater. ...

We were now going in a zigzag direction towards the northwest, and the height increased to 4 feet 6 inches, and at 1100 feet we were again crawling with a height of only 1 foot 10 inches. We should probably have suffered more from the cold than we did, had not our risible faculties been excited by the sight of our Fellah in front plunging and puffing through the water like a young grampus. [So they are trying to keep up with their villager there.]

At 1150 feet the passage again averaged in height 2 feet to 2 feet 6 inches; at 1400 feet we heard the sound of water dripping. ... At 1450 feet we commenced turning to the east, and the passage attained a height of 6 feet; at 1658 feet we came upon our old friend, the passage leading to the Ophel Shaft, [that is Warren's Shaft] and, after a further advance of 50 feet, to the Virgin's Fount [that is to the Gihon Spring].

We conclude this lecture then by talking about the difficulties of the early explorers in finding these water systems, documenting these water systems, and it's to them that we owe much of our information about the early history and archaeology of Jerusalem. We've now spent quite a bit of time looking in detail at the history and archaeology of Jerusalem in the biblical period. What I'd like to do next time is turn outside of Jerusalem and look at the northern kingdom of Israel at what everyday life was like in the northern kingdom and what we know about the history and archaeology of the northern kingdom of Israel.

Samaria and the Northern Kingdom of Israel
Lecture 6

> The governing principle of all ancient peoples .... said you worship your national deity or patron deity, but also side by side, other gods. The writers of the Hebrew Bible were against that principle.

What was going on in the kingdom of Israel, to the north, while all the things that we have been looking at in Jerusalem were going on in Judah? After the 10 northern tribes broke away from Judah and formed their own kingdom, eventually, **Samaria** became its capital, only 35 miles from Jerusalem. With these two kingdoms and their capitals in such close proximity, you can imagine that tension and rivalry developed between them.

The writers of the Hebrew Bible were pro-Judah/pro-south and anti-Israel/anti-north. They maintained that the Jerusalem temple was the only place where the God of Israel could be worshiped. And they denounced Jeroboam, founder of the northern kingdom, for setting up golden calves in the northern and southern extremities of his kingdom, at Bethel and Dan. At Tel Dan, excavations have brought to light a cultic place that at the very least was the site of some sort of shrine or temple.

With these two kingdoms and their capitals in such close proximity, you can imagine that tension and rivalry developed between them.

The House of Jeroboam is the dynasty that initially ruled over the northern kingdom. Later, Omri established himself as king; the most notorious of the northern kings of Israel was his son, Ahab, who ruled from 872–851 B.C. Ahab is infamous for, among other things, his marriage to the daughter of the king of Tyre, Jezebel, who was blamed for inducing Ahab to build a temple to the **Phoenician** deity **Baal**.

Excavations in Ahab's palace at Samaria have brought to light a wealth of ivories that are carved in the Phoenician style. It's not surprising to find these ivories in Samaria, given the close connections between Ahab and his Phoenician neighbors to the north. In fact, the Hebrew Bible refers to Ahab's "ivory house," probably indicating the numerous inlays of carved ivory that were used to decorate pieces of furniture in the palace, the sort of ivories that were found in the excavations.

We should also touch on the House of Omri's relationship with the kingdom of Moab, on the eastern side of the Dead Sea. After Omri established his dynasty, he annexed Moab. Several decades later, the king of Moab, Mesha, rebelled. Not only does the Hebrew Bible report this event, but we also have a large inscribed stone called the Mesha Stone, or **Mesha stele**, which celebrates King Mesha's victory; the stone dates to roughly 840 B.C.

Archaeology supports the Bible's stories of King Ahab's close ties to the Phoenicians.

Eventually, the northern kingdom came to an end. In 722 B.C., the Assyrians took Samaria, forcing the inhabitants of Israel to leave their land and go into exile in Assyria. The kingdom of Judah was invaded 20 years later by the Assyrians, but Judah survived this invasion under Hezekiah. In the next lecture, we'll explore daily life in Israel and Judah. ∎

Important Terms

Baal: National deity of the Canaanites/Phoenicians.

Mesha stele: Inscribed stone found in Jordan that records Mesha's revolt against one of the Omride kings in the mid-9th century.

Phoenicians: The Iron Age inhabitants of modern Lebanon, descendants of the Bronze Age Canaanites.

Samaria: Capital of the northern kingdom of Israel and, later, the name of the surrounding district, as well.

Questions to Consider

1. What are the biases of the writers of the Hebrew Bible, and what do these biases tell us about the writers?

2. What do we learn from the Hebrew Bible about the adoption of foreign religious and cultic practices by the inhabitants of the northern kingdom of Israel?

Samaria and the Northern Kingdom of Israel
Lecture 6—Transcript

We've been talking about biblical Jerusalem for a while, and in this lecture what I'd like to do is turn to look at the northern kingdom of Israel because Jerusalem of course was in Judah in the south. What was going on in the kingdom of Israel in the north while all of the things that we were looking at in Jerusalem were going on in Judah?

What I'd like to do first of all is set up this dichotomy between north and south. There actually was tension between the northern tribes and the southern tribes, and it was this tension that led to the split of the United Kingdom, the United Monarchy, after the death of Solomon. So after Solomon died in about 930 the United Kingdom split into two halves, the northern kingdom becomes known as the Kingdom of Israel. Eventually its capital is at a city called Samaria, and the southern kingdom becomes known as the Kingdom of Judah with its capital at Jerusalem. In theory at least, Jerusalem continued to be the religious center of both kingdoms with the temple built by Solomon on the Temple Mount.

In order to get an impression of how close these kingdoms were together, even though they're split apart, let's look at the distance between Samaria, the capital of the northern Kingdom of Israel, and Jerusalem, the capital of the Kingdom of Judah. The distance between these two capital cities is approximately 35 miles. These two kingdoms not only adjoin each other, they're not only neighboring, but their capital cities are also very close together. As you can imagine then there developed some tension and rivalry between these two kingdoms after Solomon's death.

One of the problems that develops between these two kingdoms is how to worship the God of Israel, Yahweh. This is a difference between two principles, inclusive Yahwism or exclusive Yahwism, something that we see actually expressed by the writers of the Hebrew Bible.

What exactly were the biases of the writers of the Hebrew Bible and what do these biases tell us about these writers? First of all we can see that the writers of the Hebrew Bible were pro-Judah, pro-south, and anti-Israel, anti-north. We can also see that they favored exclusive Yahwism, not inclusive Yahwism. What does that mean? Exclusive Yahwism says that the only God that the people of Israel may worship is the God of Israel, no other gods alongside him. That is the god to whom the temple in Jerusalem was dedicated.

Whereas inclusive Yahwism says that you worship the God of Israel as your national deity, as your patron, but side by side with that you may also worship other gods. This in fact was the common picture in the ancient world. Ancient peoples, ancient cities had patron deities or national deities who they worshiped, for example Athena, the patron deity of Athens. But side by side with those national or patron deities they worshiped other gods.

So inclusive Yahwism is the principle that basically was the governing principle of all ancient peoples in antiquity which said you worship your national deity or patron deity, but also side by side other gods. The writers of the Hebrew Bible were against that principle.

The writers of the Hebrew Bible favored the centralization of the cult over decentralization. What does this mean? It means that the only place where you may worship the God of Israel is in the Jerusalem temple. You may not construct other temples, sanctuaries, or shrines outside of Jerusalem around the country dedicated to the worship of the God of Israel. The Jerusalem temple is the only place where the God of Israel may be worshiped.

What do these biases tell us about the biblical writers? Well for one thing the centralization of cult, the centralization of the cult in the Jerusalem temple, placed religion in the control of the high priest in the Jerusalem temple, which automatically makes you suspect that the biblical writers must've been part of that group. Furthermore the high priesthood was a hereditary office in the hands of a particular family called the Zadokites, the sons of Zadok or Hebrew Zadok.

Again begins to make you wonder about where these guys are coming from. They probably have a certain interest in expressing this point of view, exclusive Yahwism, centralization of the cult in the Jerusalem temple. Furthermore, exclusive Yahwism then concentrated power in the hands of the

Jerusalem high priesthood. That is if you are not allowed to worship anyone but the God of Israel, then it means that all of the power is concentrated in the hands of the priesthood of the God of Israel, because no other gods are being worshipped therefore there are no other priests.

Centralization of the cult privileged Judah over Israel automatically because the Jerusalem temple was located in Judah, not in Israel. So it gave the Judeans, the people of Judah control and specifically the priesthood control over the Jerusalem temple, and meant that the northern kingdom, Israel, had no control over the cult if the only place where you can worship the God of Israel is in Jerusalem automatically. There are no temples, shrines, or sanctuaries located outside of Jerusalem.

So it is not surprising then when we take all of this into account. When we read the Hebrew Bible we see that the biblical writers generally express a very negative attitude towards the northern kingdom of Israel, towards its rulers, and towards the various kinds of things that they did. Generally speaking it was in the north that you find people favoring the idea of inclusive Yahwism, versus exclusive Yahwism, this idea that you can worship other gods alongside the God of Israel.

Also in the north we find the principle acceptable of establishing alternative temples or sanctuaries dedicated to the God of Israel outside of Jerusalem, because of course in Israeli would've wanted to do that because Jerusalem was in Judah, was in the other kingdom. The biblical writers there for almost universally condemn the practices of the northern kings of Israel. We see this reflected for example in this biblical passage from 1 Kings condemning one of the northern kings. "So the king," in this case is Jeroboam, "took counsel and made two calves of gold, and said to the people, 'You have gone up to Jerusalem long enough. Behold your gods, o Israel, who brought you up from the land of Egypt! So he set up the one in Bethel and the other he put in Dan; and this thing became a sin to Israel."

Notice several things about this. Jeroboam makes two golden calves, he says you have gone up to Jerusalem long enough, we don't want people continuing to go to Jerusalem. We can have our own sanctuaries here in the Kingdom of Israel, and he sets up one in Bethel and on in Dan which are the two points, the two outer most points of the northern kingdom, Bethel in the south and Dan in the north, so one at each end. The biblical writers then condemned this as a sin to Israel.

Archeology actually bears out some of this because at Tel Dan, which was located in the very northern part of the country excavations brought to light a cultic place that may've been the very site where the golden calf was set up or at the very least it was the site of some sort of an alternative shrine or a temple. The excavator Avraham Biran described this as a high place. What is a high place? This is a term actually that we get from the Hebrew Bible.

Here we have a passage from 1 Kings:

> After this episode Jeroboam did not turn from his evil way, but made again from among all sorts of people priests of the high places. Whomsoever he would, he installed to be the priests of the high places, and this thing became a sin to the house of Jeroboam, even to cut it off and destroy it from the face of the earth.

A couple of interesting things to note about this, so first of all it describes Jeroboam appointing priests of things called high places. A high place apparently is an elevated platform either for some sort of temple or a shrine or possibly for cult statues such as a golden calf that's described in the passage that we read previously.

What we have here at Tel Dan actually conforms with this description of a high place, an elevated place, for sanctuary and in point of fact the Temple Mount in Jerusalem would've qualified as a high place in the sense that it was a natural high point where the temple was located. He appoints priests to serve in this high place and this is then condemned by the biblical writers who condemn it as a sin to the House of Jeroboam. What is the House of Jeroboam? The House of Jeroboam is analogous to a phrase that we saw in an inscription in our last lecture that referred to the House of David.

When we hear this term House of Jeroboam, House of David, House of Omri, it refers to a royal dynasty. So the House of Jeroboam is the dynasty that was established by Jeroboam that rules over the northern Kingdom of Israel.

Perhaps the most notorious of the northern kings of Israel is Ahab who was King of Israel from 872 to 851. Ahab is notorious among other things because of his marriage to a woman named Jezebel. Biblical Jezebel, or in Hebrew Izabel, who was the daughter of a Phoenician king. This is actually very interesting too because here we see Ahab forming a political alliance with his Phoenician neighbors to the north in the very same way that Solomon had done. But whereas the biblical writers do not condemn Solomon, they do condemn Ahab and they really hated Jezebel.

Another interesting thing to notice, Jezebel was the daughter of a king named Itobaal or in biblical Hebrew Ethbaal, who was the king of Tyre. Notice both Jezebel's name and her father's name have an interesting element, the name Bel or Baal. Bel or Baal was the name of the national god, the patron god of the Canaanites and the Phoenicians, just as the God of Israel was the national god of the tribes of Israel and the god Dagon was the national god as described in the Hebrew Bible at least was the national god of the Philistines. The national god of the Canaanites or Phoenicians was Baal or Bel.

This name of the god then, the national god, forms part of the name of Jezebel and also her father. It's very common in antiquity for names to be theophoric, that is for names to incorporate the name of the chief deity, and that's what we see here with Jezebel. Why did the biblical writers hate Jezebel so much? Because of what she allegedly caused her husband to do, and let's read the relevant biblical passage.

> Ahab, the son of Omri, reigned over Israel in Samaria 22 years. [Notice we'll come back to this that Ahab's father was named Omri.] But Ahab, the son of Omri, did that which was evil in the sight of the Lord above all who were before him. He took as wife Jezebel, the daughter of Ethbaal, king of the Sidonians, and went and served the Baal and worshiped him. Then he erected an altar for Baal in the House of the Baal, which he built in Samaria. … Ahab did more to provoke the jealousy of the Lord, the God of Israel, than all of the kings of Israel who were before him.

First of all the biblical writers condemn Ahab for taking as a wife Jezebel, the daughter of this king of the Phoenicians, and then he erects an altar for

Baal in a temple to Baal, House of the Baal is a temple for Baal, which he builds in Samaria in the capital city. This then according to the biblical writers provokes the jealousy of the God of Israel. The God of Israel was a jealous god according to the biblical writers who would not tolerate the worship of any other gods alongside him.

In the acropolis at Samaria we have remains of the palace of Ahab. All of this episode with the palace of Ahab at Samaria and Jezebel becoming Ahab's wife and the biblical description of the House of Baal and the altar of Baal also bring to mind another famous biblical episode and that is connected with the prophet Elijah, because of course the prophet of Elijah who's wandering around the northern kingdom at this time, condemns Ahab and Jezebel for introducing the worship of Baal into the northern kingdom.

There's a lot of fighting that goes on back and forth between Elijah on the one hand and Ahab and Jezebel on the other. Just to read one passage here from 1 Kings, "When Ahab saw Elijah, Ahab said to him, 'Is it you, you troubler of Israel?' " So from Ahab's point of view, Elijah is just this troublemaker. "He answered, [Elijah answered,] 'I have not troubled Israel; but you have, and your father's house, because you have forsaken the commandments of the Lord and followed the Baals.' " Clearly Elijah is an exclusive Yahwist and he is then condemning Ahab who is an inclusive Yahwist.

Excavations at Samaria have brought to light remains associated with that palace. Among them some monumental remains, such as carved capitals which once stood atop columns, capitals that are sort of in an almost early Greek kind of a style called proto-Aeolic capitals, and also a wealth of ivories that are carved in Phoenician style. It's not actually surprising to find carved ivories in a Phoenician style in Samaria given the close connections between Ahab and his Phoenician neighbors to the north.

In fact, the Bible refers to the many ivories in Ahab's palace in a passage in 1 Kings and I quote, "Now the rest of the acts of Ahab, and all that he did, and the ivory house that he built, and all the cities that he built, are they not written in the Book of the Annals of the Kings of Israel?" Well what is the ivory house? The ivory house is apparently referring to the palace with all of its ivories. It's not referring to a palace that is built out of ivory; what it's referring to is the numerous inlays of carved ivory that were used to decorate pieces of furniture in the palace, and those are the sorts of ivories that we're looking at that were found in the excavations.

The biblical writers really did not like Jezebel and they present her in an extremely negative light. Again the reason for this is because Jezebel, from their point of view, was responsible for introducing the worship of Baal into Samaria and caused her husband then to sin. They present Jezebel's end also in a very negative way. She comes to a horrible end, and from the point of view of the biblical writers, she comes to an end that she deserves. What happens at the end with Jezebel's death? This is how the biblical account describes it.

"When Jehu came to Jezreel," Jehu by the way was an officer in the army who is responsible for a coup and he's the one actually responsible for killing Jezebel, Jezreel by the way is the place where one of the royal palaces was located, it's a site located in the north of the country, "Jezebel heard of it, and she painted her eyelashes and adorned her head and peered out at the window." So Jezebel hears that Jehu as arrived, Jehu by the way had just killed the king, Jezebel hears that he has arrived and she puts on makeup and she looks out the window. Very interesting, among the carved ivories that we have is an ivory that actually shows a woman standing and looking out of a window. We have to imagine something like this.

> As Jehu was entering the gate, she said, "Is it well, you Zimri, your master's murderer?" [Because he had killed the king already.] But he raised his eyes to the window, he Jehu raised his eyes to the window and said, "Who is on my side? Who?" At that two or three eunuchs peered out at him. "Let her drop," he said. So they let her drop, [so they throw her out the window] so that some of her blood spattered on the wall and on the horses, and he drove over her. And he went in and ate and drank.

So Jehu actually has Jezebel thrown out of the window of the palace. She splats down onto the pavement below and then he's in a horse with a chariot and he drives over her, over her body and then he goes in and he eats and drinks.

"Take care now of this cursed woman, and bury her, for she is a king's daughter," he said. He says okay she's a king's daughter we have to bury her. But when they went to bury her, they found no more other than the skull, the feet, and the palms of the hands. When, therefore, they returned and told him, he said, "This is the word of the Lord, which he spoke by his servant, Elijah the Tishbite, saying, 'In the territory of Jezreel shall the dogs eat the flesh of Jezebel, and the corpse of Jezebel shall be as dung on the face of the field in the territory of Jezreel.'"

Jezebel meets her end by being dropped out of the window, Jehu drives his chariot over her, and then so much of her is eaten by dogs, that there's nothing left to bury. And according to Jehu, as reported by the biblical writers, Jezebel then meets the end that she deserved and that was predicted for her by Elijah the prophet.

Ahab was the son of Omri. Omri was the one who established a dynasty that ruled over the northern Kingdom of Israel. This dynasty therefore is the Omride Dynasty. Ahab was a member of the Omride Dynasty. This dynasty was established by Omri in the first half of the 9th century.

One of the things that Omri did after he established this dynasty was to annex Moab. Moab remember is the territory on the eastern side of the Dead Sea. It was its own independent kingdom. Omri annexes the kingdom of Moab. Several decades later the king of Moab, who is being ruled by the Omride Dynasty and has to pay an annual tribute, rebelled against one of the Omrides, one of the kings of Israel, one of the successors of King Omri.

This episode is reported in the Hebrew Bible as follows. "Now Mesha, king of Moab, who raised sheep, used to pay the king of Israel as tribute a hundred thousand lambs and the wool of a hundred thousand rams. But when Ahab died, the king of Moab had rebelled against the king of Israel." So at some point in the 8th century the king of Moab who at this point is named Mesha rebels against the rule of the Omride Dynasty.

What is so interesting about this is this episode is on the one hand reported in the Hebrew Bible, but we also have archaeological evidence that confirms the story. This archaeological evidence takes the form of a large inscribed stone, or stele, called the Mesha Stone or the Mesha Stele. We've already talked about these big inscribed stones several times. We talked for example about the Merneptah Stele. We saw the remains of a stele that was found at Tel Dan that refers to the House of David.

What's the story with these big stele, with these big inscribed stones? They're basically the billboards of antiquity. There was no mass media in antiquity, so if you were a king and you wanted to broadcast your victory, you wanted to commemorate your victory, you would take a big stone slab and incise an inscription on it that recorded your victory. So the Mesha Stele is a victory stele recording Mesha's victory in this rebellion against the King of Israel.

The Mesha Stone was discovered in 1868 by a missionary who was wandering around in Jordan specifically at a site called Dibon, which is an ancient site. If you look at the stone you can see that it looks like it's in pieces, and in fact originally the stone was complete when it was found, but the local villagers thinking that gold was hidden inside smashed it. Fortunately before the stone was smashed by the villagers a squeeze had been made.

What's a squeeze? A squeeze is when you take a piece of paper and pound it over the inscription with water and you pull it up and you have the letters of the inscription then impressed into the piece of paper. So a squeeze had already been made, so we actually had the complete inscription even though the stone was smashed. The pieces of the stone were collected, put back together, and were taken to the Louvre in Paris where the stone is still on display today.

The stone is carved with a 34-line inscription that describes King Mesha's victory over the King of Israel and it dates to the middle of the 9th century B.C., roughly 840 BC. The inscription describes how Moab was oppressed by the King of Israel and then Mesha rebels and is victorious. It's again one of these kinds of victory commemorations inscribed on a stone slab. Let's take a look at a little bit of a relevant passage from this very important inscription.

"I am Mesha, son of Kemoshyat, the king of Moab, the Dibonite," so from Dibon. "My father was king of Moab thirty years, and I reigned after my father. ... Omri was king of Israel and he oppressed Moab for many days because Kemosh was angry with his land." And his son replaced him; and he also said, "I will oppress Moab." Several things before we go on to notice. Notice that it refers Omri originally annexing Moab, and now we're several generations later and Mesha is now king. He's the son of a guy name Kemoshyat, and it says that Omri was able to take Moab, was able to oppress and annex Moab for many years because Kemosh was angry with his land.

Who's Kemosh? Kemosh was the national god of the Moabites, the patron deity of the Moabites, and notice that Mesha is the son of Kemoshyat. So he is the son of somebody who has a theophoric name, a name with the national deity as part of it.

"In my days," that is in the days of Mesha he spoke thus. "But I was victorious over him and in his house. And Israel suffered everlasting destruction. And Omri had conquered the land of Madaba, and he dwelt there during his reign and half the reign of his son, forty years. But Kemosh returned it in my days." So due to the favor of the god Kemosh, the Moabites are able to be successful in their rebellion against Israel.

The Mesha Stone then provides a nice little piece of extra biblical confirmation for an event, an episode that is referred to in the biblical account. The Mesha Stone brings us then into the 9th century B.C. In the 9th and 8th centuries B.C. the dominant power in the ancient Near East was Assyria. Assyria was based in the northern part of what is today Iraq, the northern part of Mesopotamia. As Assyria grew stronger and more powerful, they began to expand and extend their control further and further out until finally in the 8th century B.C. they launched a series of invasions into the area of the northern Kingdom of Israel.

In the year 722 BC, the Assyrians conquered the northern Kingdom of Israel. This is described as follows in the Hebrew Bible:

> Then the king of Assyria came up against the whole land, and went up to Samaria and besieged it for three years. In the ninth year of Hosea, the king of Assyria took Samaria and carried Israel away

captive to Assyria. ... So Israel was carried away out of their own land to Assyria, as it is to this day.

So notice in 722 B.C. the Assyrians conquer the northern Kingdom of Israel. It says that they take Samaria, which is the capital of the kingdom, and they force the inhabitants of Israel to leave their land and go into exile in Assyria.

This event, the exile of people of the northern Kingdom of Israel, is the source of the Ten Lost Tribes. The Ten Lost Tribes are those tribes and their descendents who were the inhabitants of the northern Kingdom of Israel who were sent into exile by the Assyrians in 722 B.C. and who we lose touch with afterwards. We lose track of them afterwards and so then they become according to tradition the Ten Lost Tribes.

After the Assyrian conquest of Israel, the Kingdom of Judah was then invaded 20 years later by the Assyrians. But as we saw under Hezekiah they were able to survive the Assyrian invasion and the Kingdom of Judah continued to exist, but the Kingdom of Israel was no more. This then sets us up now for talking about what daily life was like in Israel and Judah.

Fortifications and Cult Practices
Lecture 7

> One of [the silver amulets dating from 600 B.C.] is inscribed in part with the priestly benediction that is known from the book of Numbers: "The Lord bless you and keep you; the Lord make his face to shine upon you, and be gracious to you; the Lord lift up his countenance upon you, and give you peace."

In this lecture, we turn from the political histories of the kingdoms of Israel and Judah to consider some aspects of their everyday life, focusing specifically on their fortifications and on the religious practices of their populations.

Some of the most distinctive features of the biblical landscape are artificial mounds called tells. Most people think that tells basically consist of layers of one city on top of another. That's only partially true. Tells exist only in certain parts of the Near East, where in the Bronze Age, a certain type of defensive system called a glacis was common. Constructing a glacis involved digging a dry moat around a town, then piling the dirt from the moat to make a tall hill that either surrounded the town or formed the foundation on which it sat, encircled by a fortification wall. It was this glacis system that retained the layers of occupation as they accumulated over the centuries, forming tells.

One of the most intriguing archaeological sites related to religion is Kuntillet Ajrud, located in the northern Sinai.

The city walls had to have gates, which of necessity were well fortified. A distinctive Israelite gateway system found at several sites consists of a passage flanked by a series of three chambers. On the outside of the gate were two towers, and the actual passage itself was flanked with the three chambers, the projecting walls of which created spaces where large, heavy doors were hung. The purpose was to set up a series of doors that could be shut and that attackers would have to batter down one after the other.

Another archaeological feature of note is a 10th-century sanctuary in the frontier city of Arad. Outside of Jerusalem but within the kingdom of Judah, this sanctuary was dedicated to the worship of the God of Israel. It includes a courtyard altar made of mudbricks and unhewn fieldstones and three rooms, the innermost of which is referred to as the Holy of Holies. In the late 8th century, the altar went out of use; in the 7th century, the sanctuary was destroyed altogether, perhaps because of religious reforms instituted by King Josiah of Judah, who centralized worship in the Jerusalem temple.

Another example of correspondence between archaeological discoveries and the Hebrew Bible is a tomb from the 7th century B.C. in Jerusalem. The only unplundered ancient tomb in Jerusalem discovered by archaeologists, it contained two tiny silver amulets inscribed with texts found in the Hebrew Bible.

One of the most intriguing archaeological sites related to religion is **Kuntillet Ajrud**, located in the northern Sinai. The finds at Kuntillet Ajrud suggest strong ties with the northern kingdom of Israel. Inscriptions on pottery refer not only to the God of Israel but also to other deities, such as a figure called **Asherah**, who is mentioned in various places in the Hebrew Bible. Josiah's reforms required that the vessels made for Asherah in the temple be burned in the Kidron Valley and ground to powder.

Having talked about some aspects of daily life in the kingdoms of Israel and Judah, we are now ready to continue our story with the events after the Babylonian destruction of the kingdom of Judah and the beginning of the Babylonian Exile. ∎

Names to Know

Asherah: A name possibly designating the ancient female consort of the God of Israel.

Kuntillet Ajrud: Eighth-century Israelite cultic site in Sinai.

Questions to Consider

1. Based on archaeological and biblical evidence, how would you reconstruct Solomon's Temple?

2. What do you find surprising about the finds from Kuntillet Ajrud?

Fortifications and Cult Practices
Lecture 7—Transcript

We've spent a lot of time talking about the Kingdoms of Israel and Judah, what were the political events that affected these kingdoms, what are the history of these kingdoms. What I'd like to do now is turn to consider some aspects of everyday life in these kingdoms focusing specifically on fortifications and on cultic practices; that is the religious practices of the populations of these kingdoms and what do we know about that through archaeology.

What I'd like to do is start by looking at fortifications. First of all one of the most distinctive features of the biblical landscape are artificial mounds called "tells." Most people are familiar with tells from reading books like James Michener's *The Source*, which actually is the story of an excavation through a made up or imaginary tell, one of these artificial mounds. Most people think that tells are formed by accumulations of one city on the other; that is building a city over and over again in the same spot which creates this artificial mound so that eventually you get a big, tall kind of a hill which basically consists of layers of one city on top of the other. That's what most people think a tell is.

That's actually only partially true. It is true that a tell is made up of layers of occupation, one on top of the other. But it's not just the building of one city on top of another, because when you think about it for a minute, tells are found in various parts of the ancient Near East, in Palestine, and in some of the surrounding areas, but they're not found in other parts of the ancient world. Have you ever seen a tell in Italy? Have you ever seen a tell in other parts of Europe or for that matter elsewhere in the world? Weren't there other places around the world where you have continuously occupied spots where cities existed for centuries and even millennia, one on top of the other? Why don't we have tells in those places?

The fact of the matter is a tell is not formed just by layers of civilization one on top of the other in the same spot over the course of a long period. They are formed specifically because of something else that we find only in certain parts of the ancient Near East and that has to do with fortifications. Specifically in the Bronze Age a certain type of defensive system became common in certain parts of the Near East. This kind of defensive system is called a glacis. What it consists of is digging a dry moat around your town or village and using the dirt from the moat, piling it up into a tall hill that surrounds your village so that either your village is in a crater surrounded by this tall hill or your village sits on top of it. The entire thing then is surrounded by a fortification wall.

What you have to imagine then is if you are coming to one of these towns or villages that is surrounded by this kind of glacis system, you would come up, you would have a big, dry moat or a big, dry ditch, and then a steep slope plastered over to hold the dirt in place, and then at the top of that steep slope you would have fortification walls and the city or the town would be inside that. Tells are formed specifically by this kind of fortification system. It was the fortification system, the glacis, which kept the layers of debris, the layers of occupation, as they accumulated over the centuries within this form of a tell which actually formed the tell.

Cities or towns that were fortified or established after this kind of fortification system went out of use, do not have the form of a tell, for example Caesarea Maritima, a classical site that we'll be spending a lot of time talking about, is not in the form of a tell even though it was occupied for centuries. Because Caesarea was not established until long after the glacis system of fortification had become obsolete.

One of the interesting things by the way about this kind of glacis system is why, in fact, did it appear? Whenever you see a certain type of defensive system introduced, it always reflects the answer, the response, to the introduction of a particular type of offensive warfare. Scholars debate what kind of offensive warfare was the glacis built in response to, was this kind of defensive system built in response to?

Let's look at it for a minute. You have this very steep plastered slope that's very smooth and slippery with the city wall on top. It could be a response to several things. One possibility that it's a response to battering rams because it would be very difficult to get a battering ram up to the top in order to break through the city wall. Another possibility, it was introduced in response to the introduction of the horse and chariot, very hard to get your horse and chariot to climb up that steep, smooth slope.

Another possibility, it was in response to mining; that is the idea is that you made it hard for the enemy to dig underneath the city wall, the fortification wall, and thereby cause the wall to collapse and enable the enemy to get into the fortifications. Basically the glacis then is a type of defensive system that is introduced in response to a specific type of offensive system of warfare. Any time you see a tell in the Near East you know that that site has this kind of fortification system.

The walls which surrounded the top of a defensive system like the glacis, these city walls of course had to have gates in them because you have to allow for people to get in and out. Gates were always the weakest part of a defensive system in any city. The gate is the easiest place to get into, and so there's always a concern with making sure that your gate if very well fortified, so you fortify it with towers for example so you can post people to fire down on anybody who is trying to approach to the gate and so on and so forth.

In the Israelite period, that is under Israelite rule, we have a very particular and distinctive kind of gateway system that is found at several sites. In fact, this kind of gateway system is found at three sites that are known to have been fortified by King Solomon. The late Yigael Yadin, the great Israeli archaeologist who was also Chief of Staff of the Israeli Army and was very interested in military history and ancient warfare, he's the one who noticed that we have a correspondence between the same kind of gateway found at three sites that are found in Solomonic levels and a passage in the Hebrew Bible which describes Solomon fortifying these three sites.

Specifically the passage is from 1 Kings and it reads as follows: "Solomon used forced labor to build the house of the Lord and his own house, the Millo and the wall of Jerusalem, Hazor, Megiddo, and Gezer." Notice the last three sites, Hazor, Megiddo, and Gezer, all of these we've talked about as originally having been Canaanite sites that eventually then were settled by the Israelites and in this biblical passage Solomon fortifies all three of them.

He noticed that at all three we have identical types of gateways and levels that can be associated with the time of Solomon. This particular gateway is very interesting because what it consists of is a passage that is flanked by a series of rooms on either side, specifically three rooms on each side of the passage. In fact, this kind of gateway also seems to be alluded to in the book of Ezekiel where it says, "There were three recesses on either side of the east gate; the three were of the same size."

So what do we have here? How did this kind of gate operate? What is the sense in this kind of gateway? First of all let me mention what we're actually looking at in terms of archaeological remains are the foundations, the stone foundations of the gate, and the rest of the gate either would've been built of stone that has not survived or of other material such as mud brick.

In fact at Tel Dan we have a complete surviving mud brick example of a gate that's very similar to this type of gate where the mud bricks were buried later on and so were preserved. Ordinarily mud bricks are not preserved, but at Tel Dan in this case because of the circumstances, the mud bricks of the rest of the gate above the foundations were preserved. We also have an Iron Age gate at Arad, in Israelite period gate at Arad, that is very similar to this type of gate, which has the chambers flanking the central passage.

What is the sense of this? What you have on the outside of the gate are two towers projecting so you could station your soldiers and maybe artillery or whatever to fire down on anybody who's trying to approach. Then you have the actual passage itself with the three chambers on each side.

What is the sense of the three chambers? The chambers are created by walls, projecting walls, that come out. You have a chamber, walls here, walls here, next chamber, walls, next chamber, walls, the projecting walls that create the chambers were places where there were originally doors. You have to imagine big, heavy, wooden doors maybe covered with metal or something like that, but big, heavy, wooden doors. The idea here is that you are setting up a series of successive doors that can be shut. So one door, two door, three door, four doors, there were four successive doors, one after the other. If you have an enemy attacking your gate, and let's imagine that they've hauled up a battering ram and they're trying to batter through the gate. They get through one door and then guess what, they've got another one they've got to batter through, and they get through that and there's another one.

You set up a series of barriers one after the other. Not only that, but in the chambers in the rooms between the doors you can have soldiers waiting, so that if they manage to get through one of the doors the soldiers are there to attack them and to keep them from going any further. So it's a defensive measure. These gates in other words were created in a way that protected, defended as strongly as possible the gate, the entrance to the city, which by definition is always the weakest part of the city's defenses.

One example of a gate of this type is found at Arad. Arad is a biblical site that is located in the southern part of the country. In fact it's in the northern Negev Desert. There's a much earlier site at Arad from the early Bronze Age, but what we are interested in is an Iron Age fortress at Arad. At Arad in the Iron Age, in the Israelite period, there was a fortress. Why was there a fortress at Arad? By the way this was at the southern part of the biblical kingdom and to the south, much further south of course was Egypt. We're basically looking at a kind of a frontier area here when we talk about Arad. At Arad we have a fortification system with a gateway similar to the type that we just looked at, but there's actually something even more interesting in the Israelite fortress at Arad and that is a sanctuary, a sanctuary that was built around the 10th century B.C., which means that it's built somewhere around the time of Solomon or maybe a little bit after Solomon and which existed then for the next couple of centuries.

Because Arad was an Israelite site located in Judah, what we have here then is an example apparently of a sanctuary outside of Jerusalem in the Kingdom of Judah that is dedicated to the worship of the God of Israel. This is something that we talked about in the last lecture, this idea of centralization of the cult versus decentralization of the cult. The cult of the God of Israel was not always centralized in Jerusalem. There was a time when there were sanctuaries and shrines around the countryside, not only in Israel but also in Judah. What we are looking at here in Arad is one of these countryside sanctuaries dedicated to the God of Israel.

What did the sanctuary here consist of? It actually consisted of the series of three elements, one after the other, starting first of all with an open courtyard that had an altar located in it that we will talk about, then three rooms, number one a hall or a broad room, a broad room means that the access is along the width rather than the length, a sanctuary consisting of a room with a small niche in it and the niche faced west, and the niche itself which was apparently the holy of holies.

Let's take a look now at the altar in the open courtyard. Before you have the actual three rooms you have this open courtyard with an altar and the altar at Arad measures 5 by 5 cubits, it's a square, which is about 2-1/2 by 2-1/2 meters. It was made of bricks, mud bricks, and unhewn field stones. That means stones that were simply picked up off of the ground and not cut at all. They're not cut at all; they're just taken as they are and built into the altar. The upper surface of this altar was plastered and had a channel to drain the blood of the sacrifices.

What's very interesting is that the way that this altar is constructed corresponds with the biblical injunction about building altars of unhewn stones. Specifically Exodus says that altars to Yahweh must be built out of unhewn stones, "for if you use a chisel upon it you profane it." In other words this altar in the Arad temple is built in accordance with the biblical law that we see in Exodus.

What do we see in the temple itself? The three successive rooms with the innermost room being this little niche that faces west that is apparently the holy of holies. In this niche, we see three steps that led to a raised platform. On top of the platform, there were three stele, three standing stones, not carved with anything. They didn't have any inscriptions or designs on them; what is called in Hebrew matzevah, a matzevah is the Hebrew term for a stele, matzevot is the plural.

This by the way we call something that we looked at way back when we talked about the Canaanites and their worship and looked at Hazor and saw a shrine dedicated to the Moon God with a bunch of standing stones. This is very common in the ancient Near East and especially in the area of Palestine to erect these sort of stele depicting apparently or referring to different gods, intended to symbolize different gods, and one of the stele was still plastered and painted red.

In addition to the stele at the top of the platform, there were two incense altars made out of stone on the lowest step. Burnt organic matter was found on top of these stone incense altars. They were actually used.

The sanctuary here at Arad was constructed in the 10th century B.C., so roughly around the time of Solomon or maybe a little later, and continued to function for a couple of hundred years. In the late 8th century, the altar went out of use. This may be connected with Hezekiah's reforms; so Hezekiah's attempts to centralize the cult. It may be at that time that the altar in the Arad temple went out of use, and then in the 7th century the sanctuary was destroyed altogether, and this apparently is connected with religious forms instituted by one of the kings of Judah whose name was Josiah.

Now what I'd like to do is consider what do we mean when we talk about Josiah's religious reforms, exactly what did Josiah do? Josiah was the King of Judah from about 640 BC until the year 609 BC. He is credited in the Hebrew Bible with instituting a reform that is described as the Deuteronomistic reform. What do we mean by Deuteronomistic? It is the reform associated with the introduction of laws recorded in Deuteronomy, the last of the Five Books of Moses. The term Deuteronomy actually is a Greek term which means the second law. What Deuteronomy does, what this book of Deuteronomy does, is it actually reiterates or repeats many of the laws that appear in the earlier Four Books of Moses.

One of the points of the Deuteronomistic reform was to eliminate the worship of other gods; that is to institute absolute exclusive Yahwism, and to centralize the cult of the God of Israel in the Jerusalem temple, that is to eliminate all of the countryside or all of the shrines and the temples were located in the countryside outside of Jerusalem, such as the one we just looked at in the Arad fortress.

How did Josiah actually do this? According to the biblical description what he did was institute these reforms as the result of a discovery. The story goes that he was having repairs done on the Jerusalem temple, and in the course of repairs a priest found a previously unknown book, one of the Five Books of Moses, a previously unknown book of law and this then is the book of Deuteronomy, and as 2 Kings says, "The high priest Kikiah informed the scribe Shaphan," remember by the way Gemaryah who is son of Shaphan, "I have found the book of law in the temple of the Lord."

What happens then the story goes is that they bring the book out, they read it to the people, and one of the points of this is then to institute these reforms centralizing the cult in the Jerusalem temple and eliminating the worship of other god other than the God of Israel. So as 2 Kings says, "He [Josiah] put an end to the false priests whom the kings of Judah had appointed to burn incense on the high places in the cities of Judah and in the vicinity of Jerusalem."

According to this account then, Josiah eliminates the sanctuaries and shrines that are outside of Jerusalem and also in the vicinity of Jerusalem leaving only the Jerusalem temple. It's apparently against this background then that the sanctuary at Arad that we just looked at, that temple at Arad, is destroyed in the 7th century.

We also have other evidence for an Israelite cult in the form of horned altars. Horned altars have been found in a number of sites, for example at Beersheba and at Megiddo. This is very interesting because we also know about horned altars from the Hebrew Bible. For example, according to biblical law it was permitted to seek sanctuary in a sacred place. If you were a refuge seeking sanctuary you could seek sanctuary and be safe if you went to let's say a temple.

So in 1 Kings we have a description, a reference to Solomon's older brother, Adonijah, and Joash, David's general "grasping the horns of the altar" in the tent of the Lord when they feared deadly retribution from Solomon. So here we have a reference to people seeking sanctuary in "the tent of the Lord by grasping the horns of the altar" and lo and behold we actually have archaeological remains of horned altars from Israelite contexts.

Another example of correspondence between archaeological discoveries and biblical descriptions of religion is a discovery from a late Iron Age tomb in Jerusalem. That is a tomb that dates to the 7th century B.C. in Jerusalem. It's a rock cut tomb. We will be talking about rock cut tombs a lot more later in the course. Specifically this is a tomb that is located northwest of the city of Jerusalem, outside the walls of the ancient city, at a site called Ketef Hinnom.

This is a tomb that was discovered and excavated in 1980 by an Israeli archaeologist and in fact it's the only example of an ancient tomb in Jerusalem that was discovered by archaeologists unplundered. It still had all of its original goods in the tomb. It had not been looted by anybody. Among the objects that were found in this tomb were two tiny little silver amulets, very thin beaten sheaths of silver that were rolled up in the form of teeny little scrolls which probably were originally worn as amulets either maybe as a necklace or a bracelet or something like that.

When these little silver amulets were unrolled they were found to be inscribed in biblical Hebrew script and in biblical Hebrew language. One of them is inscribed in part with the priestly benediction that is known from the book of Numbers, "The Lord bless you and keep you; the Lord make his face to shine upon you, and be gracious to you; the Lord lift up his countenance upon you, and give you peace." This little passage which is called the priestly benediction is inscribed on one of these little silver amulets which dates to let's say around 600 B.C.

It is the earliest example that we have of an object inscribed with a passage that is included in the Hebrew Bible. So very close to the time the Hebrew Bible was actually being edited and written down, this inscription is found on this silver amulet.

One of the most intriguing archaeological sites that we have related to cult and religion from the Israelite period, from the Iron Age, is the site called Kuntillet Ajrud, kind of a strange name to remember, but anyway that's the name of the site. It is a small site that dates to the early 8th century B.C., so a little after 900, located in the northern Sinai. It's really pretty way out there compared to the other sites that we've been talking about. It's much farther way, northern Sinai.

Exactly what is this site? It has been excavated. It seems to have been some sort of a religious center, maybe a wayside shrine, maybe caravans going by, people would stop here and there was some sort of a cult or worship going on here. And the nature of the finds at Kuntillet Ajrud suggest strong ties with the northern Kingdom of Israel. So perhaps this wayside shrine was established by one of the kings of Israel.

What do we have from Kuntillet Ajrud that's so interesting and so connected with religion and cult? The finds include plaster that was on the walls of the buildings that are painted with different kinds of figures that we're going to look at, pottery vessels that are inscribed with Hebrew inscriptions and drawings, and by the way clearly then we're talking about an Israelite population here at the site because the inscriptions are in Hebrew. Here are some of the drawings that were found on large jars called pithoi and what they include are two figures resembling the Egyptian god Bes, which are these kind of almost grotesque figures, with a lyre player nearby and five figures raising their hands in prayer. In addition to the figures resembling the Egyptian god Bes and the lyre player, there is also a cow licking the tail of a calf.

The Hebrew inscriptions on the wall plaster and pottery vessels from Kuntillet Ajrud include a whole series of very, very interesting and somewhat puzzling inscriptions. For example, "your days may be prolonged and you shall be satisfied, give Yahweh of Teman and his Asherah, Yahweh of Teman and his Asherah favored." "And when El rose up and hills melted and peaks were pounded ... bless Ba'al in day of war ... the name of El in day of war." "A[shy]o the K[ing] said: tell x, y, and z, may you be blessed by Yahweh of Shomron," that is Samaria, "and his Asherah."

Well, huh, what does this all mean? This is very interesting because remember what we see here apparently reflects northern influence and we have a reference indeed to Samaria here. Remember the principle of inclusive versus exclusive Yahwism that you may worship Yahweh but also other gods alongside him. That seems to be what we see here. So we have references not only to Yahweh, to this deity who was the God of Israel, and by Israel I mean the god of all of the Israelite tribes and their descendents, but also references to other deities. For example, something called an Asherah, which we'll talk about in just a minute.

Notice a reference to Baal, the Canaanite deity, and very interesting the name El. El actually occurs as the name of the God of Israel as a name of the God of Israel in the Hebrew Bible. But El was also a name of one of the Canaanite gods. In this context actually it's not clear to my mind whether the reference is necessarily to the Canaanite god El or to the Israelite god who here is being called El.

Another very interesting thing to notice is that Yahweh, the God of Israel here, is described in different ways. We have a Yahweh of Teman and we have a Yahweh of Samaria for example. What exactly does this mean? In the Hebrew Bible when we read about the God of Israel being worshiped in Jerusalem, it's always he is the god who dwells in Jerusalem. But if we imagine a situation where there are different sanctuaries or temples to Yahweh in different places, decentralized cult, then literally the Yahweh worshiped in those different places would be called accordingly. The Yahweh of Shomron would be the Yahweh worshiped in a temple or sanctuary in Shomron versus the one who dwells in his temple in Jerusalem, or the Yahweh of Teman would be a Yahweh worshiped in a place called Teman.

What is Teman? We don't know by the way. Is it the name of Kuntillet Ajrud? Is it the name of another site? Is it a generic name for the southern part of the country? We don't know. To my mind it's probably a site, a city, not a general area, but scholars dispute this. At any rate what we see here is a picture that is quite different than what we would expect from what we know of the early Israelites in the sense that we have a very fluid picture with the worship of different gods and goddesses and different aspects of the God of Israel, of Yahweh, and he's a Yahweh of Teman, he's a Yahweh of Shomron or Samaria. It's really not this nice homogenous neat little picture that we have in our minds of what the early Israelites were doing.

So who is this Asherah who is mentioned in the Kuntillet Ajrud inscriptions? This isn't the only place where we hear about a figure called Asherah. In fact Asherah is mentioned in various places in the Hebrew Bible. What I want to do now is examine a rather long passage associated with Josiah's reforms that discuss or describe Asherah. Let's see here what the Hebrew Bible says.

> Then the king [Josiah] commanded Hilkiah, the high priest ... to bring out of the Temple of the Lord all the vessels that were made for the Baal and the Asherah and for the host of the heavens; and he burned them outside Jerusalem in the limekilns by the Kidron, and carried away their ashes to Bethel. He also did away with the idolatrous priests, whom the kings of Israel had offered sacrifices in the high places in the cities of Judah and in the sanctuaries around Jerusalem; and to those who offered sacrifices to the Baal, to the sun, the moon, and the constellations, and all the host of the heavens. Moreover he brought the Asherah from the House of the Lord outside Jerusalem to the Kidron Valley and burned it in the Kidron Valley, and ground it to powder, and cast the powder of it upon the graves of the common people.

Obviously what Josiah is doing here is he's doing away with something that's called an Asherah. The Asherah in this passage seems to be associated with the Baal, but we have other places where Asherah is sometimes associated with the God of Israel as we see in Kuntillet Ajrud. Some scholars think that Asherah, the term Asherah, refers to the royal consort of a male deity. Baal had an Asherah, a female consort or a wife, and perhaps some early Israelites imagined the God of Israel as having a female consort in Asherah. This was very typical in the ancient world for a male deity to have a female consort.

Think for example the Greek Zeus whose wife is Hera. It may in fact be and we may have evidence here suggesting that just like other ancient peoples, at least some early Israelites conceived of their national god as having a female consort and this female consort then is referred to at least sometimes by the name Asherah. This is precisely the sort of practice that we see reflected in those female fertility figurines that we looked at when we talked about the City of David.

We have now talked about some aspects of daily life in the Kingdoms of Israel and Judah. This now sets the stage then for continuing with our story of what happens after the Babylonian destruction of the Kingdom of Judah in the year 586 B.C. and the beginning of the Babylonian exile.

Babylonian Exile and the Persian Restoration
Lecture 8

The Persian Empire was one of the most enlightened and tolerant empires of the ancient world. In contrast, for example, to the Assyrians and the Babylonians, the Persians allowed exiled peoples to return to their homelands.

In 586 B.C., the Babylonians destroyed Jerusalem and the First Temple, ending the Old Testament period, or what is also known as the biblical period of archaeology. Yet just 60 or 65 years later, the Second Temple was built on the Temple Mount in Jerusalem. In the interval, the exiles from Jerusalem dwelt in Babylon, where their response to their situation varied. On the one hand, as we see in Psalm 137, these exiles yearned for their homeland and Jerusalem. On the other hand, the prophet Jeremiah sent a letter to the exiles, encouraging them to make a life for themselves in Babylon and be content. In fact, the Jews who lived in exile became quite well assimilated among the local people. Nevertheless, they retained their separate identity, continuing to worship the God of Israel.

The Jews who lived in exile became quite well assimilated among the local people.

It wasn't too long after the destruction of Jerusalem that another power, Persia, became dominant in the ancient Near East. Immediately after capturing Babylon, the Persian ruler, Cyrus the Great, issued an edict in 539 B.C. allowing the exiles to return to Jerusalem and rebuild the temple on the Temple Mount. The homeland they returned to was divided up into Persian administrative units called *medinot* (singular: ***medinah***). The district around Jerusalem was a *medinah* called **Yahud** (i.e., Judah or Judea). To the north was a *medinah* called Samaria, the heart of what had been the northern kingdom of Israel. What had been the kingdom of Ammon was governed by a Judean named Tobias. Into this political context, the Persians sent a man named Nehemiah to govern the *medinah* called Yahud. Nehemiah was, in fact, a Judean who had attained high office in the Persian administration and had requested permission from the Persian king to be sent to Jerusalem to rebuild the city. The city that he rebuilt is small in size and population, but it included the Temple Mount with the Second Temple, consecrated in the year 516 B.C.

As Nehemiah rebuilt Jerusalem, Ezra the scribe arrived, sent by the Persian king to implement Jewish law as the law of the land. The structure of the society that he addressed was different from the one that had existed before the destruction of the city. Instead of tribes, clans or families return from exile in Babylon, and we note a new emphasis on genealogy. While in exile, these families had documented their lineage. The scribe Ezra assembled all the people together and proclaimed that anyone who had married a non-Israelite wife had to leave her. This is the first time we see a prohibition against intermarriage in Judaism.

The Jewish prohibition against exogamy began in the time of Ezra.

In competition with the returning exiles in Jerusalem, the people living in the north who had survived the earlier Assyrian conquest claimed to be the true Israel. They were not allowed to participate in rebuilding the temple in Jerusalem and worshiping the God of Israel in Jerusalem because the purity of their bloodlines was suspect. Instead, they decided to worship the God of Israel on a mountain located in the heart of the district of Samaria, called **Mount Gerizim**. These northerners eventually became known as the **Samaritans**. In the next lecture, we will examine the conquest of Alexander the Great. ■

Important Terms

medinah (pl. **medinot**): Smaller administrative districts within Persian satrapies.

Mount Gerizim: Sacred mountain of the Samaritans, overlooking biblical Shechem (modern Nablus).

Samaritans: Descendants of the population of the former kingdom of Israel who claimed descent from the old Joseph tribes (Ephraim and Manasseh).

Yahud: The Persian medinah of Judea.

Questions to Consider

1. Compare and contrast the policies toward conquered populations of the Assyrians and Babylonians, on the one hand, and the policies of the Persians, on the other. What do you think were the rationales that motivated these policies, and which kind of policy do you think was more effective in the long term?

2. What were the reasons behind and consequences of Ezra's ban on intermarriage?

Babylonian Exile and the Persian Restoration
Lecture 8—Transcript

In 586 B.C. the Babylonians destroyed Jerusalem and Solomon's temple on the Temple Mount bringing to an end the Old Testament period, what we often refer to as the biblical period of archaeology in Palestine and the end of the First Temple period. 586 BC therefore marks a cutoff point and marks the beginning of a period that we refer to as the Babylonian exile in Jewish history. Just 60 to 65 years later the Second Temple is built on the Temple Mount in Jerusalem marking the beginning of the Second Temple period.

From this point on we're going to be leaving the so-called biblical period and entering what in Jewish terms is called the post-biblical period and the Second Temple period which will occupy us now for a number of lectures. The Hebrew Bible describes the destruction of Jerusalem and Solomon's temple by the Babylonians as follows.

> In the fifth month, on the seventh day of the month—this was in the nineteenth year of King Nebuchadnezzar, king of Babylon—Nebuzaradan, the commander of the guard and a servant of the king of Babylon, came to Jerusalem and burned the House of the Lord and the King's House; and all the houses of Jerusalem.

Notice according to this description, the Babylonians destroy the "House of the Lord" which is Solomon's temple, the King's House, which is the palace by the temple on the Temple Mount, and all the houses of Jerusalem. What happens then is that the Babylonians capture the king of Judah, whose name is Zedekiah trying to escape from Jerusalem under cover of night. What do they do when they capture him and here is what the Bible says.

"Then they took the king and brought him up to the king of Babylon at Riblah; and they pronounced judgment against him. They also slew the sons of Zedekiah before his eyes and put out his eyes and bound him in fetters and carried him to Babylon." So what happens here is that the king of Judah is captured trying to escape and what do the Babylonians do? Before they blind him they kill his sons before his very eyes so that's the very last thing that he sees and then he's taken away into captivity in Babylon.

What happens then is that the Babylonians send the Judeans into exile in Babylon. So the population of Judah is sent into exile in Babylon now marking the beginning of the Babylonian exile. We have a number of documents that describe this period of the Babylonian exile.

For example Psalm 137 which reads, "By the rivers of Babylon, there we sat down, and wept, when we remembered Zion," when we remembered Jerusalem. "How could we sing the songs of the Lord in a foreign land?" How can we worship, in other words the God of Israel, in a foreign land? "If I forget you, O Jerusalem, may my right hand fail me! May my tongue cleave to my palate, if I do not remember you; if I set not Jerusalem above my highest joy!"

On the one hand we see here the yearning of these exiles in Babylonia for their homeland and for the city of Jerusalem. On the other hand we have for example a description in Jeremiah of the Babylonian exile as follows:

> These are the words of the letter which Jeremiah the prophet sent from Jerusalem to the elders among the exiles, and to the priest, the prophets, and all the people whom Nebuchadnezzar had carried into exile from Jerusalem to Babylon. ... Thus says the Lord of Hosts, the God of Israel, to all the exiles whom I carried into exile from Jerusalem to Babylon: "Build houses, and live in them; plant vineyards, and eat the fruit of them; take wives, and beget sons and daughters."

This passage from Jeremiah is very interesting because what it suggests is that Jeremiah is encouraging the exiles to settle in Babylon to make a life for themselves there and to be content. In fact that's exactly what happened. Many Jews did become very well-established in Babylonia, which was a very wealthy place to live. It was an easy lifestyle. They got settled. They began to buy houses, get jobs, and raise their children there. Basically what we have then is a period when the Jews are living in exile in Babylonia, but are really quite well assimilated among the local people.

What happens then with the Jews living in Babylonia is several interesting things. On the one hand although they did settle down and assimilate and build houses and get jobs and raise their children. They did nevertheless retain their separate identity continuing to worship the God of Israel. We know that the Jewish community in Babylonia was led by elders, apparently older people with some authority and apparently the editing of the authoritative text of the Hebrew Bible took place at this time; and by authoritative text of the Hebrew Bible I mean the Pentateuch, that is the Five Books of Moses and the books of the Former Prophets, Joshua, Judges, Samuel, and Kings.

It is also in Babylonia that we might have the origin of the institution of the synagogue, something that we will be talking about a little later in this course. The synagogue basically might have originated in Babylonia because it would've enabled these Jews living in exile to preserve their Jewish identity and to continue worshiping the God of Israel as their national deity. So many scholars think that perhaps the synagogue as an institution began to develop during the period of the Babylonian exile.

The Babylonian Empire was the dominant empire in the ancient Near East in the late 7th century and early 6th century B.C. But it wasn't too long after that that another that another power began to strengthen and that is Persia, the area that corresponds with modern day Iran. Remember that Babylonia was centered in the southern part of what is today Iraq or ancient Mesopotamia.

During the course of the 6th century B.C., Persia became stronger and stronger until finally Persia became the dominant power in the ancient Near East taking over Babylonia and also taking over many other countries as well. Eventually the Persians established a vast empire that stretched all the way from the area of southern Russia on the east through Asia Minor; that is modern Turkey, and up to Greece on the west. In fact, many people are familiar with the Persian Empire because in 490 and 480 BC the Persians mounted invasions of mainland Greece in which they were beaten back by the Greeks. It was in fact the defeat of the Persians by the Greeks that led to the ascendency of Athens as the dominant city-state in Greece in the 5th century B.C.

That actually lies a little bit outside of our story because the territory that we are talking about, the area of the Holy Land, remained under Persian rule throughout this period. In the 5th century B.C. while we have the classical period in Greece with the construction of the buildings on top of the acropolis and so on, while all of that is going on in Greece, the Holy Land is under the rule of the Persian Empire.

The Persians get kind of a bad rap in western history because of the invasion of Greece, but in fact the Persian Empire was one of the most enlightened and tolerant empires of the ancient world. In contrast, for example, to the Assyrians and the Babylonians who dealt with conquered peoples by forcing them to go into exile, the Persians did just the opposite. They allowed exiled peoples to return to their homelands, and this is actually a very interesting difference here.

The idea or the goal of these different policies was the same, to create a way of dealing with powerful local elites. The Assyrians and the Babylonians dealt with native elites, native power bases, by forcing them to go into exile thereby uprooting the native power bases and replacing them with their own people.

The Persians did just the opposite. They allowed exiled peoples to return to their homelands figuring that this would make them happy and content and less likely to rebel. In fact that's exactly what happened. That is during the vast period and space of the Persian Empire there are almost no native rebellions against Persian rule with the exception of a Greek rebellion that was actually provoked by the mainland Greeks. So the rest of the peoples living under Persian rule apparently were quite content, and it's within this context then that the Persians grant the exiled Judeans in Babylonia permission to return to their homeland.

This occurs during the rule of a Persian king named Cyrus who issues an edict in 539 B.C. allowing the Judeans to return to Jerusalem and rebuild the temple on the Temple Mount. Here is how this edict appears in the book of Ezra. "Now in the first year of Cyrus, king of Persia, that the word of the Lord by the mouth of Jeremiah might be accomplished, the Lord stirred up the spirit of Cyrus, king of Persia, to issue a proclamation throughout all his kingdom and also to put it in writing, as follows:" Very interesting by the way, notice that the way that the Hebrew Bible puts it, it's as though God, the God of Israel caused Cyrus to issue this edict. It's the act of God actually, not the act of Cyrus.

This is what Ezra says, "Thus says Cyrus, king of Persia: All the kingdoms of the earth has the Lord, the God of the heavens, given me, and he has commissioned me to build him a house in Jerusalem which is in Judah." A house in Jerusalem meaning a house dedicated to the God of Israel, i.e. a temple. "Whoever this is among you of all his people who desires to go, his God be with him; let him go up to Jerusalem, which is in Judah, and build the House of the Lord, the God of Israel, since he is the God who is in Jerusalem."

With this proclamation then the Judeans are allowed to return from exile in Babylonia and build a new temple dedicated to the God of Israel on the Temple Mount in Jerusalem. Notice this passage describes the God of Israel as the God who is in Jerusalem. This is specifically the God of Israel who dwells in Jerusalem, recalling when we talked about Kuntillet Ajrud for example in the last lecture, recalling the way that the God of Israel is variously described, Yahweh is variously described, in different locations, Yahweh of Teman, Yahweh of Samaria. Here we have the God who was in Jerusalem.

We actually have an extra biblical text which also describes edicts by Cyrus. This extra biblical text happens to be a cylinder made of clay that is impressed with cuneiform script, and it has an edict on it in which Cyrus grants various peoples permission to return to their homelands. This is not specifically the edict allowing the Judeans to return, but it is an edict which allows various peoples to return to their homelands. It's very interesting because this is an edict that's issued by Cyrus himself whereas in Ezra what we have is the Hebrew Bible's version of an edict by Cyrus.

What does this edict say?

> I am Cyrus, king of the world ... from as far as the settlements on the other side of the Tigris, where their temples have long lain in ruin, I returned the gods who lived therein to their places and provided them with permanent temples. I gathered all their inhabitants and returned them to their homes.

He's basically describing here how he then gathers together all of these exiled peoples and all of these exiled gods and allows them to return to their homes. "Daily, may all the gods whom I have brought back to their holy sites speak on my behalf for long life and plead my favor before Bel and Nebo."

Actually Cyrus apparently has a little bit of self-interest here in allowing these temples to be built to their native gods in their homelands in seeking the favor of these gods. He's hoping well I allowed these peoples to return to rebuild these temples to their gods and now hopefully these gods will grant me favor; a little bit of self-interest there.

The Persian Empire was a vast empire, it's a huge area and how do you administer a kingdom, an empire that is this big. An analogy would be in the United States today such a big place, of course it's subdivided into smaller administrative units. We have the subdivision of the 50 states, and then within the states subdivisions and counties, and then within counties townships and so on and so forth. So it was with the Persian Empire.

Because it was so big it was subdivided into smaller administrative units for the purposes of effective government. The largest subdivisions of the Persian Empire analogous to the states in the United States, but much bigger geographically speaking were called satrapies, and each one of these satrapies was governed by a satrap. The area that we're talking about, the Holy Land, was part of a very large satrapy, which was called Ebernari. It's an Aramaic word, which means the land beyond the river. Why the land beyond the river? Because from the point of view of the Persians who were over in Iran, the area of Judea is the land beyond the Tigress and Euphrates Rivers to the west of the river, so we're the land beyond the river.

Each one of these satrapies then was subdivided into smaller units called medinot, singular medinah, which might be analogous to like a county within a state, and the area that we're talking about, the area of ancient Palestine, then was divided into a number of these sort of counties or medinot. I'd like to take a look at these medinot because the subdivisions that we have here are going to remain in effect for centuries afterwards even though the governments will change. The basic subdivisions will more or less remain the same and in fact many of these subdivisions go back to the Iron Age as we'll see.

What happens then with the subdivision of Palestine? The area that had been the core of the Kingdom of Judah before 586 B.C., that is the district around Jerusalem becomes known as a medinah called Yahud, which is basically Judah or Judea. To the north of Yahud, to the north of Judea, is a medinah called Samaria, which is of course the core, the heart of what had been the biblical kingdom of Israel, the northern Kingdom of Israel before 722 B.C. What we have now, notice by the way, is a district called Samaria which is centered on a city called Samaria, the city of Samaria had been the capital of the ancient biblical Kingdom of Israel, so we have two Samarias, the city of Samaria and that city then gives its name to the surrounding district or medinah.

The area that had been biblical Edom, before 586 B.C., Edom had been a kingdom on the southeast side of the Dead Sea, the area near Petra today in Jordan. What happens after 586 B.C. is that some of the inhabitants of the biblical kingdom of Edom, that is some of those Edomites, cross the area around the southern end of the Dead Sea and settle in the southern part of what had been the Kingdom of Judah. These people are now known as Idumaeans and this district becomes known as Idumaea. So the district to the south of Judea is now known as Idumaea. The area of the biblical Kingdom of Ammon, around modern day Amman, is now a district that is governed by a Jewish, that is Judean, dynasty called the Tobiads, that is governed by a Judean named Tobias and his descendents who were called the Tobiads.

If you look at the map you will see that the coastal plane is not part of any of the districts. Instead it is divided into a series of narrow strips, and this is actually a very interesting story too. These strips of the coastal plane were under the rule of the Phoenicians. The Phoenicians are still up there to the north in the area of modern Lebanon. Because the Persians were a landlocked power, they needed the Phoenician naval power in order to fight the Greeks because the Greeks were also a naval power.

What the Persians did was to grant the Phoenician cities a degree of semi-autonomy, semi-independence, and allowed them to rule over the coastal plain of Palestine. The coastal plain is divided administratively between Phoenician cities. What happens now in Jerusalem? What happens is that under the Persians a man is sent to Jerusalem to govern the district of Judea, to govern Yahud, and this man is named Nehemiah.

Nehemiah was, in fact, a Judean who attained a very high office in the Persian administration, and was sent by the Persian king to be governor of Judea or Yahud. The book of Nehemiah describes Nehemiah being sent to Jerusalem as governor and it says as follows: "And I said to the king, 'If it please the king, and if your servant has found favor in your sight that you would send me to Judah, to the city of the graves of my ancestors, that I may rebuild it.'"

So Nehemiah requests permission from the Persian king to be sent to Jerusalem and to rebuild the city. So he is sent to Jerusalem and basically in the middle of the 5th century B.C. Nehemiah serves as governor of Yahud, and it's under him that the city of Jerusalem is rebuilt. When we look at a plan of Jerusalem what we see is that the city is now rebuilt, but it's very small in size. It looks pretty much like it did under David and Solomon consisting only of the City of David and the Second Temple on the Temple Mount, which is consecrated in the year 516 B.C.

The western hill is not part of the Persian city of Jerusalem. There's nobody living on it. Why is the population so small? Because most of the Jews preferred to remain in Babylonia where they had already settled down rather than return to Judea and try and rebuild their lives from scratch. So the population that returned to Judea to rebuild was actually quite small, and so the city of Jerusalem in the Persian period is small as well.

At around the same time as Nehemiah rebuilds Jerusalem, Ezra arrives in Jerusalem as well. Who is Ezra? Ezra is sent as a scribe skilled in the law of Moses. Ezra is not a governor of the district of Jerusalem. What he is instead is a scribe, and he is actually sent by the Persian king to implement Jewish law as the law of the land. That is by the degree of the Persian king, the inhabitants of Judah were to observe Jewish law as their everyday law, the law of their lives.

This is actually a very interesting turning point that we have here. Before 586 B.C. the religion of the 12 tribes had been called Israelite religion. It was the religion of the 12 Israelite tribes. Now with Ezra coming to Jerusalem what we have is the beginning of what we call early Judaism, the beginning of the Jewish religion, referring to the religion of the Judean families who returned to Judea and who now come back from exile in Babylonia. We have to make a distinction between Israelite religion before 586 B.C. and Judaism, early Judaism after 596 B.C.

The structure of society is now different, instead of tribes what we have now are clans or families returning from exile in Babylonia. We see this emphasis on families and on genealogy reflected in the book of Ezra where we have a chapter that begins, "Now these are the heads of families and this is the genealogy of those who came up with me from Babylon in the reign of Artaxerxes the king." What had happened is that while the Jews, the Judeans were in exile in Babylonia, these families kept genealogies documenting their lineage.

This is going to become important because what happens is when Ezra gets to Jerusalem he assembles all of the people together and he tells them as follows: "Then all the men of Judah and Benjamin assembled in Jerusalem within the three days, and all the people sat in an open square in front of the House of God, trembling on account of the occasion itself and also because of the pouring rain." It's a wonderful sentence by the way because you can just imagine they're out there and they're shivering because of the cold and the rain and they're waiting to hear what Ezra is going to say. Ezra of course is now going to tell them well this is the law that you have to observe as the law of the land.

> Thereupon Ezra the priest arose and said to them: "You have broken faith and have married foreign women to increase the guilt of Israel. Now therefore make your confession to the Lord, the God of your fathers, and do his will and separate yourselves from the peoples of the land and from the foreign wives."

This is very interesting because up until this point there was no prohibition in Judaism or in Israelite religion against intermarriage. This is the first time intermarriage is prohibited. Remember even King Solomon had many foreign wives. One of these ideals that these returning Judean exiles bring back with them is a very aristocratic notion that lineage and purity of bloodlines matter. One of the things that Ezra does is he assembles all of the people together and he says anyone who is intermarried, anyone who has married a non-Jewish, a non-Israelite wife has to leave their wives.

This is the first time that we see something like this. Probably some of those people did follow Ezra's orders, but not everybody was very happy with this new injunction, and remember Ezra is instituting here the law of the land on behalf of the Persian king.

Who does this create difficulties for? It creates difficulties actually not for the returning Judean exiles because they're the aristocratic, upper class people who had preserved the records of their bloodlines. Instead it creates problems for the lower class people who had not been sent into exile, because when we talk about the Assyrian exile and the Babylonian exile, it's not that the Assyrians and Babylonians forced everyone to leave the country and to go into exile. No, they uprooted the elite, the upper classes, because they were the ones who were in control and so the idea was to destroy the power base. The poorer people, the farmers and so on, they were left behind.

In the interim those poorer people who had been left behind, at least some of them, had intermarried with non-Jews or non-Israelites. This had happened to a much larger degree in what had been the northern Kingdom of Israel, the northern part of the country, which remember had fallen to the Assyrians in 722 B.C. So there's a very long interim here. In the meantime many of those remaining Israelites from the northern kingdom had intermarried, and when they come along and say well we're descendents of the Israelites, we want to participate in rebuilding the temple, Ezra says well no you have to divorce your foreign wives and you've intermarried and your bloodlines are no longer pure.

What happens now is that a schism is created between those people with pure bloodlines and those people who do not have pure bloodlines. A lot of this actually is based on class, upper class versus lower class, but it also goes back to the old north versus south dichotomy that we talked about that comes to the surface after the death of Solomon when the United Monarchy splits into two. This now leads us then into talking about what happens to those inhabitants of what had been the northern Kingdom of Israel when Ezra comes in and implements these laws.

These people living in the north actually claim to be the true Israel. We are in fact the original Israelites, they claimed. We have been here all along. We're descended from the old Joseph tribes in the north, from Ephraim and Manasseh. We are the true Israel, and yet they were not being allowed to participate in rebuilding the temple in Jerusalem and worshipping the God of Israel in Jerusalem because according to Ezra their bloodlines were not pure.

So what do they do? They decide that they are going to worship the God of Israel on their own sacred mountain, a mountain that is located in the heart of the district of Samaria, a mountain called Mount Gerizim. This population of the descendents of the northern Kingdom of Israel become known eventually as the Samaritans, and their major city then is a city that is at the foot of Mount Gerizim, a city that is called Shechem in the biblical period or in Hebrew Shechem, which is actually modern Neapolis in the heart of the West Bank today.

One of the main opponents of Nehemiah was the governor of Samaria whose name was Sanballat. In fact one of the things that happens is when Nehemiah comes to Jerusalem and starts to rebuild the walls, all of the other neighboring governors around start to get nervous because they didn't want Jerusalem and Judea to be more powerful than them. If you read the book of Nehemiah you see that one of his main opponents is this Sanballat who was the governor of Samaria.

Another one of his opponents was Tobiah who was the governor of Ammon. This is that Judean who was the governor of Ammon. In the book of Nehemiah then we have a description of the conflict between these various governors over the rebuilding of the wall of Jerusalem. We see that they tried to stop Nehemiah from rebuilding the walls, and there's a passage where it says Sanballat, Tobiah, and the Ashdodites, the people of Ashdod, hear that Nehemiah is trying to rebuild the walls of Jerusalem and they go forward and try to stop him from rebuilding the walls.

Nehemiah's opponent Sanballat was actually Sanballat I. Why do I say this? Because there were several Sanballats. There's another Sanballat, Sanballat III who is the grandson of Sanballat I and who lived at the time of Alexander the Great's conquest in 332 B.C. Why is this important? It's important because eventually at the time of Alexander the Great, during the time of Sanballat III the Samaritans then built a temple dedicated to the God of Israel on top of Mount Gerizim.

The high priest who officiated in this temple was actually the brother of the Jewish high priest in Jerusalem. Why is this all so important? It's because the Samaritans and the Judeans were extremely closely related. They're all descendents of the 12 tribes to one degree or another. They are all worshipping the same God, the god of Israel, but on different sacred mountains and eventually in different temples. As is typical with siblings, the closer you are the more vicious the fights can be. This was the case with the Judeans and the Samaritans.

The Judeans always viewed the Samaritans as schismatics, condemned them as schismatics. These two peoples who were so closely related fought bitterly throughout antiquity. Therefore it is not a surprise when we look at the Story of the Good Samaritan and understand it in this light which is of course reported in Luke, and here is the story.

> A man was on his way down from Jerusalem to Jericho, when he fell into the hands of robbers, and they stripped him and beat him and went off leaving him half dead. Now a priest happened to be going that way, and when he saw him, he went by on the other side of the road. And a Levite also came to the place, and when he saw him, he went by on the other side of the road. But a Samaritan who was traveling that way came upon him, and when he saw him he pitied him, and went up to him and dressed his wounds with oil and wine and bound them up.

This story which most people take at face value today seems to make it look like the Jewish priest and the Levite are bad people and the Samaritan is the good guy because he saves this guy who is lying by the side of the road beaten and left for dead. But actually what it reflects is this Judean Samaritan schism. There's a reason why the priest and the Levite cross the other side of the road. It's because according to Jewish purity laws, they could not serve in the Jerusalem temple if they had come into contact with a corpse.

The man lying by the side of the road looked like a corpse. They didn't know that he was alive. They didn't know if he was alive or dead. They couldn't take the chance. Had they come into contact with that man and if he was dead, they would not have been able to officiate; they would not have been able to perform the sacrifices in the Jerusalem temple. They were actually following biblical Jewish law and circumvented what looked like a corpse.

The point of the story is to make the Samaritan here look like the good guy. There's actually a real dig here in making a Samaritan, not someone else, but a Samaritan, the most schismatic, despised people in the eyes of the Judean, look like a good guy. We're going to wrap up here and we will now be continuing on with what happens after this with the conquest of Alexander the Great.

Alexander the Great and His Successors
Lecture 9

Alexander's conquest marked the beginning of a period that we call "Hellenistic," a term that comes from the word *Hellas*, the Greek word for "Greece."

In our last lecture, we talked about the Babylonian Exile and the return of the exiles to Jerusalem under Persian rule. In this lecture, we will discuss the conquests of **Alexander the Great**, which changed ancient Near Eastern peoples greatly—the Judeans perhaps more than others.

In the second half of the 4th century B.C., a powerful Macedonian king named Philip II consolidated control of all the Greek city-states to the south, then began preparations for the invasion of the Persian Empire. However, Philip was murdered before he could invade, and his 18-year-old son, Alexander, succeeded him. Alexander consolidated his rule and, just two years after becoming king, began his invasion of the Persian Empire. In 334 B.C. Alexander and the Persian king, Darius III, fought three successive battles, with Alexander always victorious. After the final battle in 331 B.C., Darius's own men murdered him, paving the way for Alexander to become ruler of all the Persian Empire. Alexander pushed even further, into lands that had not been subject to the Persians. After concluding his conquest, Alexander settled in Babylon, where he ruled until his death in 323 B.C.

King Darius III of Persia was defeated by Alexander the Great in 331 B.C.

In 332 B.C., during his invasion of the Persian Empire, Alexander passed through Palestine on his way to Egypt. Judea submitted peacefully to Alexander, but Samaria revolted, and we have archaeological evidence of the suppression of this revolt. After ending the Samaritans' revolt, Alexander banished them from their most important city,

Samaria, the ancient capital of the northern kingdom of Israel, which he made a Greek colony. Thereafter, the Samaritans have lived at the foot of Mount Gerizim, in what is today the city of Nablus in the West Bank.

When Alexander died in 323 B.C., his empire was divided among his generals. For our purposes, the most important generals were **Seleucus** and Ptolemy. Seleucus got the territory from Asia Minor (modern Turkey) through Syria and Mesopotamia (modern Iraq). Ptolemy got Egypt, a very wealthy country in antiquity. The Holy Land lies right between the Seleucids to the north and the Ptolemies to the south. During most of the 3rd century B.C., the Ptolemies in Egypt ruled Palestine. During most of the 2nd century B.C., the Seleucids to the north ruled it.

> **Alexander's conquest and the policies of his successors resulted in a mixture of Greek culture with the native ancient cultures.**

Alexander's conquest and the policies of his successors resulted in a mixture of Greek culture with the native ancient cultures, a mixture often referred to as "**Hellenistic**." The Ptolemies and Seleucids established many specifically Greek-style cities throughout their kingdoms, and Greek became the official language. The rulers deliberately used Greek culture as a means of unifying the diverse populations in their kingdoms. Jerusalem was not an exception to this policy. A Seleucid king, Antiochus IV Epiphanes, turned Jerusalem into a Greek **polis** named **Antiochia**. This event led to a revolt, for the Jews were not receptive to having Greek culture and religion imposed on them.

In our next lecture, we'll look at some of the native populations in the area during this period. ■

Names to Know

Alexander the Great (356–323 B.C.): Son and successor of Philip II of Macedon, defeated the Persian king Darius III and created a vast empire stretching from southern Russia and northern India through Egypt and Asia Minor. Alexander's conquests mark the beginning of the Hellenistic period.

Seleucus I (c. 355–281 B.C.): One of Alexander's generals who established a kingdom in Asia Minor and Syria (the Seleucid kingdom).

Important Terms

Antiochia: Name given to Jerusalem by the Seleucid king Antiochus IV Epiphanes (175–164 B.C.) after he refounded it as a polis.

Hellenistic: The period beginning with Alexander's conquests.

polis: A Greek or Greek-style city.

Questions to Consider

1. Who do you think has the stronger claim to being the true Israel—the Jews (Judeans) or Samaritans?

2. How did Alexander's successors attempt to establish their legitimacy as his heirs?

Alexander the Great and His Successors
Lecture 9—Transcript

In our last lecture, we talked about the Babylonian exile and the return of the Judeans from Babylonia in exile under Persian rule. In today's lecture, we are going to talk about the conquests of Alexander the Great which had an impact that lasted for centuries on the Ancient Near East and impacted the Judeans just as much if not more as other ancient peoples living in the area.

Before we get to Alexander, we have to go back and talk a little bit about what happens in Greece before the time of Alexander. In the 5th century B.C., the Persians had invaded the Greek mainland twice, in 490 and 480. After that, Athens became the leading city-state in mainland Greece. Athens was not the only leading city state. There was another dominant powerful city-state and that was Sparta. In the 5th century B.C., there were two power blocks in mainland Greece centered on the city-states of Athens and Sparta.

By the second half of the 5th century B.C. these two power blocks came into conflict with each other. A thirty year long war, called the Peloponnesian war, which ended at the very end of the 5th century B.C., and left pretty much all of Greece as a series of fragmented weak city-states with no one city-state able to gain dominance over all of the others. This remained the picture then in Greece in the 4th century B.C. until we get the rise of a kingdom located on the fringes of the Greek world in the area of modern northeast Greece, and that is the kingdom of Macedonia.

In the 4th century B.C., Macedonia was a warrior kingdom ruled by a warrior king. In the second half of the 4th century B.C., a powerful warrior king named Philip II led the Macedonians in a successful battle against the other Greek city-states. This battle was called the Battle of Chaeronea and it was fought in the year 338 B.C. After the Battle of Chaeronea, Macedonia now is the ruler, the leader, of all of the Greek city-states. Two years after the Battle of Chaeronea, Philip II began preparations for the invasion of the Persian Empire but before he could actually invade the Persian Empire, he was murdered. That occurred in the year 336 B.C.

With Philip II's murder, he was then succeeded to the throne by his son, Alexander. Alexander consolidated his position on the Macedonian throne and then continued the preparations that his father had begun for an invasion of the Persian Empire. Just two years after Alexander became king, he began his invasion of the Persian Empire. Remember that at this point, the Persian Empire reached all the way up to the borders of Greece itself.

In 334, Alexander launches his invasion of the Persian Empire, crossing the Hellespont with his Macedonian troops, and landing on Persian soil in the area of ancient Troy, northwest Turkey today. Alexander then began to march with his Macedonian troops eastwards through the Persian Empire. Of course the Persian king was not just sitting back at home watching as a foreign army invaded his country. He came out to meet and oppose Alexander in battle. Eventually, Alexander and the Persian king fought three successive battles.

The Persian king at this point was named Darius III. In each of these three battles against Darius, Alexander and his army were victorious. The final battle was fought in the year 331 B.C., and after that last battle, Darius' own men murdered him, paving the way for Alexander to become ruler of all of the lands of Persia. Alexander did not just sit back at that point. He continued to march eastwards with his troops in the lands that had not even been subject previously to the Persian Empire.

For example, Alexander marched into the area of modern Afghanistan and into the area of southern Russia and across the Indus Valley River into the area of India. Apparently, he was planning to invade the area of the Arabian Peninsula when his Macedonian soldiers simply refused to go any further.

After his conquest, Alexander never returned to his native Greece. He set up court in Babylon where he then ruled over this vast empire until his death in the year 323 B.C.

For our purposes, there are several interesting and important things that happened during the course of Alexander's conquest of the Persian Empire. Alexander's last battle was fought against the Persian king in 331. A year before that, in 332, Alexander had been marching eastwards through Syria towards Mesopotamia, towards the area of modern Iraq, when he detoured south to go to Egypt.

Why did Alexander detour to go to Egypt? Egypt in antiquity was a fantastically wealthy country, the land of the Pharaohs, the land of gold. Alexander wanted to make sure that he took Egypt. So in 332, Alexander detours south to Egypt. As he went to Egypt, that took him through the area of Palestine. So, our little neck of the woods is conquered by Alexander in 332 as he is on his way to Egypt.

While in Egypt, Alexander did two important things. Number one, he established a new city on the coast which he named after himself, Alexandria. The second thing that Alexander did was to go out into the desert to an oasis at a place called Siwa where there was an oracle, an oracular shrine, dedicated to Zeus, specifically a native Zeus worshipped as Zeus Ammon. When Alexander approached this oracular shrine, we are told the priest of Zeus Ammon came out and greeted Alexander as if he was a god.

Why is this important? It is because up until the time of Alexander, Greek rulers and leaders were not worshiped as gods, if you think about the rulers of Athens, for example, the leaders of Athens, in fact, quite the contrary. You have frequent ostracisms, for example. They were not treated all that well. Now for the first time we see the introduction of this notion that a ruler is divine among the Greeks. This notion, actually, was a very ancient notion in the Near East. Think about it, the Pharaohs and some of the ancient rulers of Mesopotamia, they are either divine or they are semi-divine. What we see here now is the beginning of Near Eastern influence on Greek culture by way of Alexander. From the time of Alexander on, he and his successors then are worshiped either as divine or as semi-divine, something that previously had been completely alien to the Greeks.

Alexander's conquest marked the beginning of a period that we call the Hellenistic period. Where does this word "Hellenistic" come from? At its root, the word comes from the word 'hellas' which is the Greek word for Greece. You may also recognize the word Hellenic, which is an adjective meaning Greek. You could say Greek food is Hellenic food, Greek architecture, Hellenic architecture.

We call this period the Hellenistic period. It has at its root a word meaning the beginning of the Greek period, but it is not exactly the Greek period. We do not call it Hellenic period. We call it the Hellenistic period. Why is that? It's because it is not exactly Greek, it is Greek-like.

What do I mean, Greek-like? Alexander's conquest marks for the first time the introduction of Greek culture into the lands of the Ancient Near East. While these lands were under the rule of the Persians, there was very little contact with an influence of Greek culture with the native cultures and with the native peoples. For the first time, the peoples of the Ancient Near East are directly introduced to and exposed to various aspects of Greek culture including Greek language, Greek food, Greek styles of architecture, Greek gods and religion, Greek theatre.

So what we see now, beginning with Alexander's conquest, is Greek influence on the native cultures and peoples of the Ancient Near East, but these cultures and peoples were very ancient, had very rich heritages of their own. They did not simply wholesale abandon their own ancient heritage in order to adopt Greek culture. No, instead what we see is an overlay of Greek culture and various aspects of Greek culture mixed with, mingled with, the native ancient cultures. It is this mixture, this mingling of Greek culture and native Near Eastern cultures that we refer to as Hellenistic, and hence we refer to this period as the beginning of the Hellenistic period.

So in 332 B.C. Alexander passed through Palestine on his way to Egypt. He probably did not go to Jerusalem despite the fact that there is a later Jewish tradition that he did. He would have had no reason to go to Jerusalem and visit Judea. He probably took the coastal road down to Egypt and passed along that way.

As Alexander passed through the country, what he did was to leave the administrative structure that had existed already under the Persians intact but replaced the Persian officials with his own men. Judea submitted peacefully to Alexander, but for some reason, Samaria did not. For some reason, the Samaritans revolted against the governor who Alexander appointed and they burned him alive. What happens then is that Alexander sends troops in to put down this Samaritan revolt.

What is interesting about this is that we have evidence of the Samaritan revolt that was found in a cave in the area of Samaria, a cave in a riverbed that is called Wadi Daliyeh. In this cave, Bedouin found over 300 skeletons lying on mats inside the entrance to the cave and with these skeletons, personal belongings. What these represent, apparently, are the remains of Samaritan refugees who, after the outbreak of the revolt, hid from Alexander's troops in this cave, were apparently discovered by Alexander's troops. The troops then built a fire at the entrance to the cave, and the people inside the cave suffocated to death. All of the personal belongings that they had brought with them remained with their physical remains, with their skeletons inside the cave, and were then discovered by Bedouin, and the cave was then excavated by archaeologists. Among the personal belongings that we have from this cave are documents, personal documents, deeds to land, personal correspondence that these people brought with them to the cave when they hid out there. These documents then give us a very valuable insight on this Samaritan population on the eve of the outbreak of the revolt against Alexander.

After the end of the Samaritan revolt, Alexander punished the Samaritans. In order to punish them, what he did was banish them from their most important city, the city of Samaria. Remember that Samaria had been the capital of the biblical kingdom of Israel way back when. Alexander now banishes the Samaritans from the city of Samaria. He settles Macedonian veterans at Samaria, so Samaria now becomes a Greek town, a Greek colony. The Samaritans now live at the foot of their sacred mountain, at the foot of Mount Gerizim in the biblical city of Shechem which today is the city of Nablus in the west bank.

We actually have more archaeological evidence for the results, the outcome of the Samaritan revolt in the city of Samaria. Excavations in the city of Samaria brought to light the original biblical, that is the original Israelite citadel at the top of the hill surrounded by its own fortification wall. When the Macedonian veterans were settled here by Alexander, they apparently refortified the citadel by adding round towers to it. These round towers are still at Samaria, can still be seen very well. They are a very typical type of round tower where the stones are laid entirely with the short ends facing out, what we call headers. If the long end is facing out it is called a stretcher, but if the short end of the block of stone is facing out, it is called a header. So all of the stones are laid in neat rows of headers.

It is very interesting that we see the addition of round towers to the ancient Israelite fortifications. This goes back to something that we have talked about already, the fact that whenever you see a new defensive system introduced, it reflects the introduction of a new offensive system of warfare. Why add round towers to the ancient fortifications? What was the point of round towers? This is something connected with events under Alexander. One of the innovations that appears in warfare in the time of Alexander and then continues through the Hellenistic period is the development of heavy artillery, that is, large, torsion machines that can throw giant cannon shot, big round boulders.

These big round boulders can be thrown at city walls for various purposes. One of the things that you do is to shoot these big stones, these big cannon shot, in order to provide cover fire for your troops that are attacking the city. You can also use these big pieces of cannon shot to batter away the city wall and specifically, to batter away at towers. If a tower is square, has square corners, those corners are going to be subject to being battered much more quickly than a round tower. They are going to be much more vulnerable than a round tower. So round towers are going to be much better at protecting your city from artillery, from cannon shot, than square towers are. So the round towers that we see added to the ancient Israelite citadel at Samaria are connected with the establishment of this new Macedonian veteran population at the site and connected with the introduction of this new type of canon shot warfare that we have, heavy artillery, beginning with the time of Alexander the Great.

In 323 B.C. Alexander died. He was still quite young. He died in Babylon. When Alexander died, there was no one person who was capable of succeeding him to the throne. What happens after Alexander dies is that a war breaks out over the succession to the throne. During the course of the next 20 years, there were prolonged wars over the succession to Alexander's throne. During the course of this period of war, Alexander's wives, he had three wives, and his offspring were killed. Eventually, Alexander's empire was divided up between various of his generals.

For our purposes, two of Alexander's generals are the most important. One general was named Seleucus. Seleucus got the lion's share of Alexander's empire. He got the territory from the area of Asia Minor, that is modern Turkey, through Syria and Mesopotamia, the area of Iraq. He established there a kingdom which was then ruled by his successors and which is called the Seleucid kingdom or the Seleucid Empire.

The other important general for us is Ptolemy. Ptolemy got Egypt, which remember was a very wealthy country in antiquity, and established a kingdom ruled by his descendents which is called the Ptolemaic kingdom or the Ptolemaic Empire. Notice where our little neck of the woods lies. The holy land lies right smack in the middle between the Seleucids to the north and the Ptolemys to the south.

As you can imagine, Palestine was a bone of contention between the Seleucids and the Ptolemys with wars being fought and with the country going back and forth. Basically, during most of the 3rd century B.C., Palestine was under the rule of the Ptolemys in Egypt. During most of the 2nd century B.C., Palestine was under the rule of the Seleucids to the north.

When Alexander's empire was divided among his generals and their successors, these successors of Alexander had a problem. That problem was establishing their legitimacy in the eyes of the population that they ruled. Why do I say that? In antiquity, generally speaking, the principle of rule was dynastic. You had a dynasty and the successors to the throne were generally related to the people who they followed. So a ruler was then succeeded by his son or by his nephew or by some other blood relative or somebody who had at least married into the family.

None of Alexander's successors were related to Alexander in any way. Their problem was establishing themselves as legitimate successors to Alexander in the eyes of the populations that they ruled over. How do you go about doing this? What they did was to imitate Alexander. Everything that Alexander had done, they did.

Why did they do this? They did this in order to make themselves seem like Alexander. If Alexander had been deified, had been worshiped as a god, well, then they too were then going to be deified and worshiped as gods. Whatever Alexander did, they followed in his footsteps. Remember that one of the things that Alexander had done was establish a new city in Egypt which he named after himself, Alexandria.

Following then in Alexander's footsteps, all of these different successors, the Ptolemys and the Seleucids established new cities around their kingdoms which they named after themselves. We have, for example around the Seleucid empire cities that are named Seleucia, and around the Ptolemaic Empire or kingdom, cities that are named Ptolemais. In fact, in the 3rd century B.C., the city of Aco, or acre, which is north of Hyfa on the Palestinian coast was renamed Ptolemais.

Establishing these cities and naming them after themselves was not just a tactic imitating Alexander. There actually was a whole other reason for this as well, a very good reason. When these successors of Alexander established cities and gave them names after themselves, what they were doing was establishing cities that were specifically Greek cities. Sometimes these cities were being established from scratch in a place where there had been no city previously.

But many times what these rulers did was to take an already-existing city or town and rebuild it. Build it so that it had new Greek style institutions, a Greek style temple dedicated to Greek gods, a Greek style school or gymnasium where the youth would be educated with a Greek education, a Greek theater where Greek plays would be performed in the Greek language. What these rulers were doing was not just establishing cities named after themselves, they were specifically establishing Greek-style cities throughout their kingdom.

Why were they doing this? They were for a couple of good reasons. First of all, if you were an inhabitant of one of these cities or towns, and suddenly you had a nice new theater to watch plays in, and a good school to send your kids to for a good education, and a beautiful temple to worship the gods in, you would be pretty grateful and loyal to that ruler. One of the points of this policy was to win the loyalty of the population by establishing these nice new cities for the people, and that actually worked very well.

There was another reason why these rulers did this, because for the most part the populations that they ruled over were pretty diverse. These were different peoples, different ethnicities, spoke different languages, worshiped different gods. These successors of Alexander deliberately used Greek culture as a means of unifying the diverse populations in their kingdoms.

Now Greek becomes the official language of their kingdoms. The youth are now being educated in the Greek manner. People are now familiar with Greek gods and with Greek customs. You have a homogenizing influence with the establishment of these Greek cities throughout the Hellenistic kingdoms.

If we look at the portraiture of Alexander and his successors, we can see again this attempt to imitate Alexander and emulate him in every way possible. There is a beautiful portrait head of Alexander that is posthumous; it was made after Alexander's death. It was found in Pergamum on the western coast of Asia Minor. What is important here is not that it depicts how Alexander actually looked, we do not really know exactly how he looked, but it depicts how people thought Alexander looked in antiquity.

Alexander is typically depicted as a young man, very beautiful, at his prime. Notice a couple of things. Notice that he has a thick wavy mane of hair on his head, so his hair is very sort of thick and wavy. He is shown as gazing up towards the heavens. Sometimes Alexander is actually shown wearing a lions mane cape on his head as we see for example on some coins. That, of course, is an attribute of Hercules—Heracles, the Greek hero. So an aspect of the fact that Alexander is divine or semi-divine being alluded to here. Of course, gazing off towards heavens, stresses his connection with the gods up in heaven.

If we look at the coins of some of Alexander's successors, both Ptolemys and Seleucids, we see something very interesting. We see that they portray themselves resembling Alexander. They too have the thick wavy mane of hair, they too are gazing up towards heaven, they bare a resemblance to Alexander. Of course, the Ptolemys and the Seleucids probably bore no resemblance to Alexander at all because they were not related to Alexander, but in antiquity the closest you got to mass media was coins. Coins were more widely distributed than anything.

Most people in their everyday lives never actually saw the ruler, never actually saw the king. What they saw instead were whatever statues or portrait busts happened to get set up, and most of them probably never even saw that, but if they didn't see anything else, they saw the portraits that were on coins. You did not know what they king actually looked like. You thought he looked like the way he is depicted on the coin.

If these rulers are depicted on coins and in other portraits looking like Alexander, you would think that that is actually what they looked like, and therefore you would conclude even though it is not being said explicitly, that if they look like Alexander, they must be related to Alexander. Another means, in other words, of perpetuating this affiction that they are like Alexander and they are Alexander's legitimate successors is having themselves portrayed looking like Alexander in art.

These Greek style cities that the Hellenistic kings, the Seleucids and the Ptolemys established throughout their kingdoms, these Greek style cities are what we call a "polis." Polis is simply a Greek word meaning a city or sometimes a city-state. Technically we refer to these Greek-style cities as a polis. We have seen that these cities were established by the Hellenistic kings throughout their kingdoms for various purposes including unifying these diverse populations but also winning the loyalty in favor of the people, because people were very happy when the king came along and made their city a Greek style city. It's very interesting that Jerusalem was not exception to this rule.

Under one of the Seleucid kings, Antiochus IV Epiphanies, Jerusalem was turned into a Greek polis. It was renamed, after the kind, Antiochia. This event, the re-foundation of Jerusalem as a Greek style city named Antiochia, is going to preface and lead up to the outbreak of a Jewish revolt against Antiochus because, of course, the Jews unlike other populations in the area were not necessarily all that receptive to having Greek culture and Greek religion imposed upon them.

We tie up here and in our next lecture, what we are going to be doing is turning to look at some of the native populations in the area during the Hellenistic period.

The Hellenization of Palestine
Lecture 10

> What is the principle of the Hippodamian town plan? This principle says that when you come to build a city, you do not just build randomly, or you do not just let the city grow organically, but you give thought before you start building as to how it will be laid out, with certain things laid out in certain places—all of this, by the way, going back to certain Greek philosophical ideals about what the ideal city should look like.

In our last lecture, we looked broadly at the effect of Hellenization, the spread of Greek culture in the ancient Near East in the wake of Alexander's conquests. In this lecture, we'll look specifically at the impact of Hellenization on the non-Jewish peoples in ancient Palestine.

In the Hellenistic period, the city of Ammon was renamed Philadelphia and made independent of Tobiad rule. The **Tobiads** continued to rule the rest of the district and established a new capital for themselves named Tyros, located midway between Jericho and Ammon (or Philadelphia) in a valley that is well watered with many natural springs. The ancient Jewish historian Josephus described a large building there decorated with animal carvings, with elegant fountains all around and, in a cliff nearby, caves converted into living and dining quarters. Dating from the early 2nd century B.C., these features are all evident in the archaeological remains at Tyros. We are not exactly sure what the large building was, but the best guesses are either a temple or a pleasure palace.

> **The most important Hellenistic city was Marisa.**

In Idumea, which had been settled by **Edomites** after the Babylonian capture of Jerusalem in 586 B.C., the most important Hellenistic city was **Marisa**. In this city dwelt not only Idumeans but also Hellenized **Sidonians** from Phoenicia. Excavations at this site have revealed a kind of city plan, introduced by the Greeks throughout the ancient Near East, called a Hippodamian town plan (associated with Hippodamus of Miletos, who lived around 500 B.C.). The Hippodamian town plan was based on the principle that cities should not be built randomly or simply allowed to grow organically; instead, certain structures should be laid out in certain places. This type of planning can be traced back to Greek philosophical ideas about what the ideal city should look like. The area within the city walls is divided by a grid of north/south, east/west streets, and parts of the city are zoned for such purposes as industry, worship, education, and commerce. Also, the burial caves evidence Alexandrian influence in their layout and decoration, and the names in these tombs of local Idumeans and Hellenized Sidonians reveal that, in later generations, members of families adopted Greek names rather than their local native names.

Hellenistic influence on the Phoenicians is also evident along the coast. At Tel Dor, for example, excavations have revealed an imported marble image of Hermes. The city has a Hippodamian town plan, but interestingly, we also see houses built with a typically Phoenician kind of construction called pier-and-rubble masonry.

It's interesting that this Hellenistic culture is found among some of the native non-Jewish populations in Palestine. In our next lecture, we will consider the impact of Greek culture on the Jewish population of Judea. ∎

Important Terms

Edomites: The Iron Age inhabitants of the area southeast of the Dead Sea.

Marisa (Hebrew, **Maresha**; Arabic, **Tell Sandahannah**): Main city in Hellenistic-period Idumaea, inhabited by Idumaeans and Hellenized Sidonians.

Sidonians: Natives of the Phoenician city of Sidon (in modern Lebanon).

Tobiads: A Judean dynasty that governed the district of Ammon in the Persian and Hellenistic periods.

Questions to Consider

1. What would be the significance of the Qasr el-Abd at Iraq el-Amir if it was indeed a temple?

2. What does archaeology tell us about the impact of Hellenization on local Semitic (non-Jewish) populations?

The Hellenization of Palestine
Lecture 10—Transcript

In our last lecture we looked at Alexander's conquests and the policies of Alexander and his successors, the Ptolemys and the Seleucids and the effect of Hellenization, the spread of Greek culture on the area of the Ancient Near East in the wake of Alexander's conquests. What I would like to do in this lecture is look specifically at the impact of Hellenization, Greek culture, on the native peoples of ancient Palestine, not the Jews, not the Judeans, but the other non-Jewish peoples in the area of ancient Palestine.

We are going to start specifically with a site located in the area of ancient Ammon, remember the biblical kingdom of the Ammonites located in the area of modern Amman and Jordan. This area, in the Persian period, was the medinah the district of Ammon. It was governed by a Judean named Tobias and later by Tobias' successors who are called the Tobiads.

In the Hellenistic period, that is after the conquest of Alexander, the city of Ammon, which is modern day Amman and Jordan, which by the way in the Hellenistic period was renamed Philadelphia, that city was made independent of Tobiad rule. The rest of the district, then, was ruled by the Tobiads but not the city of Ammon itself, it was independent.

The Tobiads, then, establish a new capital city for themselves, not the city of Ammon, but another city in the district. This new capital is at an ancient site called Tyros or today called by the Arabic name Iraq el-Amir. We have archaeological remains of the capital city of the Tobiads at Iraq el-Amir. It is a site that is located today approximately midway between Jericho and Amman in Jordan. The area of the capital is spread out in a valley which is very well watered, lots of natural springs. The buildings that were built by the Tobiads in this capital city are described by Josephus, the ancient Jewish historian.

Specifically, Josephus describes what was built by one of the Tobiads, a man named Hyrcanus. Hyrcanus was one of the successors of that original Tobia. He lived in the early 2nd century B.C. Let us now consider and look closely at Josephus' description of what Hyrcanus built at this capital city, ancient Tyros modern Iraq el-Amir.

So Josephus says "He [Hyrcanus] also erected a strong castle (baris), and built it entirely of white stone to the very roof, and had animals of prodigious magnitude engraved upon it. He also drew around it a great and deep canal of water." So notice here that Josephus here describes Hyrcanus building a strong building which he calls in Greek a "baris" of white stone carved with animals and surrounded by water.

"He also made caves of many furlongs in length, by hollowing a rock that was over against him; and then he made large rooms in it, some for feasting, and some for sleeping and living in." So Josephus describes caves that were made into living and dining quarters surrounding this strong building called the "baris."

Josephus says,

> He introduced also a vast quantity of waters which ran along it, and which were very delightful and ornamental in the court. But still he made the entrances at the mouth of the cave so narrow, that no more than one person could enter by them at once. Moreover, he built courts of greater magnitude than ordinary, which he adorned with vastly large gardens. And when he had brought the place to this state, he named it Tyros. This place is between Arabia and Judea, beyond Jordan, not far from the country of Heshbon.

When Antiochus IV Epiphanies, the Seleucid king became king, Hyrcanus committed suicide. Apparently, political reasons, he was aligned with the wrong side so in 175 B.C. Hyrcanus committed suicide. At Iraq el-Amir we have archaeological remains that seem to correspond with Josephus' description of the buildings that were built by Hyrcanus. Very interesting, by the way, some of these buildings are unfinished, which corresponds with what we know that Hyrcanus committed suicide when Antiochus became king. So apparently at that point not all of the building had been finished being built.

The major building that is located at Iraq el-Amir today is a building that seems to correspond with the baris, this strong building made of white stone and carved with animals that Josephus describes. Today, this building, which is apparently the ancient baris, is called by the Arabic name the Qsar el-Abd. It is a large rectangular building that was originally two stories high, had porches at either narrow end, and four towers in the corners. The building still stands today pretty much to its original two-story height, in fact, you can still see windows in the original second story level. It is a very large building. What is so interesting about it is that it corresponds with Josephus' description of having animals carved in decoration around it.

The building, when you approach it today, is surrounded by springs and is so big that it dwarfs people who walk around it. One of my favorite shots shows a couple of friends sitting by one of the blocks of stone in the walls of this building which gives a sense of its immense size. Again, this corresponds nicely with Josephus' description.

The animal friezes, the animal decorations, the carvings of animals are still on the building as well. As you walk around the building, you can see various kinds of animals, many of them felines, including some which decorate the base of the building and have holes in the mouth. Why do they have holes in the mouth? Because, apparently, these were originally fountains that had water spouting out of the mouth. Notice very nicely that the artist who carved these stone reliefs of the animals took advantage of the natural rock which is modeled, which is different colors, and corresponds with the spots that you might see in the hide of a feline like a leopard, for example.

Furthermore, we have remains in the cliffs surrounding the Qasr el-Abd of caves. Caves which correspond again with what Josephus describes of caves being converted into living quarters and dining quarters. One of the caves is inscribed by the entrance with the name Tobia. Remember that Hyrcanus was a member of the Tobiad Dynasty.

One of the big questions about the Qasr el-Abd is what exactly was it? The Greek term "baris" is usually translated as we saw castle or fortress. The fact that this building has towers at the four corners does in fact give it the look of a fortress or a fortification. But when you look at the entrances to the building, the porches on either side, you can see clearly that they were not protected, they were just open entrances. Clearly this could not have functioned as a fortress. It may have been described by Josephus with a word that means "fortress" but it really could not have functioned as a fortress. Besides, notice all the decoration with the animal reliefs and the fountains with the water, that does not really fit a fortress. So if it is not a fortress, what is it?

Some scholars have suggested maybe it was a temple. Because we have other temples in Syria that have a similar arrangement with the towers at the corners that originally led up to a two-story level and the roof. Some scholars think maybe it was a temple. If it was a temple, it is very important because it would be a temple that was built by a Jewish Dynasty. It would then be an example of a Jewish temple of the Second Temple period located outside of Jerusalem. That would be very rare.

It is not actually completely unattested. It would not be unique because we know that there were other Jewish temples outside of Jerusalem in the Second Temple period. Specifically there were a couple in Egypt. One at a site called Elephantine and another at a site called Leontopolis. There were in fact Jewish temples in antiquity in the Second Temple period outside of Jerusalem, but we do not have archaeological remains of those temples. If this was in fact a Jewish temple outside Jerusalem, it would be the only example we have where we have archaeological physical remains of that building.

The identification of a temple is also problematic. Some scholars have suggested well it does not actually fit a temple either; in fact, it does not look like either a fortress or a temple. It instead looks like a palace, a pleasure palace. This suggestion has been made in particular by an Israeli archaeologist named Ehud Netzer.

Let us now consider another part of the country and another native population. We are going to turn now to Idumea. Remember that in the Persian Period, Idumea was a district which was inhabited by the descendents of the biblical Edomites who were called Idumeans.

Before 586 B.C. this area had been the southern part of the kingdom of Judah, but from the Persian period on, it now becomes known as Idumea. The population is not Jewish at this point, it is Idumean. Before 586 B.C. when this area was still part of the kingdom of Judah, the most important city in this area in the southern part of Judah was Lachish, which we talked about when we talked about Hezakiah because Lachish was destroyed by the Assyrians before they came and besieged Jerusalem in 701 B.C. So Lachish had been the most important city in this area before 586 B.C.

In the Hellenistic Period, the most important city in the area is the city of Marisa. Marisa is the ancient Greek name of this city. The Hebrew name is Maresha and we will see that it has actually another name in Arabic. What was the population of this city, of Marisa, in the Hellenistic Period? They were Idumeans but in addition to Idumeans, Hellenized Sidonians, that is Phoenicians from the city of Sidon who were Hellenized, who had adopted Greek culture. What we have here is a non-Jewish population consisting of Idumeans, descendents of biblical Edomites, and Hellenized Sidonians, Hellenized Phoenicians.

Marisa is the Greek name of the site, Maresha in Hebrew, but in Arabic the name of this site is Tell Sandahannah. That is a strange name but it is actually an interesting name. How did it get that name, Tell Sandahannah? In the Middle Ages, the crusaders built a church nearby that was dedicated to St. Anne and part of that church still stands today on a hill near the site of Marisa. The Church of St. Anne eventually gave its name to the site in Arabic, because Sandahannah is a corruption of Santa Anna. So in Arabic, the site then takes the name of the nearby church dedicated to St. Anne, Santa Anna.

Marisa has a very interesting excavation history. It was excavated back in 1900 by two British archaeologists named Bliss and Macalister. In 1900 Palestine was part of the Ottoman Empire. When Bliss and Macalister came to excavate at Marisa, they had to get a permit from the Ottoman authorities. The Ottoman authorities gave them a permit but with a condition, on condition that they leave the site looking as they had found it. So what did Bliss and Macalister do? They started to dig, they took the top of the site which is actually a tell, a mound, and they started to dig. Very soon as they started to dig, they started to come down on the walls of buildings.

What did they do? Every time they started to come down on walls that defined a room, they would dig out the interior of the room and throw the dirt onto one of the four walls and clear the other three walls. Then when they finished the excavation, they took all of the dirt that was piled on the fourth wall of every room, and backfilled, piled it back into the room. So today, when you go to Marisa, to the top of the site, there is nothing to see because it was all backfilled in 1900. In fact, the only plan that we have of the ancient site is the plan that Bliss and Macalister made when they excavated in 1900.

If we look at this plan of the site that they made in 1900, what do we see? We see several very interesting things. First of all notice that the town is enclosed by a fortification wall, it is rectangular in shape with square towers coming out. Within this area of the fortification wall, we can clearly see two streets that are running east/west through the city and three streets that are running north/south. In other words, what we see are streets creating a grid of blocks with the streets running north/south and east/west and intersecting each other at right angles, therefore dividing the city into blocks of buildings.

Furthermore, if we look at this plan of the city carefully, we can see that in the center of the city is an open area with two big open squares, and on the right-hand side of the city is another big open area with a building in the middle. What we are seeing here at Marisa is the introduction of a new kind of city plan associated with the Greeks. Specifically what we see at Marisa is something called a Hippodamian town plan.

When the Seleucids and Ptolemys built Greek style cities through their kingdoms, they built them with a typical Greek style city plan that is called a Hippodamian town plan. This kind of town plan is called Hippodamian because the ancient Greeks associated it with a man named Hippodamus of Miletos who apparently lived around 500 B.C. Now whether Hippodamus of Miletos really invented this kind of city plan, we do not know, but the ancient Greeks associated him with it and therefore it becomes known as a Hippodamian town plan. When Greek style cities begin to be built throughout the Ancient Near East after Alexander's conquests, they are often built then with a typical Greek style plan which is this Hippodamian town plan.

What is the principle of the Hippodamian town plan? This principle says that when you come to build a city, you do not just build randomly, or you do not just let the city grow organically, but you give thought before you start building as to how it will be laid out with certain things laid out in certain places, all of this, by the way, going back to certain Greek philosophical ideals about what the ideal city should look like.

So one characteristic of a Hippodamian town plan is that the inside of the city, the area within the walls, is divided into blocks by a grid of streets that run north/south and east/west. Another principle of Hippodamian town planning is the idea of zoning. The idea that you reserve certain parts of the city for certain purposes. Your industrial area, your cultic area, the education area, the commercial area, and we see that here at Marisa. We see a Greek style city plan with a grid of streets running north/south, east/west, and in the very center of the city, a large open space which was the marketplace of the city, the commercial heart of the city, which is what is called in Greek, an 'agora' which simply means a big open area where people can congregate and conduct commerce and people can set up stalls and sell whatever it is that they are selling, usually this area then bounded by various public buildings.

On one side of the city here, we then see another big open space, clearly a public space with a building in the middle. If you look closely you can see that that building is divided into three rooms. That building is a temple. Because the population of this city was not Jewish, this was a temple dedicated to non-Jewish gods, presumably a triad of gods, that is three different gods suggested by the division of the temple into three room. What we see here at Marisa, then, is Greek influence on the layout of this city in the Hellenistic period.

If you go to Marisa today and you walk around the top of the site, there is nothing to see, but more recent Israeli excavations on the slopes outside the city wall have uncovered some very interesting things, including extramural houses, that is suburban houses located outside the walls. These houses are very nicely built. This was apparently a population that was affluent. The houses are large, they are built of stones. Inside the houses are entrances to underground caves. In fact, the slopes of the tell are literally honeycombed with caves that were cut by hand into the soft chalk. All of this area around Marisa are hills of very soft chalk, so soft that you can actually carve into it with your fingernail.

These caves were made from quarrying rock. That is the rock that was used to build the houses in the town was quarried and what you had left then were caves that were underground. These caves were then used for various purposes. We have caves that were used as storage areas, for example cellars for storing food and cisterns for storing water because it remains cool underground. We have industrial installations in the caves including olive presses. We have dove cotes or columbaria. Some of the caves were even used for burial, as tombs.

Let us take a look at a couple of examples of these. For example, we have a cave with an olive press. Olive presses actually have two main parts to them. The first part consists of having to take the olives and crush them. That is the first part of the process, so we see a crushing stone for crushing the olives. The second part is then taking the crushed olives and gathering them up into a basket and then pressing the basket with the crushed olives so that the olive oil comes out. We are looking here at a cave with the area for the press and the olive oil would come out. In fact, notice that in the middle of the press, there is an area carved on the wall where there is a little altar where perhaps some offerings could be made either to ask the god for a good harvest or perhaps to thank the god for a good harvest.

Apparently, from the number of olive presses that we have at Marisa, we can deduce that the production of olive oil was a major component of the local economy. In fact, it has been estimated that the 20 olive presses at Marisa would have produced 270 tons of olive oil per year, far more than the local people would have needed, so clearly they were producing olive oil for the purposes of selling on the market and exporting it.

In addition to the olive presses, we have caves at Marisa that were used at dove cotes, for raising doves. These are called columbaria caves, coming from the Latin word columbus, or dove. These caves were used for raising doves or pigeons that could be used for various purposes. You can use the guano, for example, from the birds for agriculture for fertilizing your fields. You can use doves and pigeons as carrier birds. You can use them for food, that is, you can eat them. You can use them for purposes of worship, that is, you can offer them to gods.

There are over 60 columbaria caves at Marisa with a total of some 50,000 to 60,000 little niches carved on the sides of the walls which were used for actually holding the birds. The largest columbaria cave at Marisa is called the Suk in Arabic which means the marketplace. The inside of this cave is absolutely overwhelming. You go into it and you just have rows and rows and rows of these little niches carved into the walls of the caves where the birds originally were kept. Notice, by the way, that the niches start relatively high up on the walls. That was to keep the birds away from predators, so cats and other kinds of predators on the ground would not be able to reach the birds.

This suggests then that the economy of Marisa was based largely on raising pigeons and doves and the production of olive oil. Hence we see this very affluent settlement.

Some of the caves at Marisa were used for burials. The most famous of the burial caves is a cave that was discovered in 1902. What happened actually at that time is some local villagers found the cave and reports of this cave reached Jerusalem, and a couple of scholars, French scholars in Jerusalem, rushed down to Marisa and recorded the paintings in the cave. It is a good thing because the paintings that decorate this cave were afterwards completely destroyed. Today, they have been reconstructed. So you can go into the cave and see modern reproductions, but the paintings eventually were completely destroyed and the record that we have of them is the record that was made by these two scholars who rushed down in 1902.

What we have here is a very interesting kind of burial cave. It is cut into bedrock. It has several halls. The halls of the cave are lined with long narrow niches for individual bodies. These individual niches are called loculi, that is a Latin word plural, singular, loculus. This is very interesting. This is the first example that we have of a burial cave in Palestine with these kinds of niches, with these loculi which is going to become very popular and common afterwards, but this is the first appearance that we have.

Where do loculi come from? This idea of loculi comes from the great center of the Hellenistic world Alexandria. Alexandria was the cultural capital of the Hellenistic world. Apparently what we see here is influence from Hellenistic Alexandria on the burial customs of the local population.

We also see that in the paintings in this tomb. Where running above the loculi, we have a continues painted frieze, a continuous painted strip which shows, among other things, a man on a horse hunting and a man behind him blowing a trumpet. Then a very, very strange series of animals, some of which are real but just exotic types of animals, but some of which are imaginary, for example, fish with elephant trunks and animals that look like they came out of a Dr. Seuss book, for example.

What is the story with these animals? Where is this coming from? What we see here, again, is Alexandrian influence. Not only was Alexandria the cultural capital of the Hellenistic world, but it was also the seat of, of course, the great library and a zoo. A zoo where various exotic animals collected from around Africa were kept. Picture books of these exotic animals circulated around the Hellenistic world and served as a source of inspiration and art.

Apparently what we see here is some of that influence, that is this notion of decorating, in this case a tomb, with pictures of exotic animals and in some cases imaginary animals. To us, at least, they are imaginary, but I should mention by the way that in antiquity people believed that these sorts of animals, these kinds of hybrid animals actually existed.

So again, the layout of this tomb and the decoration of the tomb, reflect Hellenistic influence on the local population which in this case are local Idumeans and Hellenized Sidonians. We even see that in their names because sometimes their names are inscribed next to the burial niches. We can even see that in later generations, members of families adopted Greek names rather than their local native names.

We also have Hellenistic influence on the Phoenicians living along the coast. One example of a Phoenician city is Tel Dor. This is a wonderful example of a Hellenized Phoenician city. The site of Tel Dor has been undergoing excavation for a number of years.

Among other things, the excavations have brought to light remains of houses of the Hellenistic period which, again, reflect a Hippodamian town plan. So we can see elements of a Hippodamian town plan in the layout of the city with a grid of streets. But very interesting in these Hellenistic Phoenician houses we also see a very distinctive type of architecture.

Look at the way these houses are built. You can see that the walls are build with alternating stretches of rubble, that is uncut field stones, and nicely cut ashlar, nicely cut stone. So you have sections with rough stones, nice smooth stones, rough stones, nice smooth stones. This kind of construction is called pier and rubble masonry. What is so interesting about it is, it is characteristic of Phoenician architecture.

Not only do we see it here at Dor and at other Phoenician sites, but we even see it at Carthage in Tunisia, North Africa which was originally founded as a Phoenician colony and there too we see this very distinctive type of Phoenician architecture.

Among the Hellenistic remains that have come to light is a marble head of a little statue called a Herm. First of all, marble in and of itself is not local. We do not have any marble native to Palestine. So automatically you know that this had to have been imported. What exactly is a herm? This head is the head of a herm, but what exactly is a herm? Herm is short for Hermes. Hermes is the Greek name of this god. You might know him as the Roman Mercury. You are probably familiar with him best because today people who sell flowers often use the symbol of this god as the icon with the little wings on the hat and the little wings on the feet. Because, of course, today we associate Hermes as the messenger god which he was in antiquity. But he was also other things in antiquity. One of the things that Hermes did in antiquity was mark boundaries or borders between things. So you often find statues of Hermes, called Herms, set up at the entrances to places.

I show a picture of a Herm, a statue of a Herm, from the Greek island of Delos marking the entrance to the marketplace there. Notice that very typically these Herms are such that only the head is carved. The body is just a plain pillar, and the only part of the body that is carved on the pillar are the genitals that is the only part that is represented. The rest of it is just a plain pillar because among other things, Herms were also associated with fertility.

What is so interesting here is that we then see the influence and the impact of Greek that is Hellenistic culture on some of these native non-Jewish populations in Palestine. In our next lecture, we are going to turn and consider the impact of Greek culture on the Jewish population of Judea.

The Maccabean Revolt
Lecture 11

> It is ironic that, although the Maccabees are renowned for having opposed the attempt to impose Greek culture and religion on the Jews, ... as soon as they become the rulers, we begin to see them adopting various aspects of Greek culture.

In 167 B.C., the Seleucid king Antiochus IV Ephiphanes issued a decree ordering the Jews to abandon the observance of Jewish law and follow Greek customs, threatening death to the disobedient. Many Jews complied readily. The Jerusalem temple was now rededicated to the Greek god Zeus, and sacred prostitution was practiced there. In reaction to this radical change in the law of the land, a revolt was initiated, led by a village priestly family called the Hasmoneans (also Maccabeans, after the word for "hammer"). The patriarch of this family, Mattathias, killed another Jew who was about to participate in a pagan sacrifice and the royal officer overseeing the sacrifice.

The Maccabean family began collecting relatives and friends to form the core of a 6,000-strong insurgency. Mattathias soon died, and the Hasmonean army was then led by Judah, the third son, and his brothers, Simon, Jonathan, John, and Eleazar. Judah searched out and slew Jews who had abandoned the law and scored important military victories against royal troops. Antiochus IV died in 164 B.C.,

Mattathias, patriarch of the Hasmonean family, began the Maccabean revolt.

and his son Antiochus V rescinded his father's edict, allowing the Jews to freely observe their law. They rededicated the temple to the worship of the God of Israel, an event commemorated by the modern Jewish holiday of **Hanukkah**.

After this rededication, the Maccabees renewed the revolt to gain complete independence from the Seleucids. Eleazar was killed, but in 161 B.C. Judah won a significant battle against the Seleucids. At about the same time, he also made a treaty of alliance and friendship with the Romans, a treaty that was renewed several times. In 160 B.C., Judah died in battle, and leadership passed to Jonathan, who established himself in 152 B.C. as ruler of Judea by supporting Alexander Balas in his struggle for the Seleucid throne. Alexander rewarded Jonathan by appointing him as both a semiautonomous ruler over his people and their high priest. For the first time, a secular ruler served in the Jerusalem temple—contrary to Jewish law, which said that a man with blood on his hands could not be a priest in the temple.

> **The result in Galilee was a Judaized population, mixed probably with some settlers from Judea.**

In 142 B.C., Jonathan was killed through treachery, to be succeeded by the last of the five brothers, Simon, who gained complete independence from Seleucid rule. In 134 B.C., he was succeeded by his son John Hyrcanus I, who began to expand the kingdom by conquering Idumaea, Samaria, and parts of Transjordan. In Samaria, John Hyrcanus I destroyed the temple on Mount Gerizim. In Idumaea, he permitted the conquered to remain only if they had themselves circumcised and observed Jewish laws. Among the Idumaeans who converted was Antipas, the grandfather of Herod the Great.

John Hyrcanus died in 104 B.C., succeeded briefly by his son Aristobulus I, the first Hasmonean to call himself king. Aristobulus I conquered Galilee and the Golan to the north and, like his father, strongly encouraged the native populations to convert to Judaism. The result in Galilee was a Judaized population, mixed probably with some settlers from Judea.

The stage was now set for the late history of the Hasmonean kingdom and its annexation by the Romans, which we will talk about in our next lecture. ■

Important Term

Hanukkah: Jewish holiday commemorating the rededication of the Jerusalem temple to the God of Israel in 164 B.C.

Questions to Consider

1. What were the consequences of the edict outlawing Judaism issued by Antiochus IV Epiphanes?

2. How did the Hasmonean kings deal with conquered non-Jewish peoples, and what were the consequences of this policy?

The Maccabean Revolt
Lecture 11—Transcript

In our last lecture we looked at the impact of Greek culture Hellenization on the need of non-Jewish populations of Palestine, but what happens when Hellenism, when Greek culture is introduced to Judea? Remember that the Seleucid king Antiochus IV Ephiphanes turned Jerusalem into a Greek city called Antiokia, but that was not all that he did. In the year 167 B.C., Antiochus IV issued a decree and this is how it reads in the first book of Maccabees.

Antiochus "wrote to his whole kingdom that all should be one people and that all should give up their particular customs," and by the way, remember that is one of the reasons why the Hellenistic successors of Alexander liked to introduce Greek culture and spread Greek culture throughout their kingdoms was in order to use it as a unifying force among their diverse populations. We see that represented here, that he is introducing Greek culture now in order to make everyone one people and everybody should give up their own particular customs. "All the gentiles accepted the command of the King. Many even from Israel gladly adopted his religion. They sacrificed to idols and profaned the Sabbath."

Notice by the way that according to first Maccabees, there were even many Jews who were happy to adopt Greek culture; why not?

> And the king sent letters by messengers to Jerusalem and the towns of Judah. He directed them to follow customs strange to the land, to forbid burnt offerings and sacrifices and drink offerings in the sanctuary that is in the Jerusalem temple, to profane Sabbaths and festivals, to defile the sanctuary and the priest, to build alters and sacred precincts for idols to sacrifice swine and other unclean animals, and to leave their sons uncircumcised.

In other words, Antiochus IV forced the Jews to abandon the observance of Jewish law, biblical Jewish law, and follow Greek customs which were completely foreign and contrary to Jewish law.

So first Maccabees goes on, "they were to make themselves abominable by everything unclean and profane so that they would forget the law and change all the ordinances. He added, 'and whoever it does not obey the command of the King shall die.' " So the implication of this is that Jews must now by law, by the command of the King, follow Greek customs and Greek religion and cease observing Jewish law and Jewish religion. The Jerusalem temple was now rededicated to the Pagan Greek god Olympian Zeus and prostitution was practiced there, sacred prostitution. Similarly by the way, the Samaritans requested that their temple on Mount Gerizim be rededicated to Zeus Hellenios. Both temples of the Jewish god were now rededicated to the god of Israel were rededicated to the Greek god Zeus.

The consequence of Antiochus' decree means that Judaism was now outlawed, and that means that observing Jewish law was a crime punishable by death. This is directly contrary to what had been the case before. From the time of the Persian restoration, Jewish law had been the law of the land. Remember that Isriah comes and institutes Jewish law at the command of the Persian king. So from the time of the Persian restoration on, the Judeans had observed Jewish law as the law of the land. What this means is that if you were a Judean, a person of Judean origin or heritage, you were then obligated to worship the god of Israel as your national god and observe the laws of the god of Israel, the laws in the Torah as the law of the land. What Antiochus IV does that is so radical is abolishes that, and he now makes Greek law and Greek religion and Greek customs the law of the land as opposed to Jewish law and Jewish customs. This is very, very different from what the Jews had been used to before.

Antiochus IV's decree was actually accepted by many members of the Jewish population, but not by all of them, and what happens is a revolt now breaks out against Antiochus which is led by a Jewish priestly family not from Jerusalem but from a village outside of Jerusalem. A village called Modiin, which today is located about halfway between Jerusalem and Tel Aviv. This local priestly family, this village priestly family was called the Hasmonean family, or sometimes called the Maccabean family and the revolt actually begins in 167 B.C. when the patriarch of this priestly family, a local priest named Mattathias, kills another Jew who is about to participate in offering a sacrifice to a Greek God and also executes the officer of Antiochus IV who is overseeing the sacrifice, and that then marks the beginning of this revolt against Antiochus IV.

The revolt is then led by Mattathias and his sons, the most famous of his sons, and the one who is instrumental at the beginning of the revolt, is his third son whose name is Judah sometimes nick-named Judah Maccabee, which means Judah the hammer. So we hear Judah Maccabee with about nine others got away to the wilderness and kept himself and his companions alive in the mountains as wild animals do. They continued to live on what grew wild so that they might not share in the defilement. So the revolt starts with Judah Maccabee fleeing to the mountains, taking refuge in the mountains with some of his companions, and actually living on wild plants so that they would not have to eat impure food, the impure food of the Greeks, which of course was not permitted according to biblical Jewish law; and so both first and second Maccabees describe mass flight to the wilderness. "Judah, who was also called Maccabeus ["the hammer"], and his companions secretly entered the villages and some of their kinsman and enlisted those who had continued in the Jewish faith so they gathered about 6,000 men."

With the outbreak of this revolt then, the Maccabean family collects family members, relatives, friends, and they start to form a core of a rebellious unit. At the very beginning of the revolt, Mattathias who was already an old man died, and the Hasmonean army then, this family is led by Judah, the third son, and his four brothers Simon, Jonathan, John, and Eleazar. We read in Maccabees,

> He [Judah] searched out and pursued the lawless; he burned those who troubled his people. Lawless men shrank back for fear of him. All the evildoers were confounded and deliverance prospered by his hand. He went through the cities of Judah; He destroyed the ungodly out of the land and thus he turned away wrath from Israel. (1 Maccabees)

This is a very interesting passage actually because it describes Judah Maccabee searching out and perusing lawless people. Who were the lawless people? Lawless people are those who do not observe or obey the law. Which law, in this case it is referring to Jewish law. Actually what this reflects is that we have here, at least at the very beginning of the revolt, a situation that can be characterized as a civil war. With some Jews going ahead over to the Greek side and observing the Greek customs, they are the lawless ones, according to first Maccabee, and Judah and his followers perusing them, calling them lawless because they are not observing Jewish law. It is basically those who are observing Jewish law versus those who are not; a state of civil war.

The Hasmoneans collected a small army and scored a series of important military victories against Antiochus IV and his troops. In 164 B.C., Antiochus IV died and was succeeded to the throne by his young son Antiochus V. And Antiochus V then issued a very important edict which says as follows,

> King Antiochus [AntiochusV] to his brother Lysias, greeting. Now that our father has gone on to the gods, we desire that the subjects of the kingdom be undistrubed and caring for their own affairs. We have heard that the Jews do not consent to our father's change to Greek customs but prefer their own way of living and ask that their customs be allowed them.
>
> Accordingly, since we choose that this nation will also be free from disturbance, our decision is that their Temple be restored to them and that the live according to the customs as their ancestors. You will do well, therefore, to send word to them and give them pledges of friendship so that they may know our policy and go on happily in the conduct of their affairs. (2 Maccabees)

So notice that Antiochus V in 164 B.C. issues an edict which rescinds the edict of his father and allows the Jews to go back and freely observe Jewish law without fear of persecution. The situation now reverts back, and not only that, but the temple, the Jerusalem temple, is now restored to the Jews having of course in the interim been rededicated to Olympian Zeus.

The temple is now restored to the Jews and it is allowed to be rededicated to the God of Israel to the worship to the God of Israel, and before we go on, notice again too that 2 Maccabees here in this edict refers to the customs of the Jews as being the customs of their ancestors. We will see that this figures in later when we talk about the Roman view of Judaism as being an ancestral religion, an ancient ancestral religion, so here Antiochus V is allowing the

Jews to return to the customs of their ancestors and returning the temple to them.

Judah and his brothers seized control of the Jerusalem temple and restored the sacrificial cult according to tradition. In the middle of December, in the year 164 B.C. they cleaned the temple out. They rededicated it to the worship of the God of Israel and it is this, event the rededication of the Jerusalem temple to the God of Israel in 164 that is commemorated by the modern Jewish holiday of Hanukkah, and we celebrate the holiday of Hanukkah today by lighting a candelabrum called a menorah which recalls one of the lamps in the ancient Jerusalem temple. The ancient Jerusalem temple had candelabra that had seven branches, and to celebrate the holiday of Hanukkah Jews now light a candelabrum that has nine, and that is what is called a Hanukkah menorah.

The conflict between the Maccabees and the Seleucids did not end in 164 B.C. In fact after the rededication of the Jerusalem temple, the Maccabees started the revolt up all over again. This time with the purpose of gaining complete independence from the rule of the Greek Seleucid kings. This rebellion then goes on for a number of years with several different sons of Mattathias leading it. At the beginning, Judah was the leader of this rebellion, and in 163 B.C. his brother Eleazar was killed in a battle and Judah was defeated in that battle, but 161 B.C. Judah scored a big battle, won a big battle, against the Seleucids.

It is at about that time that Judah wins this big battle against Seleucids that he also signs a treaty of alliance and friendship with the Romans. This is actually also very interesting. What are the Romans doing in this picture here? We are now in the middle of the 2nd century B.C.; what is happening with the Romans? At this point, the Romans have been expanding their control outside the Italian peninsula and moving further and further into the Eastern Mediterranean into the area of the Hellenistic kingdoms. As the Romans moved into the area of the Eastern Mediterranean, their interest was in taking over various territories. These were the territories of course of the Hellenistic kingdoms, the Ptolemies and the Seleucids.

From the point of view of the Romans then, anybody who is an enemy of the Ptolemies and the Seleucids is going to be a friend of theirs, because that is going to help weaken the Ptolemies and the Seleucids and make way for the Romans to come in and take over. It is against this background of politics that the Romans then sign a treaty of alliance and friendship with Judah and his brothers, and this is a treaty of alliance and friendship that was renewed several times over, over the course of time. Here is what the treaty, as we have it says, "And Judas chose Eupolemus, the son of John, and Jason, the son of Eleazar, and sent them to Rome to establish and friendly relations and an alliance with them," with the Romans. So Judah chooses a couple of guys and sends them to Rome sort of as his emissaries to sign this treaty, "And they went to Rome though the journey was very long." Sure it is a long trip from Judea to Rome, "And they went into the Senate house and answered and said," so these two emissaries who are sent by Judah appear before the Roman Senate and say, "Judas, who is called Maccabeus, and his brothers and the Jewish people have sent us to you to make an alliance and firm peace with you so that we may be enrolled as allies and friends of yours." So the treaty is preserved in 1 Maccabees; so very interesting, a very early alliance then between the Romans and the Maccabees or Hasmonean family.

In 160 B.C. Judah was killed in battle, and what happens after Judah is killed in battle, the leadership of the revolt is then taken over by one of his brothers whose name is Jonathan. Jonathan established himself as ruler of Judea by exploiting a struggle over the Seleucid throne, and this then happens in the year 152 B.C., so what we are seeing here under Judah and his brothers is sort of a successive progression. What starts out as a revolt sparked by Antiochus' attempt to impose Greek culture and Greek religion on the Jews and outlaw Judaism ends up becoming a process whereby the Jews establish complete independence from Seleucid rule over the course of a series of events. So in 152, Jonathan, Judah's brother, who has taken over leadership of the revolt, manages to establish himself as ruler of Judea. He does this because at this point there is a weakness among the Seleucids and he exploits that, and what he does is he supports one of the people who is fighting for control of the Seleucid throne. In return that guy, whose name is Alexander Balas, supports Jonathan as ruler of the Jews. Specifically here is what we have preserved as the treaty or support between Alexander Balas and Jonathan.

"King Alexander [Balas] sends greetings to his brother Jonathan. We have heard that you are valiant warrior and fit to be our friend. Now we have today appointed you to be high priest of your nation and to be called a friend of the king." So this step in 152 is that Jonathan is appointed high priest and he is also a friend of the king, which means that he has a certain degree of autonomy. Notice a very important thing about this little passage here. Alexander Balas not only appoints Jonathan to be a ruler, sort of a semi-autonomous ruler over his people, but he also appoints him high priest.

What has happened here is a very interesting sequence of events because the Hasmonean family, although they were a priestly family, previously had not been high priests in the Jerusalem temple. They were a village priestly family. Now for the first time members of this family become priests serving in the Jerusalem temple. First of all, we have the introduction here of a family that previously had not had any official capacity in the Jerusalem temple, but more than that, we also have now for the first time among the Jews and even among the Israelites a situation where a secular ruler is also officiating as high priest in the Jerusalem temple.

This actually is contrary to Jewish law. That is why for example David and Solomon—Solomon when he built the temple—he appointed somebody else to be priest in the Jerusalem temple. He never officiated as priest in the Jerusalem temple, because according to Jewish law, if you have blood on your hands you are not supposed to be a priest in the temple. Jonathan, of course, as leader of the revolt had been fighting battles so he was a secular leader, a secular ruler, but now he is also going to be a priest in the temple and this is going to create a deep schism in Jewish society. The fact that the Hasmoneans now begin to serve not only as secular rulers but also as high priests in the Jerusalem temple is something that is going to cause a deep division and a lot of opposition among certain sectors of the Jewish population. This is something that we will be talking about much more when we get to the story of the dead sea scrolls in the site of Camron.

In 142 B.C., Jonathan was killed through an act of treachery, and what happens when he killed then is that the last of the five brothers whose name is Simon takes over from Jonathan, and it is under Simon that the Jews gain complete independence from Seleucid rule. By the time Simon died in 134

B.C., an independent Jewish kingdom had been established in Palestine under the rule of this family, the Hasmonean family, a kingdom that we therefore refer to as the Hasmonean kingdom. What we have just talked about then is a remarkable series of brothers who led the Jewish population on a journey towards complete independence from Greek Seleucid rule. This family then established a dynasty where Judah Maccabee and his brothers were succeeded by their sons.

When Simon died in 134, he was succeeded to the throne of this independent kingdom by his son John Hyrcanus I who ruled from 134 to 104 B.C. When the Hasmoneans first gained independence from Greek rule, the area that constituted their kingdom or territory was the area of the Judea, that relatively small territory around the city of Jerusalem. Over the course of the decades after the death of Simon with the various Hasmonean kings, the Hasmoneans expanded the boundaries of their kingdom through territorial conquests, and so this begins already with John Hyrcanus I who conquered Idumaea, the territory to the south, Samaria, the district to the north, and also territories in Transjordan on the other side of the Dead Sea and the Jordan River.

Notice that John Hyrcanus I conquers among other things Samaria, and very, very interesting—so this is the first time now that Judeans conquering, come into control of Samaria and guess what they did? John Hyrcanus I destroys the Samaritan temple on Mount Gerizim. Remember that Judeans viewed the Samaritans as schismatic and their temple as schismatic, so the first thing that they do when they conquer the Samaritans is to destroy their temple on Mount Gerizim. There could be only one temple dedicated to the Jewish god, that is the one in Jerusalem, not the one in Samaria.

John Hyrcanus I also forcibly converted people to Judaism, specifically he converted the inhabitants of Idumaea and other non-Jewish territories to Judaism as we are told by Josephus. "He [John Hyrcanus] permitted them to remain in their counties so long as they had themselves circumcised and were willing to observe the laws of the Jews." This is actually a very interesting thing. First of all, John Hyrcanus did not forcibly convert the Samaritans. To the contrary, the Samaritans were not converted to Judaism. The Samaritans, it is weird, they are schematics, but they are already worshiping the god of Israel, so the Hasmoneans destroy the Samaritan temple on Mount Gerizim but the Samaritans are not forcibly converted to Judaism. The other native peoples though who were conquered by the Hasmoneans are forcibly converted to Judaism.

Actually, Josephus' passage indicated that we given a choice. They were permitted to remain in their country as long as they had themselves circumcised and were willing to observe the laws of the Jews. What does this mean? Your choice was if you were non-Jewish and you were conquered by the Hasmoneans, you could either leave or if you wanted to stay, you had to convert, you had to become circumcised, and you had to observe the laws of the Jews.

This is a very interesting policy that has been the subject of a lot of controversy. Why did the Hasmoneans forcibly convert non-Jewish populations to Judaism? First of all, there might have been an element here of security, that is they were conquering peoples who were different, so if want to be secure within your boundaries, if everybody is Jewish, it is going to be more secure than if you have various populations. I actually think personally that what the Hasmoneans were doing here was a sort of Hellenization, but they were doing it not with Greek culture and religion but with Jewish culture and religion. That is, they were doing the very same thing that Hellenistic kings did to the peoples within their kingdoms. The Hasmoneans were using Jewish culture and religion as a means of unifying different population within their kingdoms, and so just as Antiochus IV had tried to impose Greek culture and religion on the Jews, so now the Hasmoneans impose Jewish culture and religion on non-Jewish populations including the Idumaeans.

This business with the Idumaeans is actually very interesting because one of the Idumaeans who was forcibly converted to Judaism by the Hasmoneans at this time was a man named Antipas. Antipas was the grandfather of Herod the Great. We are going to talk a lot about Herod the Great, and there is always a lot of controversy. Herod was Jewish, part-Jewish, how was he Jewish, well actually he was half-Jewish on his father's side of the family through forced conversion. His grandfather was one of these Idumaeans who had been forcibly converted to Judaism.

When John Hyrcanus died he was succeeded to the throne by his son Aristobulus I who ruled only very briefly from 104 to 103 B.C.; although very, very interesting thing to note, notice his name, Aristobulus the first. John Hyrcanus has a name that is a little bit Greek, Hyrcanus is somewhat Greek sounding, but John is a Jewish name, but Aristobulus I is a completely Greek name. It is ironic that although the Maccabees are renowned for having opposed the attempt to impose Greek culture and religion on the Jews, that is what they are known for, as soon as they become establishment, as soon as they become the rulers, we being to see them adopting various aspects of Greek culture.

By this point, Aristobulus I is simply using a Greek name, and also other aspects of Greek culture were adopted by the Hasmonean rulers. These Hasmonean kings were not necessarily very nice people. In fact a lot of them were pretty ruthless. Aristobulus, in order to take over the throne when his father died, had his mother and brothers imprisoned, and while in prison his mother actually starved to death and he had another brother put to death because he did not want him to be able to take over the throne. These guys were actually pretty ruthless, just because they were Jewish kings does not mean that they were necessarily all the good or all that nice.

Aristobulus I was also the first Hasmonean to call himself by the title of king, so up until this point really technically, the Hasmonean kingdom, was not yet a kingdom, technically speaking, even though it was it was a little independent entity. Aristobulus is the first one to take that title of king. As I just said, he used his Greek name instead of his Hebrew name, which was Judah. Aristobulus I like John Hyrcanus I also increased the size of the Hasmonean kingdom. He increased the kingdom by conquering territories to the North, specifically Galilee and the Golan, and like John Hyrcanus I, Aristobulus I forcibly converted the native populations to Judaism. The native population in the North was a people called Ituraeans.

Under Aristobulus I, these people are forcibly converted to Judaism and Galilee now becomes Jewish. This is actually a very interesting point too. It is interesting because it leads us into the story of Jesus of Nazareth, because 100 years after Aristobulus' conquest of Galilee, we read in Mark, "In those days Jesus came from Nazareth of Galilee." So this raises the question what was Jesus' background? What was in fact the background of this population in Galilee beginning with Aristobulus' conquest? What we apparently have is sort of a native population that is Judaisized, converted to Judaism, mixed probably with some people who came from Judeah and settled in the north and mixed with the native Judaisized population.

It is against this background that we will come back to reconsider later in the course what was Jesus' linage or background, and what do we know about this, and what do we know about Galilee in the time of Jesus. So Aristobulus I's conquest of Galilee actually sets the stage for beginning to consider the background and the linage of Jesus who came from Nazareth in Galilee. We have reviewed here the establishment of an independent Jewish kingdom in Palestine as the result of an uprising against Antiochus IV and his attempts to impose Greek culture and religion on the Jewish population and the eventual growth and expansion of that independent Jewish kingdom up until the reign of Aristobulus I at the very end of the 2nd century B.C.

This now sets the stage for considering the continued history of the Hasmonean kingdom and its eventual annexation by the Romans, which we will talk about in our next lecture.

The Hasmonean Kingdom
Lecture 12

> In other words, the people at Qumran who deposited the Dead Sea Scrolls in the nearby caves mocked this other group of Jews, the same group that rebelled against Alexander Jannaeus, as those who seek the easy way out in the observance of Jewish law. ... Who is this group, then, the seekers of smooth things? This is a name that the group at Qumran gave to the Pharisees.

We ended our last lecture with the Hasmonean king Aristobulus I, who ruled from 104 to 103 B.C. Aristobulus I was a ruthless man who imprisoned his brothers, killing one of them, and allowed his mother to die of starvation in prison. When Aristobulus I died of an illness, his widow, Salome Alexandra, freed his brothers and married one of them, Alexander Jannaeus. This was a **Levirate marriage**, in accordance with Jewish law. Unfortunately, Alexander Jannaeus would also be high priest and could marry only a virgin; thus, the marriage violated the law.

This violation was not to be his last. Alexander Jannaeus was a ruthless ruler who frequently disregarded the Jewish law and, therefore, aroused a great deal of opposition. Once, during the feast of Tabernacles, Alexander Jannaeus, acting as high priest, poured holy water on the ground instead of on the altar; the people became upset and threw at him the citrons they held as part of the ceremony. In response, Alexander Jannaeus massacred 6,000 of the pilgrims.

Eventually, the **Pharisees** had had enough and organized a revolt; for help, they turned to the nearest outside power, the Seleucid king, Demetrius III. Demetrius then invaded, but the rebels suddenly had a change of heart, abandoning Demetrius and returning to Alexander Jannaeus. Unfortunately for them, Alexander did not forgive them. According to one of the Dead Sea Scrolls, he crucified 800 of them, slaughtering their wives and children before their eyes as they suffered on their crosses, while he banqueted with his concubines.

Alexander Jannaeus died in 76 B.C., succeeded by his widow, Salome Alexandra. She ruled the Hasmonean kingdom rather well while her older son, John Hyrcanus II, served as high priest. When Salome Alexandra died in 67 B.C., the office of king should have fallen to John Hyrcanus II, but a younger son, Aristobulus II, also wanted to be king. A civil war broke out between the brothers, who both turned for help to an outside power, Rome. Soon, the Romans would simply step in and take over the Hasmonean kingdom.

> **Soon, the Romans would simply step in and take over the Hasmonean kingdom.**

At around the same time, just to the south, a people called the **Nabateans** were prospering. An Arab people, they had established caravan routes through the desert, and using those routes, they brought to the Mediterranean coast expensive items from the east, such as myrrh and frankincense. With time, this lucrative trade had made the Nabateans wealthy, as is evident in the ruins of their capital, **Petra**, presently in Jordan southeast of the Dead Sea. At this desert site appear a colonnaded street, large temples dedicated to various Nabatean gods, and a Greek-style theater cut into one of the sides of the cliffs, indicating Hellenistic influence. Most spectacular are the rock-cut tombs, miles of them, in some cases with facades cut to create the illusion of three-dimensional buildings.

Miles of rock-cut tombs create a beautiful landscape in Petra.

Our exploration of the Hasmonean kingdom and the Nabatean kingdom to its south now sets the stage for a look at some of the Jewish groups that came into existence during the Hasmonean period. ■

Important Terms

Levirate marriage: Biblical law requiring a man to marry his brother's widow if his brother was childless.

Nabataeans: An Arab people who created a kingdom in the area of modern Jordan, the Negev, and the Sinai from the mid-2nd century until A.D. 106.

Petra: Capital of the Nabataean kingdom, located to the southeast of the Dead Sea in modern Jordan.

Pharisees: Jews of the Late Second Temple period who were moderately prosperous and known for their strict observance of Jewish purity laws.

Questions to Consider

1. Considering the cruelty and atrocities carried out by Hasmonean kings, such as Aristobulus I and Alexander Jannaeus, and their blatant disregard for the observance of biblical law, why should Jews commemorate the Maccabean revolt by celebrating Hanukkah?

2. Knowing that Herod was half Idumaean (his father's side) and half Nabataean (his mother's), what would you expect from him in terms of cultural and religious orientation?

The Hasmonean Kingdom
Lecture 12—Transcript

In our last lecture, we talked about the Maccabean revolt and the establishment of an independent Jewish kingdom ruled by the Maccabees and their successors called the Hasmoneans. We talked about some of the earliest Hasmonean rulers, ending with Aristobulus I who ruled from 104 to 103 B.C. I would like to pick up with Aristobulus I today and look at him some more, and the rest of the Hasmonean kings up until the end of the Hasmonean kingdom when it's nixed by the Romans. Then I would like to finish up the lecture by looking at one of the very important neighboring peoples of the Hasmoneans, and that is the Nabateans.

If we go back to remind ourselves of what we were talking about with Aristobulus I, remember that he was a ruthless man who became king by imprisoning his brothers, killing one of them, and imprisoning his mother who died of starvation while she was in prison. He was also a Hellenizer preferring to use his Greek name Aristobulus instead of his Hebrew name; and like his predecessor, he continued to increase the size of the Hasmonean kingdom through territorial expansion. This is one of the very important things about the policy of the Hasmonean kings, that they enlarge the size of their kingdom through territorial conquests and forced the non-Jewish peoples, who they conquered, to convert to Judaism or leave the country.

Among the peoples who were forcibly converted by the Hasmoneans were the Idumaeans to the south and the Ituraeans, the inhabitants of Galilee and the Golan to the north. So what happens after the time of Aristobulus I? Aristobulus I died in 103 B.C. of an illness, and when he died, his widow, whose name was Salome Alexandra, freed Aristobulus brothers from captivity because they were still in captivity, and then she married one of them. This actually sounds like a bit of a peculiar policy that the widow frees the brothers and then marries one of them, but in fact it is in accordance with Jewish law.

Biblical Jewish law says that when a brother dies without leaving any heirs, the widow of that man should then marry one of the brothers. Let us actually read the biblical passage which is from Deuteronomy,

When brothers reside together, and one of them dies and has no son, the wife of the decreased shall not be married outside the family to a stranger. Her husband's brother shall go in to her, taking her in marriage, and performing the duty of a husband's brother to her, and the firstborn whom she bears shall succeed to the name of the deceased brother, so that his name may not be blotted out of Israel.

Again this is according to Deuteronomy. This kind of marriage where a widow marries one of the brothers of her husband is called levirate marriage, and so when Salome Alexandra, the widow of Aristobulus, married Aristobulus' brother she was actually acting in accordance with this biblical law.

Of course the idea of the biblical law originally was that a family line should not come to an end because a brother dies without leaving any heirs. In this case, Salome Alexandra marries one of Aristobulus' brothers, a brother whose name was Alexander Jannaeus; and Alexander Jannaeus now becomes the next Hasmonean king. It sounds as though this all was in accordance with biblical law, but in fact by marrying Salome Alexandra, Alexander Jannaeus actually was breaking biblical law because on the one hand Deuteronomy mandates this sort of levirate marriage, this marriage between a brother of a man who died and his widow, but on the other hand there is another law in the Hebrew bible that prohibits this particular circumstance. This law is in Leviticus and it says, "He, the high priest, shall marry only a woman who is a virgin. A widow or a divorced woman or a woman who has been defiled, a prostitute, these he shall not marry."

So what is the problem here? On the one hand yes, Alexander Jannaeus was supposed to marry his brother's widow in accordance with Deuteronomy, but because the Hasmonean kings also assumed the office of high priest, there was a law that prohibited a high priest from marrying a widow. So in this case, that law should have superseded the principle of levirate marriage, and Alexander Jannaeus should not have married his brother's widow in this particular case. Again although there was a general principal of levirate marriage, in the particular case of Alexander Jannaeus, because he was high priest, there was another law that prohibited him specifically from marrying a widow, and therefore he should not have married Salome Alexandra. Basically what this means is that Alexander Jannaeus, when he becomes Hasmonean king, violates biblical Jewish law by marrying his brother's widow.

Alexander Jannaeus in general was a ruthless ruler. He ruled for quite a long time from 103 B.C. until 76 B.C. He was a ruthless man as we will see, and he also acted frequently with disregard for the observance of biblical Jewish law; and Alexander Jannaeus' actions therefore aroused a great deal of opposition among the Jewish population. There were already wide sectors of the Jewish population that believed that the Hasmonean king should not be acting also as high priest, but Alexander Jannaeus' blatant disregard for the observance of biblical Jewish law aroused much more opposition and especially among a particular group called the Pharisees, who we will be talking about some more in this lecture and also in our next lecture.

One example of Alexander Jannaeus' disregard for Jewish law occurred during the holiday of Sukkot, which is the Feast of Tabernacles, a holiday that occurs usually around our month of October. As part of the ceremony, observing this festival, Jews hold a bundle of branches of different species together with a large bumpy citrus fruit called a citron which is like a big bumpy lemon, and as part of the ceremony observing this particular festival, the Feast of Tabernacles, the bundle of branches and the citron are waved together.

The holiday of Sukkot, the Feast of Tabernacles, was one of the pilgrimage holidays to the Jerusalem temple, and so we have to imagine then that every year on this holiday masses of Jews would go to Jerusalem and congregate in the temple, and as part of the observance of this festival, would wave these branches and the citrus fruits, the citrons, in their hands. One year during the observance of this festival, Alexander Jannaeus, acting as high priest, poured holy water on the ground instead of on the altar, and this got all of the pilgrims upset, and what happens according to Josephus, "For at a festival which was then celebrated, when he stood upon the altar [he being Alexander Jannaeus] and was going to sacrifice, the nation rose up against him and pelted him with citrons." So when Alexander Jannaeus poured the water on the ground instead of on the altar, everybody got upset and started to throw their citrons at him. "At this he flew into a rage and killed about 6,000 of them." Alexander Jannaeus got so upset that he then massacres

6,000 of the pilgrims. So Alexander Jannaeus is somebody who did not act in accordance with Jewish law and who acted ruthlessly and mercilessly against his enemies, and we see this over and over again.

It is not surprising then that a number of years later, a Jewish revolt breaks out against Alexander Jannaeus, so some sectors of the Jewish population were so upset at him that they rise up and revolt, and who do they turn to for help, they turn to the nearest outside power which is the Seleucid king, and at that point the name of the Seleucid king was Demetrius III. So these Jewish rebels turn to Demetrius III for help. Demetrius then invades, and what happens when he invades Jerusalem? The rebels suddenly decide, maybe we do not really want to go back to Seleucid rule; maybe we would prefer a bad Jewish king over a good Greek one. So they stop the revolt, they abandon Demetrius and the go back to Alexander Jannaeus. The problem is that Alexander Jannaeus was really mad at the rebels, and so he decides to take revenge on them and to punish them for the revolt.

We have a reference to Alexander Jannaeus' punishment of the Jews in a Dead Sea Scroll that is called the Pesher Nahum. The Pesher Nahum is commentary on the prophetic book Nahum, and here is what the relevant passage says and we are going to sort of go through it carefully in order to understand it. "Interpreted, this concerns Demetrius, king of Greece, who sought on the counsel of those who seek smooth things to enter Jerusalem." We are going to be talking a little more about Dead Sea Scrolls in another couple of lectures, but let me just preface by saying that in the literature from Cumron in the Dead Sea Scrolls, when you have books that are commentaries, what they will do is they will cite the original biblical passage and then they will give the interpretation.

So what we are looking at here is an interpretation of a specific passage from the book of Nahum where the interpretation starts, interpreted, this concerns Demetrius, the King of Greece. The relevant passage in the book of Nahum actually does not say anything about Demetrius king of Greece; the person who wrote the interpretation, the Pesher on Nahum, however, interpreted this particular passage as relating to Demetrius, King of Greece.

What we have here then is a passage from this biblical book that was interpreted by the person who wrote the Pesher as relating to this episode where Demetrius invades Jerusalem because some sectors of the population sought his help in their rebellion against Alexander Jannaeus, and specifically this particular passage here is starting, interpreted, this concerns Demetrius, King of Greece, who sought on the counsel of those who seek smooth things to enter Jerusalem. In other words, the group of Jews, the rebels, who invited Demetrius in are described here in the Pesher Nahum as those who seek smooth things. That group of Jew is described here as those who seek smooth things.

I emphasize this because we will come back to talk about what this means. What is this group who seeks smooth things? So the passage continues, "But god did not permit the city to be delivered into the hands of the kings of Greece, from the time of Antiochus until the coming of the rulers of the Kittim," that is the Romans. So the way the author of this document interpreted things, God intervened and did not allow Jerusalem to be delivered into the hands of Demetrius. In fact, he did not allow Jerusalem to be delivered again into the hands of a foreign power until the Romans come along, and Romans in this document are titled Kittim, a biblical term that is used here as sort of a cover term for Romans.

So in the Pesher Nahum then from Cumron, we have a reference to this invasion of Jerusalem by Demetrius because he was invited by the Jewish rebels who were rebelling against Alexander Jannaeus. After the revolt ended then, Alexander Jannaeus decided to take action against and punish the rebels for having rebelled against him, and Josephus, the ancient Jewish author, describes this event and describes Alexander Jannaeus' punishment as follows. "He [Alexander Jannaeus] brought them [the rebels] back to Jerusalem; and there he did a thing that was as cruel as could be." So this is how he punishes the rebels. "While he feasted with his concubines in a conspicuous place, he ordered 800 of the Jews to be crucified, and slaughtered their children and wives before the eyes of the still-living wretches."

In other words, Alexander Jannaeus punishes the Jewish rebels by crucifying them, and while they are writhing in agony on their crosses, he slaughters their wives and children before their eyes and all of this while he is banqueting with his concubines. So again, obviously Alexander Jannaeus was not a very nice person; he was quite ruthless. Interestingly, this same episode, the crucifixion of these rebels, is referred to in the Pesher Nahum, that same document from Cumron that we talked about that is a commentary on the biblical book of Nahum, and here is what the relevant passage in the Pesher Nahum says. "Interpreted, this concerns the furious young lion," and there is no doubt furious young lion here is referring to Alexander Jannaeus, "[who executes revenge] on those who seek smooth things and hangs men alive."

So he took revenge on his group of rebels here in the Pesher described as "those who seek smooth things," and what does he do, he hangs them alive. Hanging them alive means he crucifies them, so this document refers to the same episode of the crucifixion of Alexander Jannaeus' opponents as we read about in Josephus so it is very interesting. We have a document from Cumron and we have a description in Josephus that pretty much described this event in the same way. That still leaves us hanging with the seekers of smooth things. What is this group, those who seek smooth things?

One of the interesting things about the Dead Sea Scrolls is that a lot of times when they refer to real people or groups of people, they refer to them not by their real names but by nicknames, and usually the nicknames are puns. Those who seek smooth things is a pun, a name for a particular group. So the people who lived at Cumron and deposited the scrolls in the nearby caves referred to another Jewish group, specifically in this case the group that rebelled against Alexander Jannaeus, by the title "those who seek smooth things." In order to understand the pun we actually have to go into Hebrew a bit. Seekers of smooth things in Hebrew is *dorshay halakot*; those who seek smooth things, *dorshay halakot*. *Dorshay* is seekers. Smooth things, *halak, halakot*.

This is a pun on another Hebrew term that is very close seekers of the law, *dorshay halakhot*. So *halakot* is smooth, *halakhot* is the law. So in other words, the seekers of smooth things is a pun for a group of people who seek to observe the law and mockingly the people at Cumron are referring to this group not as those who seek to observe the law but who seek smooth things. Well, what does this mean? Those who seek smooth things means those who

177

seek the easy way out, who look for the easy observance of the law rather than the correct observance of the law.

In other words, the people at Cumron who deposited the Dead Sea Scrolls in the nearby caves mocked this other group of Jews, the same group that rebelled against Alexander Jannaeus, as those who seek the easy way out in the observance of Jewish law. They, the people at Cumron, saw themselves as observing the law in the right way, which was a stricter observance of law, while this group, the one that rebels against Alexander Jannaeus, they mock as those who seek the easy way out, the seekers of smooth things. Who is this group then, the seekers of smooth things? This is a name that the group at Cumron gave to the Pharisees. Specifically the group that rebels against Alexander Jannaeus and that is then punished by Alexander Jannaeus with crucifixion and that is described in this document, the Pesher Nahum, as those who seek smooth things, that is the Pharisees, and remember that one of the groups that was especially opposed to Alexander Jannaeus' disregard for the observance of Jewish law was the Pharisees.

Alexander Jannaeus dies in 76 B.C. and then he is succeeded to the throne by his widow, Salome Alexandra, and she rules the Hasmonean kingdom until 67 B.C. when she dies, and this is actually very interesting too because here we have an example of a Hasmonean queen ruling. By the way, of course, Salome Alexandra as a woman automatically was disqualified from serving as high priest in the Jerusalem temple. The high priest in the Jerusalem temple could only be men, and so Salome Alexandra ruled the Hasmonean kingdom as queen but her older son served as the high priest while she was in office, and Josephus actually gives Salome Alexandra kind of a glowing review with a little bit a qualification sort of saying, she was great even though she was a woman and here is what he says.

> She died, after reigning nine years, and she lived in all seventy-three. She was a woman who showed no signs of the weakness of her sex for she was sagacious to the greatest degree in the ambition of governing and demonstrated by her deed at once that her mind was fit for action.

So all together she was a good queen, she was a good ruler, despite being a woman. Salome Alexandra then served as queen and her older son, John Hyrcanus II, served as high priest. When Salome Alexandra died in 67 B.C., the office of king should have fallen to her older son, to John Hyrcanus II, the problem is that Salome Alexandra had a younger son named Aristobulus II who was very ambitious and who also wanted to be king. So what happens after Salome Alexandra's death is that a civil war breaks out over the struggle to the throne between her two sons, and it is this civil war that eventually leads to the downfall and collapse of the Hasmonean kingdom, because eventually both of these of these sons during the course of the civil war are going to turn to an outside power for help, that power being Rome, and what is going to happen eventually is that the Romans then will simply step in and take over the Hasmonean kingdom. The Hasmonean kingdom falls as a result of the struggle over the throne between the two sons of Salome Alexandra.

By the time the Hasmonean kingdom reaches its height, which is roughly around let us say, 100 B.C. or a little afterwards, what we have is then a sizable kingdom that goes all the way up in the north through Galilee and the area of the Golan Heights. It includes territories on the eastern side of the Jordan River and the Dead Sea, through the area of the Judea and including Idumaea. It is actually quite a sizable kingdom in the end and includes much of the area that is today within the borders of the state of Israel and the Palestinian territories, and even some area that today is in the country of Jordan, excluding part of the Negev desert.

Who was living in this territory while the Hasmoneans had their kingdom? What I would like to do now is turn to look at the peoples living here to the south of the Hasmoneans kingdom, bordering on the Hasmonean kingdom, and talk about them. The people who directly bordered on the Hasmonean kingdom were a people called the Nabateans. The Nabateans were a Semitic people, specifically actually they were an Arab people, their language, the Nabatean language, is an early form of Arabic. Originally the Nabateans were nomads in the desert and wandered desert routes through the near East to the Mediterranean coasts.

Originally when we first started hearing about them which is roughly let us say six century B.C., we hear about them establishing a series of caravan routes with trading posts along the way through the desert, and what they would do with these caravans is bring expensive items from the East, for example myrrh, frankincense, things like that, perfumes. They would bring these costly items by caravans through the deserts to the Mediterranean coasts, and then from the Mediterranean coasts, these expensive luxury items were shipped to the various Hellenistic kingdoms and other kingdoms around the Mediterranean basin. This was a very lucrative trade, this trade in these luxury items, and you have to imagine these caravans of various kinds of pack animals going through the desert. These are precisely the kinds of items that are very small, lightweight to carry, not breakable, but earn a lot of money once you get them to their destination.

Over the course of the centuries, the Nabateans established a very lucrative trade and began to amass quite a bit of money. Eventually some of the trading posts along the caravan routes turned into permanent settlements, and over the course of the centuries, these permanent settlements turned into towns and cities. By the second and 1st centuries B.C., the Nabateans had established a kingdom in the area through which their caravan routes passed. The area of the Nabatean kingdom eventually came to include much of what is today Jordan, much of what is today the Negev desert, and most of the Sinai Peninsula. The main outlet for the Nabatean trade was the port of Gaza on the Southern Palestine coast which you will recall was originally one the Philistine cities.

By the 2nd and 1st centuries B.C. when the Nabateans established this kingdom, they then also established a Monarchy that ruled over this kingdom, and they established then a capital city for their kingdom at a place called Petra, which is today in Jordan, to the southeast of the Dead Sea. Many of you might be familiar with the city of Petra because of its landscape which is absolutely spectacular. On the one hand, it is an extremely bleak desert landscape but it is spectacular because it is mountainous, and not only is it mountainous, but the mountains are made out of a red-colored sandstone. Into this sort of bleak but very rugged red sandstone landscape, the Nabateans established their capital city.

If you go to Petra today, you can still wander around it, and in fact it is one of these world heritage sites today that is protected, and as you approach Petra, one of the things that strikes you again is how utterly barren this landscape is. One of the things that the Nabateans did was to establish a very sophisticated water technology which enabled them to survive in desert conditions, and not only survive and store water in these sorts of desert conditions, but even cultivate land in these desert conditions.

When you go to Petra today and you wander around, and it is an enormous site, you see different parts of the city. There are places where there are houses and not surprisingly many of the houses are very affluent. Some of them are beautifully decorated for example with wall paintings. Even though we are in the middle of the desert, we see things like a colonnaded street, large temples, which were dedicated to various Nabatean gods, including a temple that has been coming to light over the last number of years with an archaeological expedition from the United States, the Great Temple at Petra.

There is a theater which is cut into one of the sides of the cliffs, a Greek-style theater, and very interesting to notice already that we see here Greek or Hellenistic influence on the Nabateans. So even though they are a desert people, originally a Nomadic people, by the time they settle down and build their capital city at Petra, we see a great deal of Hellenistic influence on them, just as we see Hellenistic influence on the other native peoples in this area.

By far the most spectacular thing about Petra and what it is best known for are the rock-cut tombs, miles and miles and miles of tombs that are cut into the cliffs. Many of these tombs consist of simple openings which led in to one or more caves where bodies were originally buried, but in some cases, the facades of the tombs have been cut in beautiful ways to depict buildings so it makes it look as though you have a three-dimensional building in front of you when, in fact, what you have is a façade where the face of the bedrock has been cut.

The most famous of the rock-cut tombs at Petra by far is the tomb that we are going to look at here. It is a tomb that is reached when you first go into Petra. In order to go into Petra actually, you have to go through a very long, narrow, windy canyon which is called the Siq. When you reach the end of this canyon, you begin to see in front of you the beginnings of one of these rock-cut tombs, and by far the most spectacular one of these rock-cut tombs, and here it is, it is called The Khazneh, that is a modern Arabic name, which means the treasury. Looking at this rock-cut tomb—which by the way might be familiar to you from the movie Indiana Jones and the Last Crusade, in that movie the Holy Grail is supposedly in this structure, which it is not of course, but anyway, you might have noticed it in the movie—what we see in this rock-cut tomb is an attempt to imitate a façade of a building to make it look like a Greek-style temple.

Again, look at the Greek or Hellenistic influence here on the Nabateans. The quality of this particular rock-cut tomb though indicates that it must be Royal, not only the quality but also the location of it. The fact that everybody who goes into Petra, the first thing that you see when you emerge from the Siq is this in front of you, so the location and the quality of this tomb indicate that it must be royal, it must be the tomb of one of the Nabatean kings. Which one we are not sure, possibly Aretas IV, who was the Nabatean king at around the time of Jesus, so late 1st century B.C. early 1st century A.D., possibly that is the king who was originally buried in this tomb.

Unfortunately because the tombs are open and people have wandering around in them now for centuries and centuries, all of the tombs are looted out of their original contents so we cannot say for sure now who was buried there but best guess is that it was somebody like Aretas IV.

Although we focus on Petra as the most famous example of a Nabatean city and rightfully so, the Nabateans established other permanent settlements in other parts of their kingdom. In fact, there were a series of Nabateans cities located around the Negev desert. One of them is at Avdat, or the original Nabatean name Oboda, which is in the middle of the Negev desert. There what we have is the original Nabatean acropolis which originally had a temple on top of it, surrounded by houses, and we have other settlements like that located around the Negev desert. All of these permanent settlements, even though they are in the middle of the desert, were agricultural settlements because the Nabateans developed a sophisticated technology which enabled them to grow agricultural produce even under these harsh desert conditions.

When we look at other aspects of Nabatean culture, we can see very clearly some of the Greek or Hellenistic influence reflected for example in sculpture, reliefs, and statues. The Nabateans in terms of material culture are perhaps best known for their pottery, spectacular pottery which is literally eggshell thin, fired very, very hard and decorated with beautiful abstract floral and geometric designs. It is impossible to mistake this for any other kind of pottery.

The neighbors of the Hasmoneans to the south were these Nabateans, and the Nabatean kingdom then continued to exist until the year 106 A.D. when it was annexed by the Roman emperor Trajan. What we have looked at here now is the Hasmonean kingdom, the Nabatean kingdom to its south, and this now sets the stage for talking some more about some of the Jewish groups that it came to exist during the course of the Hasmonean period.

Pharisees and Sadducees
Lecture 13

> The Sadducees believed in complete human free will, so no intervention at all by God; there is complete human free will. The Pharisees, on the other hand, emphasized both divine omnipotence—God is all knowing and all powerful—alongside human freedom and responsibility.

In our last lecture, we saw that Alexander Jannaeus's failure to observe Jewish law aroused the opposition of certain groups in Jewish society, and we mentioned the Pharisees and the community at **Qumran** associated with the Dead Sea Scrolls, which we will identify as the Essenes. Historical sources indicate a third major group, the Sadducees. In this lecture, we will focus on the Pharisees and Sadducees.

All three groups had separated themselves from the rest of Jewish society because they believed that the traditional values had been corrupted and that only they were practicing the law correctly. Events of the 2nd century B.C., including the revolt against Antiochus IV Epiphanes and the establishment of the Hasmonean kingdom, seem to have contributed largely to the formation of these groups.

> **They believed that the traditional values had been corrupted and that only they were practicing the law correctly.**

The Sadducees originally were a branch of a large family called the **Zadokites**. Solomon had appointed a man named Zadok to officiate as high priest in the temple, and from his time, all of the high priests who officiated in the Jerusalem temple traced their ancestry back to Zadok. In the early 2nd century B.C., right before the Maccabean revolt, the Zadokite family lost control of the temple priesthood. This extended broke into three branches: One branch established a temple in Egypt at Leontopolis, eventually closed by the Roman emperor Vespasian in 73 A.D; another branch helped found and at least initially led the community that settled at Qumran; and a third branch stayed in Jerusalem, accommodated with the ruling powers, and became part of the

Jerusalem elite by the late 1st century B.C. This last branch was what we know as the Sadducees, but eventually, the term applied to anyone belonging to the upper class and connoted a political and religious conservatism.

The Pharisees included some of the lower ranks of priests, craftsmen, small farmers, and merchants. They were known for their recognition of oral tradition in addition to written law. Because many of the laws in the Hebrew Bible applied to situations that no longer existed, these men, who were learned in Jewish law (**rabbis**), interpreted it for their time and passed down their interpretations to disciples.

These two groups differ on some important theological issues. For example, the Sadducees did not believe in life after death because it was nowhere explicitly mentioned in the Five Books of Moses. The Pharisees, in contrast, developed a tradition that some sort of afterlife follows death. Again, the Sadducees believed in complete human free will, without divine intervention, whereas the Pharisees believed in human free will but also in the foreknowledge of God. (We will see that the Essenes believed that everything is preordained by God.)

In the next lecture, we will visit the community that lived at Qumran and deposited the Dead Sea Scrolls in caves there. ■

Important Terms

Qumran: Ancient settlement by the northwest shore of the Dead Sea, surrounded by caves in which the Dead Sea Scrolls were found.

rabbi ("my master"): Originally, a Hebrew term of respect for someone learned in biblical Jewish law.

Zadokites: Descendants of Zadok, high priest in the time of Solomon.

Questions to Consider

1. What is a sect?

2. What sorts of issues divided the various sects of the Late Second Temple period?

Pharisees and Sadducees
Lecture 13—Transcript

In our last lecture, we talked about the Hasmonean kingdom, and the fact that the failure of Alexander Jannaeus to properly observe Jewish law aroused the opposition of certain groups in Jewish society. Specifically we mentioned the Pharisees, and we also referred to the community at Qumran associated with the Dead Sea scrolls. What I would like to do now is talk about some of these Jewish groups that emerged during the Hasmonean period, and specifically in this lecture focus on what we know about the Sadducees and the Pharisees.

First of all, where does our information come from about these groups? Our major sources of information are Josephus, the Jewish historian of the 1st century A.D., the books of 1 and 2 Maccabees which are apocryphal books, that is that they are included in the Catholic canon of Sacred Scripture but not in the Jewish or Protestant canons, the Dead Sea scrolls from Qumran, the New Testament, and rabbinic literature. These are our major sources of information about the Pharisees and the Sadducees.

Josephus, who was a very important source of information, calls these groups haireseis which is a Greek word, singular hairesis. The Latin equivalent of the Greek word hairesis would be the Latin secta. Automatically, you can see that our word heresy comes from the Greek word haireseis, and you can see that our word sect comes from the Latin word secta. So when we read Josephus in translation and we read that he refers to these groups as heresies or sects, it automatically raises certain associations for us today, and the reason is that today heresy and sect or sectarian are words that have a negative connotation.

Why do these words have a negative connotation today? Because today we refer to groups that do things that are illegitimate or that we disapprove of as sects, and we refer to illegitimate practices or unrecognized practices which we do not approve of heresies. The fact that these words today have negative connotations is actually a very Christian concept. Originally in Greek and in Latin, that is in the time of Josephus, haireseis/heresy and secta/sect had no negative connotations at all. It is only later in the early church that the church fathers begin to use these terms in order to denigrate their opponents, but originally they were neutral terms.

We can contrast these terms today, heresy, sect/sectarian with the word denomination. If we refer to a group that we approve of that is recognized as a legitimate group within let's say a larger church, we would refer to that as a denomination, but if we refer to a sect, we refer to a practice as sectarian or as a heresy, then clearly it is something that we disapprove of. We go into this in order to point out that when we read about haireseis or about secta in Josephus, we must then remove the modern negative connotations that these words have today and instead understand that they are simply neutral words that in Greek and in Latin referred to schools of thought or philosophical schools or different groups or movements without any of the disapproving connotations that we might read into it from a modern point of view.

What were the major Jewish sects of the Second Temple period, the late Second Temple period, and what do we know about them? First of all when we refer to these groups, we must describe them as groups that separated themselves from other groups largely because they felt alienated, and they felt alienated because these groups believed that the traditional values had been corrupted. One of the characteristics then of Jewish sects of the late Second Temple period of these various groups is that they separated themselves from the rest of Jewish society and believed that the traditional values had been corrupted, and they believed that only they were practicing Judaism in the right way. So one of the characteristics then of these groups, of these sects of the late Second Temple period, is that each one of them believed that they were doing things the right way and the others were not doing things the right way.

Josephus refers specifically to three sects in the late Second Temple period, and he says as follows, "Indeed there exist among the Jews three schools of philosophy," three *haireseis* in Greek, "the Pharisees belong to the first, the Sadducees to the second, and to the third belong men who have a reputation for cultivating a particularly saintly life, called Essenes." In this lecture we are going to be focusing on the first two, the Pharisees and Sadducees, and we will talk about the Essenes in the lectures after this.

When Josephus says that there are three philosophical schools or three haireseis or three of these groups in Judaism in the late Second Temple period, he is undoubtedly simplifying a more complex situation. That is, undoubtedly there were other groups and movements that existed in late Second Temple period Judaea beginning in the Hasmonean period, but Josephus does not mentions them. He mentions only Pharisees, Sadducees and Essenes. Why do I say this? I say this because there is a debate among scholars as to how many different groups existed in the late Second Temple period Judaism, and what the major groups were. Some scholars think that although there may have been other groups, there were really only three main groups: Pharisees, Sadducees, and Essenes, because these are the ones that we hear of repeatedly in our sources.

Whereas other scholars argue that our sources are only partial in terms of the information that they provide, and that there must have been a wide range of groups that existed in Jewish society and indeed in some sources, different sources, we get hints of other groups because occasionally other groups are referred to. So there is a question about how complex the picture was. How many different groups and movements and sects there were in late Second Temple period Judaea, but for our purposes we are going to focus on the ones that appear to be the major ones. The ones that we have at least the most information on and those are for now the Pharisees, Sadducees, and then later we will also talk about the Essenes.

These sects, Pharisees, Sadducees, and Essenes, seemed to have originated and crystallized by the middle of the 2nd century B.C., and in fact, it is the events that lead up to the formation of the Hasmonean kingdom, the outbreak of the revolt against Antiochus IV of Epiphanies culminating with the establishment of the Hasmonean kingdom that seemed to have contributed largely to the formation and crystallization of these groups. Remember that there were some sectors of the Jewish population that opposed some of the practices of the Hasmoneans, including the fact that they serve not only as kings but also as high priests, and these sorts of divisions of opinion apparently contributed to the formation of these different groups, of these different sects.

What do we know then about the Sadducees? The Sadducees are a group that on the one hand is well known in the sense that most people have heard of Sadducees, but on the other hand we have a problem in terms of our information about them. Our major sources of information on the Sadducees are all hostile to them, and in fact, our sources of information about the Sadducees are all external sources. That is, we have no sources of information about the Sadducees that come from the Sadducees themselves. They come from people or sources that were not part of the Sadducees movement and that were hostile to the Sadducees and so present them in a negative light.

What are these sources? Josephus talks about the Sadducees, and he describes himself as a Pharisee, so he is not a Sadducees but a member of another group, the New Testament, which is also hostile to Sadducees, and rabbinic literature, the literature of the later rabbis, which is allied with the Pharisaic movement or grows out of the Pharisaic movement. So in other words, all of our sources of information on the Sadducees are external to the Sadducees and are hostile to the Sadducees, and therefore present them in a biased light and generally tend to present the Sadducees in a negative light.

What then do we actually know about the Sadducees and about their origins? The Sadducees were a branch of a larger family called the Zadokites. Who exactly were the Zadokites? Way back, centuries before the late Second Temple period, when Solomon had built the first temple on the Temple Mount in Jerusalem, he had appointed a man named Zadok, Hebrew Zadoq, to officiate as high priest in the temple. From that point on, all of the high priests who officiated in the Jerusalem temple traced their ancestry back to Zadok and became known as the Zadokite family.

By the 2nd century B.C. this Zadokite priestly family was a very extended family. Through a series of complicated events right before the outbreak of the Maccabean revolt, the Zadokite family lost control of the priesthood in the Jerusalem temple and the priesthood was taken over, usurped by other priestly families that were not Zadokites, and from that point on, the Zadokites never again regained control of the priesthood in the Jerusalem temple. This Zadokite priestly family, which at this point is very extended, branches off. Different branches of the family go and do different things.

One branch of the family, called the Oniads, establish a temple at a place in Egypt called Leontopolis, and they and their descendents officiated at this temple in Egypt until it was closed by Vespasian in the year 73 A.D. Another branch of the Zadokite family was instrumental in founding and at least initially leading the community that evidentially settled at Qumran and deposited the Dead Sea scrolls in the nearby caves. Yet another branch of this Zadokite family stayed in Jerusalem, accommodated with the ruling powers, and eventually morphed into group that becomes known as the Sadducees. So in other words the Sadducees are one branch of the Zadokite family, and in fact the word Sadducees and Zadokite in Hebrew are basically the same word, and they then become part of the Jerusalem elite in the late 1st century B.C. and 1st century A.D.

Who were these people then, these Sadducees, of the late Second Temple period? They are therefore members of the elite, which means that they are priestly families by definition, and other members of the Aristocracy. Although originally the Sadducees are a branch of the Zadokite family, eventually the term comes to refer to the members of the upper class in Judaea and especially in Jerusalem in the late Second Temple period. So they are the high priests, they are the Aristocracy, and therefore not surprisingly, both politically and religiously, they were conservatives because they were the elite. They were the upper classes. They had it good. Anybody who has it good is going to want to preserve the status quo, and therefore is going to be a conservative. So both politically and religiously they were conservatives.

What does it mean when I say they were religious conservatives? Political conservatives is clear. They like to keep the status quo, things as they are, but what does it mean religious conservatives? It means that they were opposed to religious innovations. Their opposition to religious innovations, to introducing new things in religious practice, is going to be diametrically opposite to what we will see among the Pharisees.

Who are the Pharisees? This is another group where it is a little bit difficult to define them at first. The word Pharisees is a word that actually we do not know where it originally comes from. In Hebrew, the Pharisees are the proscheme. The name Pharisee in Hebrew therefore comes from a Hebrew word, apparently Parash, which means to separate. Actually we are not positive that is the root of the name but it likely is. So the word Parash, the root of this name Pharisees, means to separate. What does it mean, the separate ones, the ones who separated themselves? Why were they called that? What did the separate themselves from? We do not actually know why they were called that. Did they separate themselves from the Sadducees, from the high priests and the elite? Did they separate themselves from the Hasmoneans to whom they were largely opposed? Did they separate themselves from the rest of the population considering that the rest of the population to be too lax in the observance of Jewish law? We do not know; all of those are possible; we just do not know for sure.

What is interesting is that they did not actually call themselves Pharisees, they referred to themselves by other names. When they called each other by a name, they did not say hey over there you Pharisee. They said hey, haver, friend, or they would call each other scribes or sages, and sometimes they called each other by the term rabbi. This term rabbi, which is today a loaded term, means something very different from a modern rabbi. When we say modern rabbi today, it is somebody who has undergone an official process of ordination and generally leads or officiates in a synagogue, but originally the term rabbi is a title which literally means my teacher or my master, and it is a title of respect that you would give to somebody who is an authority in Jewish law, who is learned in Jewish law, so they would often call each other by the term rabbi, my master, my teacher.

If the Sadducees were the elite, the upper classes, who were the Pharisees? The Pharisees came from very diverse backgrounds. They came from both rural areas and from urban areas. They included some of the lower ranks of priests, not the high priests, but some of the other kinds of priestly families, craftsman, small farmers, and merchants. Basically what we have here, and I hate to use this term because it is so anachronistic, but it is what would be analogous to kind of middle-class or maybe an upper middle-class, that is group that is not among the very poor but also not among the wealthiest classes, but fairly comfortably off.

At this point, I want to actually caution and say that I presented a very sort of black and white picture of Pharisees and Sadducees, but we have to remember that the picture was much more complicated than this. Not necessarily every person who was a high priest or a member of the Jerusalem elite would of considered themselves the Sadducees, and not everyone who was from this sort of upper middle-class background would of consider themselves a Pharisees. The picture is more complex than this, but generally speaking, the groups do roughly correspond with these kind of socioeconomic groups.

What are the Pharisees known for? One of the major things that they are known for is their recognition of oral tradition in addition to written law, and what do I mean there? The core of the Hebrew bible is the Pentateuch, the Five Books of Moses, or what Jews call the Torah. The Five Books of Moses contain the laws that the god of Israel gave to his people and which they were expected to live their lives according to. By definition, if you were a Jew, a Judean, in antiquity, you then worshiped the god of Israel as your national deity, as your patron god, and lived your life according to the laws that he gave his people in those Five Books of Moses; fair enough, that is a pretty basic element.

What is new about the Pharisees? In addition to the observance of this written law, the Pharisees added an element of oral tradition, and why is this? The Hebrew bible, the Five Books of Moses in particular, had been compiled and edited now centuries before the late Second Temple period, and already by this time, and it is even more of the case today, many of those laws applied to situations which no longer existed because times change and there is human progress and technology changes. Over the course of time, if you want to continue to live your life according to the laws in the Five Books of Moses, you are going to need to do a certain degree of interpretation and adaptation of those laws in order to make them fit the current situation.

To give you a very anachronistic example from today, nowhere in the Five Books of Moses does it say that you may not flip a light switch on the Jewish Sabbath, on Saturday. What the Hebrew bible says, what the Pentateuch says is that you may not light a fire on the Sabbath. Once electricity was invented, Judaism had a problem; nowhere in the bible does it refer to electricity. So modern rabbis went back and interpreted the biblical passage that says that you may not light a fire on the Sabbath to refer also to electricity, and thereby Jews who observe Jewish law, biblical law, will not flip a light switch on the Sabbath because that turns on the electricity.

What do the Pharisees do? They develop an oral tradition where these rabbis, that is these men who are learned in Jewish law, study the biblical passages, study the biblical laws, and interpret them and begin to pass down their interpretations to generation of disciples or students. This body of oral tradition or oral interpretation becomes the characteristic feature of the Pharisees and distinguishes them from some of the other groups of the late Second Temple period.

Let us now take a look at some examples of the differences between these groups as reported by our various sources. Let us see first of all what Josephus says here about the Sadducees. He says, "But the doctrine of the Sadducees is this: that souls die with the bodies, nor do they regard the observation of anything besides what the law enjoins them." So notice Josephus says that the Sadducees simply will not accept anything except what is written exactly in the law, in the torah, in the Five Books of Moses, and as part of this they believe that souls die with the body, which means that there is no life after death. Why do they believe that there is no life after death? They believe that because the Sadducees said nowhere in the Pentateuch is there an explicit doctrine of the resurrection of the dead after death, so therefore they believe that souls die with the bodies because there is no reference to anything but that in the Hebrew bible.

Josephus says about the Pharisees on the other hand, "They also believe that souls have an immortal vigour in them, and that under the earth there will be rewards or punishments, accordingly as they have lived virtuously or vicious in this life." The Pharisees according to Josephus believe exactly the opposite. They developed a tradition that after death there is in fact some sort of an afterlife, and this is diametrically opposed to what the Sadducees believed, and the Sadducees rejected this because there is no explicit doctrine of such in the bible.

Very interesting, we actually see this also reflected in Acts of the Apostles where it says, "For the Sadducees hold that there is no resurrection and that there are no angels or spirits, while the Pharisees believe in all three." So notice that according to Acts also that the Sadducees do not believe in a resurrection, the Pharisees do, and by the way, here it says the Sadducees also believe that there no angels or spirits and the Pharisees believe that there are angels or spirits.

Another one of the differences between these groups is the doctrine of free will. To what extent is there human free will? The Sadducees believed in complete human free will, so no intervention at all, by god there is complete human free will. The Pharisees, on the other hand, emphasized both divine omnipotence, God is all knowing and all powerful, alongside human freedom and responsibility. Josephus says for example, "And when they determine that all things are done by fate," this is the Pharisees, "and they do not take the freedom from men of acting as they see fit; since their notion is, that it has pleased God to make a temperament, whereby what he wills is done, but so that the will of men can act virtuously or viciously."

That is actually a little bit confusing so it is a little hard to understand here what Josephus is saying. We actually have an early rabbi, Rabbi Akiba, who puts in much more simply. The is what the Pharisees believe: All is foreseen but free will is given. In other words, people have free will to choose what they are going to do but because God is all knowing, he knows what you are going to choose to do before you even do it. So this is the Pharisees doctrine, which is that there is human free will but there is also an element here of God knowing what is going to happen.

When we get to talk about the Essenes, we will see that they actually believe that there is no human free will at all. They believe that everything is preordained by God, so we have three points of a spectrum here: Sadducees at one end believing in complete human free will; Essenes at the other end, no human free will; and the Pharisees somewhere in the middle in this case.

With which sect did Jesus usually engage in debate? If you go through the gospels you will see that the group that is mentioned over and over again are the Pharisees, and this then if we take at its most literal reading would suggest that Jesus engaged most in debate with the Pharisees. However, this is debated by scholars. Why is it a subject of contention among scholars? The canonical gospels as we have them today were written down pretty much after the destruction of the temple in 70 A.D. Mark which is the earliest maybe 60 to 70 A.D., but pretty much what we have dates to after

70 A.D. Where is the problem? The problem is that these groups apparently disappear or cease to exist after 70, so by the time the gospel accounts are written, these groups pretty much have disappeared.

I actually have to qualify this a minute and say that in recent years some scholars have suggested that although we do not hear about these groups after 70, maybe actually they did continue to exist for a while after 70, and so maybe the gospel accounts are not completely anachronistic in that regard; this is a little bit problematic. It is also problematic because we cannot define precisely the relationship between the Pharisees and the rabbis after 70. After 70 the dominant group, the dominant religious authority in Judaism become the rabbis and there is clearly some sort of a relationship between the rabbis after 70 and the Pharisees before 70 because they have a same sort of view of the practice of Jewish law, which is that is it is okay to use this body of oral tradition in order to interpret the written law and to practice Judaism.

Somehow the rabbis after 70 seemed to grow out of the Pharisaic movement before 70, and it may be in fact that some of the other movements also continue to exist in some form after 70. There is a whole problem here with how long these groups continued to exist after 70, in what form they continued to exist, and this is the problem in trying to then relate the groups that we know about with the gospel accounts. If we take the gospel accounts at face value, it looks like Jesus is usually engaging in debate with the Pharisees, so there could be two logical explanations for this. Number 1 either Jesus really does debate the Pharisees more than any other group, and the gospels are therefore more or less accurate, or the other possibility is—and this is what some scholars think—that Jesus is portrayed as debating the Pharisees because by the time the gospels are being written after 70, the only major group that really is continuing to exist is the Pharisaic movement, which is morphing into the rabbis.

This is kind of a conundrum actually. There is actually no solution to this question. It is an ongoing debate among scholars. I will actually say that I think that without saying that the gospels are completely historically accurate, but to my mind it is most likely that Jesus really was debating mostly with the Pharisees because the Sadducees are the upper classes there in Jerusalem and they would not have been debating with Jesus when he is up in Galilee, and the Essenes, well they are a marginal group that we will see that probably was not debating with Jesus' movement. So of the movements that we know about actually, most logically it would have been the Pharisees who Jesus was engaging in debate with. Anyway, this is what the gospels portray; usually Jesus is engaged in debate with the Pharisees.

Let us take a look at an example of a passage of where is Jesus is engaged in a debate. "The Pharisees gathered about him, Jesus, with some scribes," and there is whole other question, who are these scribes right? Are they a different group, are they part of the Pharisaic movement, are they Sadducees, a whole other question.

> The Pharisees gather about him with some scribes who had come from Jerusalem. They had noticed that some of his disciples ate their food without first giving their hands a ceremonial washing to purify them. For the Pharisees and all the Jews observe the rules handed down from their ancestors, and will not eat until they have washed their hands in a particular way, and they will not eat anything from the market without first purifying it by sprinkling it. ...
>
> And the Pharisees and the scribes asked him, "Why do your disciples not observe the rules handed down by our ancestors, but eat food without purifying their hands?" [And this what Jesus says to them:] But he said to them, "It was about you hypocrites that Isaiah prophesied so finely in the words, 'This people honors me with their lips, but their hearts are far from me; in vain do they worship me, teaching human precepts as doctrines,' [that is a quote from Isaiah]. "You abandon the commandment of God and hold to human tradition."

And this of course from Mark. This is actually very interesting, Jesus of course, his response is you are hypocrites because you observe the law with your lips by words but not with your hearts, but then he goes on and he says that they are worshiping God by teach human precepts as doctrines and holding to human tradition. What is this reflecting? This is actually very interesting. It is a criticism of the Pharisaic observance of oral tradition versus written law. So what Jesus is saying is your criticism of us, that we are not washing hand before eating, is based on a tradition that has no basis in the written law, it is one of your oral traditions; therefore, it is a human doctrine that has nothing to do with the laws of God, and that is how Jesus responds to the criticism of the Pharisees, according to this passage in Mark.

With this we are going to wrap up our discussion of Pharisees and Sadducees, and we will now continue next time with the community that lived at Qumran and deposited the Dead Sea scrolls in the nearby caves.

Discovery and Site of the Dead Sea Scrolls
Lecture 14

> Here is a wonderful example of correspondence between our literary sources, both Dead Sea [Scrolls] and outside literary sources, which ... describe communal meals being held by the members of this community ... and the archaeological evidence where we clearly see evidence of communal meals practiced by this community.

In our last lecture, we talked about the major groups or sects that developed in the Late Second Temple period in Judea, focusing especially on the Pharisees and Sadducees. In this lecture and the next three, we'll discuss a group that many scholars identify with the Essenes, that is, the community that lived at Qumran and deposited scrolls in the nearby caves.

Qumran is located on the northwest shore of the Dead Sea, south of Jericho and east of Jerusalem. In 1946–1947, Bedouins discovered in caves at Qumran pottery jars, some of which contained ancient parchment scrolls. These scrolls made their way onto the antiquities market, and soon scholars realized that scrolls had been found near the site of Qumran. It had already been surveyed, but a new expedition was conducted in the 1950s to excavate the site and explore the caves nearby for more scrolls.

The remains of more than 900 different scrolls were found in 11 caves.

Eventually, the remains of more than 900 different scrolls were found in 11 caves. These remains were mostly fragmentary: One cave yielded more than 500 different scrolls, strewn on the floor of the cave, where they had disintegrated into thousands of small fragments. Scholars literally spent decades sifting by hand through these fragments, trying to determine which pieces belonged together. This task is now done, and all of the Dead Sea scrolls have been fully accessible to the public for well over a decade.

The excavation of the site of Qumran itself revealed a settlement that had been established around 100 B.C. and was destroyed by earthquake in 31 B.C., by fire in 9 B.C. or a little later, and finally, by the Romans in A.D. 68. This Hasmonean site is very small and evidences no private dwellings. Instead, all of the rooms in the settlement were used either for communal purposes or as workshops. If most or all of the members of this community lived nearby in huts or tents, then the population could reasonably be estimated at 100 to 150.

This complex included a two-story watchtower, what was probably a scriptorium of sorts, a communal dining room, many workshops, an extensive water system, and a large cemetery nearby. The place was visually modest: Walls are made of mostly uncut fieldstone, floors are either dirt or rough flagstone, and there is no interior decoration, no stucco.

In our next lecture, we will look at some of the other interesting features at Qumran, including peculiar animal bone deposits, the potter's workshop, the water system and pools, and the large adjacent cemetery. ∎

The ruins of Qumran, destroyed in A.D. 68 by the Romans. Many of the Dead Sea Scrolls were likely created or copied by the community here.

Questions to Consider

1. Why did conspiracy theories arise about the Dead Sea Scrolls soon after their discovery?

2. One of the questions frequently posed in the popular media is: Who wrote the Dead Sea Scrolls? Does the identification of a room at Qumran as a "scriptorium" help us answer this question?

Discovery and Site of the Dead Sea Scrolls
Lecture 14—Transcript

In our last lecture, we talked about the major groups or sects that developed in the late Second Temple period in Judea focusing especially on the Pharisees and Sadducees. What I would like to do now and in our next couple of lectures is talk about a group that many scholars identify with the Essenes, that is the community that lived at Qumran and deposited the scrolls in the nearby caves.

What we are going to start out by doing is talking about the initial discovery of the Dead Sea scrolls, and the exploration of the site of Qumran. We are then going to go around the site of Qumran and look at some the major features that make the site so unique, and then we will talk about what the Dead Sea scrolls are and how they relate to the site of Qumran and what they tell us about this particular group.

First of all, where is the site of Qumran located? It is located on the northwest shore of the Dead Sea, to the south of Jericho and to the east of Jerusalem. To give you a sense of scale, today it is about a half an hour drive from Jerusalem down to Qumran. The area around Qumran consists of rugged cliffs that go steeply down to the shore of the Dead Sea. Qumran is located, by the way, in an area that many people refer to as the West Bank. That is the territory that was under the rule of the government of Jordan from the time the state of Israel was established in 1948 and up until the 6-day war in 1967 and since then, of course, it has been under Israeli control.

What is the story of the initial discovery of the Dead Sea scrolls? There are many different versions of the story, and I am going to give you just a very simplified version which is that one day a Bedouin boy wandered into a cave in the vicinity of site of Qumran. This occurred in the winter/spring of 1946/1947. When the Bedouin wandered into this cave, which we call Cave 1 at Qumran, he reportedly saw a row of tall cylindrical pottery jars covered with bowl-shaped lids. The Bedouin boy called to other members of his tribe. They came and opened up the jars; found that most of the jars were empty, but at least a couple of the jars contained ancient scrolls, which the Bedouin removed from the cave apparently on several different occasions.

Eventually the Bedouin removed seven complete or nearly complete scrolls from Cave 1 at Qumran.

The Bedouin, of course, did not know that these were ancient scrolls. In fact because the scrolls were written on parchment, which is processed animal hide, it looked to them like pieces of old shoe leather and so they did the logical thing; they took these scrolls and offered them for sale to a man who worked as a cobbler, a shoemaker in the area of Bethlehem. That man's name was Kando. Kando purchased the seven scrolls from the Bedouin. Kando also did not know that these were ancient scrolls, but he could see that there was writing on some of them. He could not read the writing, but he thought that maybe the writing was ancient Syriac. You see, Kando was a member of the Syrian Orthodox Church in Jerusalem.

He took four of the scrolls and offered them for sale to the Patriarch of the Syrian Orthodox Church in Jerusalem at that time, a man named Athanasius Yeshua Samuel. Athanasius Yeshua Samuel purchased those four scrolls from Kando for the sum of 24 British pounds sterling, which was equivalent to approximately 100 U.S. dollars at that time. The other three scrolls that Kando had he offered for sale to somebody else, a man named Eleazar Lipa Sukenik. Who was Eleazar Lipa Sukenik? He was an Israeli biblical scholar and archaeologist based at the Hebrew university of Jerusalem. On November 29, 1947, coincidentally by the way the very same day that the U.N. voted in favor of the establishment of the state of Israel, Sukenik traveled to Bethlehem to see the three scrolls that Kando was offering for sale, and Sukenik arranged to purchase them. I should add parenthetically here that Sukenik was apparently the first scholar to recognize what these scrolls were, because you have to realize that the Dead Sea scrolls had surfaced at this point on the antiquities market, these scrolls from Cave 1, without anybody knowing where they had been found, where they came from, what their date was, or whether they were even authentic ancient scrolls. Sukenik was the first to realize that these were authentic ancient scrolls dating to about the time of Jesus, and he arranged to purchase those three scrolls from Kando.

In the meantime at the Athanasius Yeshua Samuel had purchased his four scrolls as an investment hoping to turn around and make a profit off of reselling them. He tried for a number of years to resell his four scrolls without any success on the markets in the Middle East, and eventually gave up and brought them to the United States and put them for sale in the U.S. On June 1, 1954, Athanasius Yeshua Samuel placed an ad in the Wall Street Journal advertising his four scrolls for sale, and the ad actually says, "The Four Dead Sea Scrolls, biblical manuscripts dating back to at least 200 B.C. are for sale. This would be an ideal gift to an educational or religious institution by an individual or group."

It just so happened that when the ad appeared in the Wall Street Journal, Sukenik' son Yigael Yadin was in the United States on a fundraising mission. Yigael Yadin, of course, eventually became a very famous archaeologist later excavating among other things, the site of Masada and eventually served as Chief of Staff of the Israeli army. Well, it just so happened that when Athanasius Yeshua Samuel placed his ad in the Wall Street Journal, Yadin was in the U.S. on a fundraising mission, someone brought to his attention the ad in the Wall Street Journal, and through the aid of middle man, Yadin was able to arrange for purchase of those four scrolls. By the way Athanasius Yeshua Samuel received $250,000 for the four scrolls so he actually did make a nice profit off of his investment.

So eventually all seven scrolls from Cave 1 came to be in the possession of the state of Israel and subsequently the state of Israel built a special building on the grounds of the Israel museum in Jerusalem called the Shrine of the Book to house and display the seven scrolls from Cave 1. If you ever been to Jerusalem and visited the Shrine of the Book, those are the scrolls that you saw on display there.

Because the scrolls from Cave 1 had been deposited in jars, they were in a good state of preservation and were either complete or nearly complete, and therefore were relatively easy to read, and so for all intents and purposes by the middle of the 1950s, all seven scrolls from Cave 1 had been fully published. The subsequent controversies surrounding delays in the publication of the Dead Sea scrolls have nothing to do therefore with the scrolls from Cave 1 at Qumran. They have to do with scrolls from other caves at Qumran as we are going to see.

By the late 1940s, scholars realized that these scrolls had come from somewhere in the area of the Dead Sea, and they had pinpointed the location as being in the area of the site of Qumran. Qumran was a small archaeological ruin that was known. It had already been surveyed and visited by various people, but nobody paid any attention to Qumran until scholars realized that scrolls were being found in the caves around this site. So by the late 1940s, early 1950s, scholars realized that the scrolls had been found in the vicinity of the site of Qumran and an archaeological expedition was then organized to Qumran. By the time this expedition was organized and took place, we are now in the 1950s, and what has happened in terms of the larger political background? Well the British mandate of Palestine ended, Palestine was partitioned, the state of Israel was established, and now Qumran lay in the territory that was under the rule of the government of Jordan.

When the expedition of Qumran was conducted in the 1950s, it was conducted under the auspices of the government of Jordan, and, by the way, the political situation at the time explains why there were no Israeli or Jewish scholars involved in the original publication team of the Dead Sea scrolls. It goes back to the political situation at the time of the original discovery.

Instead the expedition to Qumran was organized and led by a French biblical scholar named Roland de Vaux, who was affiliated with the French school of biblical studies and archaeology in Jerusalem, the *École biblique et archéologique*. From 1951 to 1956, De Vaux led an exhibition to Qumran that had two main components. Number one to systematically explore all of the caves in the vicinity of Qumran to see if whether there were anymore scrolls to be found, and number two to excavate the site of Qumran itself.

What did De Vaux find in terms of scrolls in caves? Eventually scrolls were found in 11 caves surrounding the site of Qumran which we number Caves 1 through 11. All together, these 11 caves yielded the remains of over 900 different scrolls, but in most cases what we have here are not 900 complete scrolls but small fragments surviving from what had once been complete scrolls.

Archeologists found about half the caves and Bedouin found the other half of the caves. But the Bedouin the best caves, and one of the caves that Bedouin found—and it is interesting that they found it and not the archaeologist because it was literally right under the noses of the archaeologists as they digging—was Cave 4. Cave 4, which actually is two caves, 4 A and 4 B, yielded over 500 different scrolls, but unlike in Cave 1 where the scrolls had been deposited in jars; in Cave 4 the scrolls were lying strewn on the floor of the cave and they had disintegrated into thousands of little fragments.

The subsequent controversy surrounding delays in the publication of the Dead Sea scrolls have nothing to do with scholarly conspiracies or Vatican conspiracies or any other kind of conspiracies but really have to do with the fragmentary nature of these scrolls and especially the massive fragments from Cave 4 where scholars literally spent decades sifting by hand through these little fragments trying to figure out which pieces belong together, which kinds of documents they belong to, and all of this in an era before the advent of the computer. I should add parenthetically that as of now all the of Dead Sea scrolls are fully published, and all of the Dead Sea scrolls have been fully accessible to the public for well over a decade, so nobody can claim any longer that there are still secrets hidden in the Dead Sea scrolls or conspiracies to hide information in the Dead Sea scrolls.

The other component of De Vaux's expedition to Qumran was to excavate the site of Qumran itself, and we are looking at a photograph of the site of Qumran, which is a small ruin that sits on a natural terrace overlooking the Dead Sea, and specifically we are looking here from west to east, and as we look across the Dead Sea what we see on the other side are the mountains of Moab, that is the mountains in Jordan. What did De Vaux find when he excavated this small ruin? He found a settlement that was established roughly around 100 B.C. That means that the settlement at Qumran was established during the Hasmonean period.

This settlement then existed until the year 31 B.C. when it was destroyed by an earthquake. We will actually look at evidence of the earthquake damage and De Vaux was able to pinpoint the date of the earthquake precisely to the year 31 B.C. because the ancient Jewish historian Josephus tells us that a strong earthquake hit the area of Jericho in the Year 31, and De Vaux was able to match that up with the archaeological remains.

After the earthquake, the community cleaned up the settlement, rebuilt the buildings, and continued to live there until another destruction. Somewhere around the year 9 or 8 B.C. or maybe a little later when the site is burned down by a fire, a fire that apparently was set by a human enemy so somebody came and destroyed the settlement, after that, there is a short period of abandonment maybe lasting only one winter season, the community comes back, cleans up the site and continues to live there until the year 68 A.D. when the settlement is destroyed by the Romans at the time of the first Jewish revolt against the Romans.

In terms of chronology, what we are looking at is a settlement that is established roughly around 100 B.C. and exists until the year 68 A.D., so a settlement that is established during the Hasmonean period, continues to exist through the period when the Romans come in and take over, through the reign of Harod and his successors, and up until the first Jewish revolt against the Romans in the year 68 A.D.

What did De Vaux's excavations uncover in terms of the settlement at Qumran? We are looking at a plan of the settlement, which is a settlement that is remarkable in many ways. It is really quite unlike anything else that we have. One of the things that is interesting about this settlement is that it is very small and compact in size, and we will see that when we look at some pictures of it. Another interesting thing about this settlement is that there are no private houses in the settlement, no private dwellings. Instead all of the rooms in the settlement were used either for communal purposes, for example communal dining rooms, or as workshops.

I know what you are thinking. If there are no private houses in the settlement, where did the people live, i.e., where did the people sleep? As we look at the settlement, we will see that some of the rooms in the settlement originally were two stories high. It may be that some of those second story rooms where used as bedrooms. If you think that all of the members of this community lived, slept, only inside the settlement, there is so little space for bedrooms at the second-story level that you would have to estimate a very small population, maybe 10 to 15 people, but if you think as I think following De Vaux that most if not all of the members of this community lived, that is slept, not inside the settlement but outside of it, in tents, in huts, and in some of the caves around the outside of the settlement, then you can reasonably estimate a larger population of somewhere around 100 to 150 people.

A small compact settlement, rooms used for communal purposes or workshops, what are some of the rooms that we are going to looking at in particular? We are going to look at a structure in the middle of the north side of the settlement that was a two-story high watchtower. Why put a watchtower in the middle of the north side of the settlement? It's very logical, because just like today in antiquity most people coming to Qumran would have come from the direction of the north, that is from the direction of Jerusalem in Jericho, so you put a watchtower there on your north side. You can post guards, and by the way, that watchtower could be isolated by drawbridges all around it so you can also take refuge in the watchtower if you are being threatened by an enemy.

From the watchtower, we will then look at a room that is right in the middle of the settlement, a room that De Vaux identified as scriptorium or writing room, and we will talk about why he identified it in that way. We will look at the largest room in the settlement which is located on the south side. De Vaux identified this room as an assembly hall because it is the largest room, and he identified also as a communal dining room, because in the room adjacent to it he found a pantry of dishes, and we will look also at the pantry.

We will look at one of the many workshops that dot the settlements specifically the potter's workshop. We will look at the extensive water system that runs through the settlement, with many pools for storing water. We will look at a large cemetery on the plateau to the east of the settlement, and then we will talk about what the Dead Sea scrolls are and how they relate to all of these archaeological remains.

Let us start first of all with the tower. Here is a view of the tower as it looks today and you can see that there is now a modern wooden staircase that goes up to the second story level. When people come to Qumran today, you can climb up those steps and go to the original second story level of the tower, and it is a great thing to do because when you stand up there, you find yourself looking out over the settlement of Qumran. I always like to say that I love to take people to visit Qumran because whenever they get there, they are always disappointed, and they are always disappointed for a couple of reasons. Number one, most people who visit Qumran do it as part of a day trip from Jerusalem down to the Dead Sea. First thing in the morning they leave Jerusalem and go south to Masada and visit Herod's palaces on Masada, which visually are spectacular, and then start heading back north up along the shore of the Dead Sea, stopping in and getting maybe lunch and for a swim in the Dead Sea, and then hitting Qumran late in the afternoon on the way back up to Jerusalem. First of all, people have been to Masada and been overwhelmed by that, and you get to Qumran and this is it, and most people of course are super-psyched to see Qumran because pretty much everybody has heard about the Dead Sea scrolls and want to see where they were found.

You get to Qumran, you climb up to the top of the tower, you look over the settlement, and what do you see in front of you? You see this very small, compact, and visually very modest settlement. Notice that walls are made of rubble, that is field stones that were not cut or maybe roughly cut for the corners. Notice that the floors are either dirt floors or rough flagstone pavement. There is no interior decoration. There are no wall paintings. There are no mosaics. There is no stucco, so a very small plain and unimpressive looking settlement.

As we stand on top of the tower and we look down below us, we can see some of the rooms that we talked about in our plan before. Specifically, immediately below us, we can see the room that De Vaux identified as the scriptorium, or writing room, which I am going to come back to in just a minute. We can see the dining room/assembly hall, the communal dining room and assembly hall that the southern end of the site which is sort of off at an angle here, and opening onto it, the pantry with the dishes. The potter's workshop is not visible, it would be up in a corner, and the cemetery is completely off to the left or to the east of the site in our view here. When you stand at the southern end of the settlement just outside of the buildings and look down below you, you can see Cave 4. One of the remarkable things about Qumran is how close Cave 4 with all of its 500 different scrolls is to the settlement itself, very close by.

Let us now talk about the scriptorium. In the middle of the settlement is this room that De Vaux identified as a scriptorium or writing room. Why did he identify it as a scriptorium? It is because of the furniture that he found in this room. The furniture, which I am going to show you in a minute, comes not from the room as you see now but actually comes originally from a second story level. In other words the scriptorium is one of the rooms in the settlement that originally was two stories high. The furniture that I am going to show you was originally at the second story level.

When the settlement was destroyed by the Roman in 68, it burned, and the second story level collapsed, fell down onto the ground, and De Vaux then picked up the pieces of furniture, had them picked up, had them put back together and what did he find? He found long, narrow tables and benches make of mud brick and covered with plaster. The reason why De Vaux identified this room as a scriptorium or writing room is because in addition to the furniture, he found these things mixed in with the debris. These are inkwells. The picture of the inkwells makes them look very large but they are small. They are little things. Mixed in with the debris, he found inkwells, and because of the inkwells De Vaux identified this room as a scriptorium.

Sounds perfectly logical, and you might then think that the scribes sat on the benches and wrote at the tables they way that we do today. De Vaux's identification of this room as a scriptorium has been the subject of a lot debate because the furniture probably did not work that way, and here is the problem. The custom of sitting at a table to write the way that we write today is a custom that developed later in history. It developed specifically in medieval monasteries with Monks sitting and copying things at tables. Typically in the ancient world when scribes wrote, they squatted with the material in their laps. Scholars have objected to De Vaux's identification of this room as a scriptorium on the grounds that the scribes would not have sat on the benches and written at the tables the way we might think they would have.

Some scholars then have suggested well maybe the furniture worked a little bit differently. Maybe the scribes sat on the tables, rested their feet on the benches and wrote with the material in their laps like that. The problem with that is the tables are concave underneath. They are only made of mud brick.

If you sit on them they are going to crack and collapse under your weight, so that explanation really is not satisfactory either. Some scholars have suggested, well maybe De Vaux was wrong, maybe this room was not used as a scriptorium, maybe it was used for some other purpose. Maybe, some scholars have suggested, this room was used as a dining room, a triclinium, where you reclined to dine on the benches and ate at the tables.

The problem with that is the benches are so narrow, they are only 40 cm wide, that if you try to recline and dine on them, you are going to roll off, so that does not work either. So what exactly was this room? I think that De Vaux was right in identifying it as a scriptorium. First of all, there are the inkwells. Inkwells are extremely rare finds on archaeological excavations in Israel. I personally have sorted through thousands and thousands and thousands of buckets of pottery from various excavations around Israel and I have only found until now one example of an inkwell, so they are very, very rare finds.

The fact that De Vaux found inkwells mixed in with the debris suggests that they was some writing going on in this room, and not only that, let us think for a minute about what they were writing. They were not writing books, codices. They were writing scrolls, and to write a scroll what you have to do is to take the individual pieces of processed animal hide, parchment, and line them up side by side to make a scroll. These long, narrow tables would be ideally suited for the preparation of the scroll. So I think that De Vaux was right, and if that is the case, then we can reasonably suggest that some of the Dead Sea scrolls might have been written or copied in this room.

I deliberately say some of the Dead Sea scrolls and not all of the Dead Sea scrolls because there is no doubt that some of the Dead Sea scrolls were brought to Qumran from somewhere else. How do we know that? We know that because some of the Dead Sea scrolls antedate the establishment of the settlement. Some of the Dead Sea scrolls were written before the settlement was established, so clearly some of the scrolls had to have brought to Qumran from other places, but it may be that some of the scrolls were written or copied at Qumran, and in this case the best candidate for where that activity was taking place is this room which De Vaux identified as a scriptorium.

Here is a picture of the dining room/assembly hall and the pantry as they looked today. De Vaux identified this room as a communal dining room because of the pantry of dishes found next to it, and as an assembly hall because it is the largest room in the settlement. The pantry today of course is empty of the dishes that it originally had contained, but at the time of excavations what De Vaux found in this room were stacks of dishes, specifically stacks of over a 1,000 pottery dishes.

There are a couple of interesting things about the pottery dishes that De Vaux found in the pantry. First of all, they are lying stacked on the floor in neat piles but broken. Here is some of the evidence of the earthquake of 31. Originally those dishes were stacked on wooden shelves lining the walls of this room. When the earthquake of 31 hit, what happened? The shelves sort of started to tremble then boom fell on to the floor. The dishes fell, broke, could not be fixed, and so after the earthquake, what they did was to wall off this part of the room and simply left the broken dishes like that, and that is how the archaeologists found them.

The other interesting thing about these dishes to notice is that they are all what we call open shapes: plates, cups, bowls. So we do not see cooking pots, we do not see storage jars, and what is interesting about this is that these open shapes—plates, cups, bowls—are precisely the kinds of dishes that you would use to dine off of, to set your table with. The presence of so many dishes stacked in the pantry suggested to De Vaux that communal meals must have been held in the room adjacent to this, and so De Vaux identified that large room not only as an assembly hall but also as a communal dining room.

One of the very interesting things about this is that we learn from the literature of this sect that one of the central aspects of their lifestyle was having communal meals. Everybody who was a full member of this sect participated in communal meals, so what we see here is a wonderful example of correspondence between our literary sources, both Dead Sea and outside literary sources, which refer to or describe communal meals being held by the members of this community or members of this sect, and the archaeological evidence where we clearly see evidence of communal meals practiced by this community.

We have now started on our archaeological tour of Qumran, looking at the tower, looking at the scriptorium or writing room, looking at the communal dining room and pantry of dishes. In our next lecture, we are going to continue our tour of the site of Qumran, and we are going to look at some of the other interesting features including peculiar animal bone deposits, including one of the workshops, the potter's workshop. We are going to talk about the water system and pools at Qumran, and the large adjacent cemetery.

The Sectarian Settlement at Qumran
Lecture 15

> Becoming ritually impure in Judaism has nothing to do with being bad, being sinful, being evil—nothing at all to do with that. It is simply a mechanical category that means you are ritually impure. It is something that happens to everyone in the course of everyday life. ... The Hebrew Bible also designates how to purify yourself if you become ritually impure.

In this lecture, we continue our tour of the settlement at Qumran, looking at some of its distinct features. Among the peculiarities of the settlement at Qumran are the many animal bone deposits. An analysis of these bones has indicated that all the animals represented are kosher species. This is a phenomenon that is unique to Qumran. Before we look at one possible explanation for these animal bone deposits, we have to know a little more about the group that lived at Qumran.

An analysis of these bones has indicated that all the animals represented are kosher species.

Scholarly consensus is that the community at Qumran was part of a larger movement initially founded and led by dispossessed Zadokite priests. Believing that the current priesthood in the Jerusalem temple was impure, because the priests were usurpers, and that the sacrifices were polluted, the Zadokite priests withdrew, forming an alternative community. Every full member of this sect lived his everyday life as if he was a high priest officiating in the Jerusalem temple, and apparently, partaking of communal meals was a substitute for participation in the temple sacrifices. The bone deposits mirror the designated areas outside of the temple compound in Jerusalem for the disposal of sacred refuse from the sacrifices.

The priestly lifestyle of the occupants also explains the extensive system of pools for storing water at Qumran. Evidence shows that a channel was built to bring water from a nearby riverbed during the few flash floods that occur in winter. Did the community at Qumran need to drink all the water it stored, or were some of the pools used as Jewish ritual baths? Indeed, some of the pools have steps. Not everybody needed to be ritually pure on an everyday basis, only the priests. Ritual purity applies very specifically to entering the presence of God. All Jews, no matter who they were, took it for granted that they should ritually purify themselves before entering the Jerusalem temple, before entering the presence of God. It is no surprise, then, that we find such a large number of pools at Qumran.

Remains excavated in Qumran's cemetery point to an overwhelmingly male community.

On the plateau to the east of the settlement is a large cemetery that consists of 1,100 graves. Only 46 of these graves have been excavated, but almost all of those are graves of adult men. The three exceptions are adult women, no children or infants at all. We have an admittedly small sample that nevertheless suggests that the community at Qumran was one overwhelmingly of men, not an ordinary community consisting of families.

This picture goes along with information that we have about this sect from other sources, which we will talk about together with information from the Dead Sea Scrolls in our next lecture. ■

Questions to Consider

1. What is the concept of Jewish ritual purity, and how is it reflected in the archaeological remains at Qumran?

2. Did the Qumran community offer animal sacrifices?

The Sectarian Settlement at Qumran
Lecture 15—Transcript

In our last lecture, we started with an introduction to Qumran and the Dead Sea scrolls by talking about the initial discovery of the Dead Sea scrolls and the exploration of the site of Qumran and then looked at some of the buildings that de Vaux uncovered in his excavations at Qumran including the tower and the communal dining room and pantry with dishes, and the so-called scriptorium or writing room.

What I would like to do now is pick up where we left off, continuing our tour of the settlement at Qumran looking at some of its distinct buildings and features. This will then lead us into a discussion of what the Dead Sea scrolls are and how they relate to the settlement of Qumran.

One of the peculiarities of the settlement at Qumran are animal bone deposits. In open air spaces around the outsides of the buildings, de Vaux found deposits of animal bones. We can see the animal bone deposits coming to light in the excavations. Well, what exactly are these animal bone deposits? An analysis of the animal bones indicated that all of the animals represented in these deposits are kosher species of animals. That means species of animals which it is permitted to eat according to biblical Jewish law. So, for example, there are sheep, cow, goat. But, for example, no pork represented at Qumran. There is no pig among the animal bone deposits. Very interesting, by the way, there is also no poultry represented among the animal bone deposits, even though, of course, poultry is permitted according to Jewish law.

An analysis of these animal bone deposits indicated that these animals had been slaughtered, butchered. The meat had been cut into chunks. The chunks of meat had been boiled or roasted. The meat had been eaten off of the bones. Then the bones were placed on top of the ground in the open air spaces around the outsides of the buildings and either placed inside pots or covered with pieces of broken pottery.

How do we explain this phenomenon? We do not have any other archaeological site where similar deposits of animal bones have been found. This is a phenomenon that is unique to Qumran. I believe that there are two reasonable possible explanations for the animal bone deposits which means that there are other explanations that are not reasonable.

What would these be? Well, one possibility is that what we have represented here are the remains of animal sacrifices. Apparently these are not the remains of animal sacrifices. Why are they not? We have no indication from the literature of this sect, the sect that lived at Qumran, that they rejected the basic biblical principle that you can only offer animal sacrifices in the Jerusalem temple and that they would have or did animal sacrifices somewhere else. We have no evidence that they sacrificed animals outside the Jerusalem temple even though, as we will see, they themselves did not participate in the sacrifices offered in the Jerusalem temple.

Also, we have no evidence, no physical remains of an altar for animal sacrifices at Qumran. If they are not the remains of animal sacrifices, what are they? De Vaux suggested that these were the remains of special ritual meals that were eaten by the community. I think that de Vaux's explanation is correct, but it lacks explanatory power. That is, even if de Vaux is right, that these are the remains of special ritual meals that were eaten by the community, it does not explain why they deposited the bones in this very peculiar manner.

So what is the explanation for this? Now I am going to tell what I think is the reason for the animal bone deposits, but in order to get to that, I now have to tell you a little bit about the group that lived at Qumran.

The community that lived at Qumran was part of a Jewish sect that was originally established by, that is originally founded by, and at least initially led by dispossessed Zadokite priests. Remember that the Zadokites were a high priestly family that had controlled the priesthood in the Jerusalem temple until the first half of the 2nd century B.C. when the priesthood was taken over by other priestly families that were not Zadokites.

When that event occurred, some members of this family established the sect that later settled at Qumran, at least some of which settled at Qumran. There were members that lived in other places too aside from Qumran. So what we have here are members of a larger movement that initially is founded by and at least initially led by dispossessed Zadokite priests.

This group believed that the current priesthood in the Jerusalem temple was unfit to serve and was impure because they were usurpers, and that by way of extension, the sacrifices offered in the temple and the temple itself were polluted. They therefore refused to participate in the sacrifices offered in the temple, withdrew, forming themselves, that is their community as a substitute temple.

Every full member of this sect lived his everyday life as if he was a high priest officiating in the Jerusalem temple. It was a priestly community, that is, a community living a priestly lifestyle but without a temple. In the interim, until they regained control of the Jerusalem temple, they apparently considered participation in their communal meals to be a substitute for participation in the temple sacrifices.

Everything I have just told you is not my original scholarship. This is generally what scholars believe about the sect that lived at Qumran. How does this then relate to the animal bones that we have at Qumran? Well, let us think for a minute when we talk about animal sacrifices in the Jerusalem temple or in any ancient temple for that matter. What went on? Generally speaking, what happens is you have a lot of animals being brought up, the animals are being slaughtered, butchered. The meat is being cut into chunks. Depending on the type of sacrifice, either all of the animal is burned on the altar, that is all of the animal is offered to god, for example, a Holocaust offering, or in some cases, parts of the animal are burned on the altar offered to god, and the rest of the meat is cooked an eaten by the priest and the people.

When we imagine this gigantic esplanade, this gigantic plaza with the temple building in the middle of it—by the way, other ancient temples around the Mediterranean world in the Near East—what we have to imagine is a lot of banqueting going on. People are eating the animals that were being offered for sacrifice. They are cooking the meat and they are consuming the meat on the spot. The meat, by the way, was cooked and eaten on the spot because in antiquity, once an animal was slaughtered, there was no way of preserving it. So you cooked the meat and you at it on the spot. When we think about this big temple esplanade, we have to imagine a lot of people up there and what are they doing? They are eating meat.

You have had your sacrificial portion of meat, you participated in the sacrifice, you got your meat, you ate it. What do you do with the parts that you cannot eat? The bones, the gristle, all that stuff, what do you do with it? You cannot just take it home and toss it out with the rest of the kitchen garbage. It is part of a sacrifice, but it has to be disposed of, it is refuse. Well, apparently, there were around the outside of the temple compound in Jerusalem, specially designated areas for the disposal of sacred refuse from the sacrifices.

Let us zip back to Qumran. Here we have a community which is living as if it is a substitute temple with every full member living his everyday life as if he is a priest officiating in the temple and participation in their communal meals being considered a substitute for participation in the temple sacrifices.

What I think is going on at Qumran is that even though technically these are not sacrifices, in terms of the idea of what is going on, it is something very similar. They are then disposing of the remains of the animals consumed at these meals in a manner analogous to the way the meat consumed in the Jerusalem temple was disposed of afterwards.

I think de Vaux was right, these are the remains of special ritual meals, but I also think there is a very specific reason for why the animal bones were deposited in this manner and which explains why we do not have analogous deposits at other archaeological sites.

One of the workshops that dots the settlement at Qumran happens to be a potter's workshop which has a couple of kilns for firing pottery in it. It is very interesting that we have a potter's workshop at Qumran. Why is this interesting? First of all, it explains why we have certain types of pottery that are found basically at Qumran but nowhere else. One of the things that archaeologists do when we study pottery from any given archaeological excavation is to see where else has pottery like this been found.

One of the very interesting things about Qumran is that there are certain types of pottery that are very distinctive to Qumran and that are basically found nowhere else. One of these distinctive types of pottery are the tall cylindrical jars covered with bowl shaped lids that were found in the caves with the scrolls, in Cave 1, and are found in other caves with scrolls and other caves around Qumran in general and inside the settlement itself. Why are they distinctive to Qumran? They are because apparently they were being manufactured there.

Another interesting thing about having a potter's workshop at Qumran is that it is not really an intuitive place to have a potter's workshop, that is you have a problem with fuel. Where are you going to get all of your fuel from in order to light the fires that you need to burn the pottery in the kilns, to fire the pottery in the kilns. It is not really a logical place to establish a potter's workshop. So the existence of a potter's workshop at Qumran, well, there has to be a specific reason for it. The reason for it apparently is connected with this group's observance of the Laws of Purity, the biblical Laws of Purity which we are going to discuss.

These Laws of Purity actually come up right away when we talk about the water system at Qumran. There is a very extensive system of pools for storing water that runs through the settlement. The water system at Qumran has been the subject of a lot of controversy. The reason is Qumran is located in the desert. There is very little rainfall; there are no freshwater springs immediately in the vicinity. If you want to live at Qumran year-round, you are going to have to store enough water for the purposes of survival.

The question is: Did the community at Qumran need so much water as was stored in all of the pools or could it be that some of the pools were used for another purpose? Specifically, could it be that some of the pools were used as Jewish ritual baths, what is called in Hebrew, a miqvah, plural, miqvaot.

I agree with Roniricht who is an expert on ancient ritual baths that ten of the pools at Qumran should be identified as ritual baths, as miqvaot. Here is the question: How do we identify a pool as a ritual bath versus a pool that is used for storing drinking water, that is, a cistern? How do you tell the difference?

Well, the major feature that identifies some of the pools at Qumran as ritual baths are the broad sets of steps that go from the top to the bottom.

Why does this identify a pool as a ritual bath? It does because if you are in the desert and your main concern is with storing drinking water for the purposes of survival, you are not going to take up valuable volume in the pool with these broad sets of steps which also, by the way, take more effort to cut. You are not going to take up that valuable volume. You are only going to have broad sets of steps going from the top to the bottom, if, what, if you need the steps to go up and down, in and out of the pool. If you are going up and down the steps in and out of the pool, then by definition you are immersing yourself in the water which means it is a ritual bath.

Furthermore, some of the pools at Qumran, some of these ritual baths, have other features that make no sense in a cistern. For example, some of the pools have low partitions running down the steps. These low partitions make no sense in a cistern but make good sense in a miqvah, in a ritual bath. The idea being that the bather went down one side of the partition impure, immersed himself in the water, and came back up on the other side, purified. I have just referred to what is probably the central governing principle of the community that lived at Qumran, and that is the principle of Jewish ritual purity.

This is a principle which is poorly understood by most Westerners, at least today, including most Jews today. Let us take a minute now to talk about this idea of Jewish ritual purity which is so central to the lifestyle of this community. What is this all about? The Hebrew bible designates certain things and certain natural processes as causing ritual impurity.

I use the word "things" deliberately because the things that cause ritual impurity as designated by the Hebrew bible today appear to us to be quite random. They range from things like touching mildew on the walls of a house to touching a lizard to touching a corpse. And certain natural processes cause impurity, for example, for a man having a nocturnal emission or for a woman having her menstrual period.

These things cause a person to be ritually impure. Becoming ritually impure in Judaism has nothing to do with being bad, being sinful, being evil, nothing at all to do with that. It is simply a mechanical category that means you are ritually impure. It is something that happens to everyone in the course of everyday life. These things are absolutely unavoidable.

The Hebrew bible also designates how to purify yourself if you become ritually impure. The way to purify yourself actually varies depending on who you are, for example, priest versus layperson, and what kind of impurity you incurred, for example, some kinds of impurity are worse than others.

The worst of all is corpse impurity which involves a very long and complicated process of purification afterwards. Remember that story of the good Samaritan and the priest and the Levite who detour around what appears to be a dead body, because afterwards to purify yourself from corpse impurity, it is a very, very complicated process. Of course, as a priest and a Levite, you would have to be especially concerned about that.

The way to purify yourself depends on who you are and what kind of impurity you've incurred. For most kinds of ritual impurity and for most people, the way to purify yourself is to immerse yourself in a pool of undrawn water and wait for the passage of a certain amount of time. What does it mean a pool of undrawn water? It means water that has been put into a pool not by mechanical means but naturally. So, for example, springs, streams, rivers, the Jordan River, lakes, a pool of water left standing after a heavy rainfall, all of those can be used for the purposes of ritual immersion.

When it says the pool cannot have been filled mechanically it means that you cannot take a pool and fill it with a hose or take buckets of water and empty the buckets into the pool. You cannot do that. You can dig a pool and you can then dig a channel and allow water to flow naturally through the channel into the pool, but you cannot fill that pool through mechanical means.

I would like to say God did not make things easy on the Jewish people. Look at where we are. We are not in North Carolina here, my home state, nice and green, lots of water. We are in the middle of the Middle East here, it is the desert. So if you are observing the laws of Jewish ritual purity on a regular basis, you are going to have to provide for pools for the purposes of ritual immersion. That is exactly what we see here at Qumran.

At this point, I can just imagine what many of you must be thinking. Oy vey, what a pain to be a Jew, every time I touch one of these random things or have one of these unavoidable natural processes, I become ritually impure and have to run off and dunk myself in a pool of undrawn water. Actually, that is not the way it works.

You see, it was not necessary for most Jews to be ritually pure on an everyday basis. In fact, most Jews were not ritually pure on an everyday basis. This notion of ritual purity applies very specifically to coming into contact with a divine presence. That is, it was necessary to be in a state of ritual purity when you entered the presence of God. Otherwise, for most Jews on an ordinary basis, it was not necessary to be in a state of ritual purity all the time.

What was the focal point for coming into contact with a divine presence in early Judaism? That was the Jerusalem temple. All Jews, no matter who they were, and including, by the way, Jesus and Paul, took it for granted that you ritually purified yourself before entering the Jerusalem temple, before entering the presence of God.

Again, for most Jews, otherwise on an everyday basis, if you are not going in and out of the temple, you do not have to be ritually pure except for one category of ancient Jews who did have to worry about maintaining a higher degree of ritual purity on an everyday basis. Who would that be? Of course, that was the priest.

Now zip back to Qumran. Here we are looking at a settlement that was inhabited by a community living a priestly lifestyle. The community literally conceived itself as a substitute temple with every full member living his everyday life as if he is a priest officiating in the temple. Is it any surprise then that we have such a large number of ritual baths and large sizes of ritual baths to accommodate the members of this community over the course of a year? Is it any surprise then? No, it's not a surprise. This is as clear an expression as you can get of this group's concern with the maintenance of a high level of Jewish ritual purity.

Another interesting thing that we can see in this particular ritual bath, this particular pool, is that there is a crack running down the middle of the steps.

In fact, the steps are split and one side of the steps literally dropped. Here we see more evidence for the earthquake of 31. When the earthquake hit, the steps of this pool literally split down the middle and one side dropped.

I know what else you must be wondering. Well, she just said that we are in the middle of the desert, there is very little rainfall, there is no fresh water springs in the area. Where did they get all the water from to fill these pools? What the community at Qumran did was to build a water system to bring water from a nearby riverbed.

The site of Qumran sits on a terrace, an actual terrace overlooking a riverbed. This riverbed is called Wadi Qumran. Wadi is Arabic for riverbed. Now like 99.9 percent of the riverbeds along the shore of the Dead Sea, Wadi Qumran is a dry river bed. That is, most of the time it has no water flowing in it. But on very rare occasions, in the winter, maybe once or twice a year in the winter, if you have enough rain falling, not at Qumran but in the mountains behind Qumran, what happens, the ground becomes saturated with water and the water begins to concentrate and flow in these dry river beds down to the Dead Sea in the form of flash floods.

What the community at Qumran did was to take advantage of this natural principle and they built an aqueduct, a water channel going from the settlement back to Wadi Qumran to bring the water in times of flash floods. We are going to take a look at this water system but before I go on, let me point out another very interesting thing.

As I just said, you usually have flash floods very rarely in the winter and only in the winter because it does not rain otherwise. So you might have one or two flash floods a year, which means that the pools at Qumran were filled and replenished only maybe once or twice a year. The rest of the time, that was it. That was the water that you had. So over the course of the life of this community, people repeatedly immersed themselves in those ritual baths.

What I am trying to point out here is that the concept of Jewish ritual purity has nothing to do with hygiene and cleanliness in the modern sense of the word. The water could be dirty, but if it was a ritual bath, it was considered pure enough to immerse yourself in. In fact, I believe that probably this practice spread disease if anything, rather than preventing disease and sickness.

Today, when you go to Qumran, you can actually follow the line of the aqueduct back to where it starts in Wadi Qumran. By aqueduct, I do not mean the Pont du Gard, it is not one of these aqueducts, Roman style aqueducts on arches or something like that. What you have is a relatively modest channel dug into the ground to bring water to the settlement from the riverbed. You can follow the line of this channel back to where it starts. This idea of flash floods is somewhat alien to most people living in North America today, unless maybe you live in the American Southwest.

I have a couple of pictures showing what flash floods actually look like that I took. I happened to be in Israel in the winter of 2005. It is very dramatic because you can see huge amounts of waters flowing through these riverbeds, and what is very interesting is that it is not raining along the shore of the Dead Sea. It is raining back in the mountains on the way to Jerusalem. But so much rain has fallen that the water has concentrated in these ordinarily dry river beds and is flowing down to the Dead Sea in the form of flash floods with a particularly dramatic example of a flashflood flowing over the highway just south of Ein Gedi here at Nahal Arugot.

Today when you visit Qumran, you can actually walk back along the line of the aqueduct, the line of the water channel, and I always take people to do this when I am at Qumran because it is a fun thing to do. As you follow the line of the channel, you reach a point where there is a solid cliff and then a tunnel cut into the cliff, because at this point they reach the cliff and in order to continue the line of the channel, the line of the aqueduct, they have to cut through the rock of the cliff. You can crawl through this channel on your hands and knees. I always make people do this because it is kind of fun.

When you emerge from the other side of the tunnel, you find that you are still following the line of the aqueduct, and at the moment when you emerge from this tunnel and you look straight ahead of you, what you see is a waterfall which, again, ordinarily is a dry waterfall, but in times of flashflood would have water flowing through it.

What they did was to build a dam at the base of the waterfall, and in the time of a flash flood, then the water would rise up behind the dam and would begin to flow into the channel. The water then would flow out to the settlement. We can see the channel as it comes from the area of Wadi Qumran and the cliffs behind the site out to Qumran, and the channel then flows into the settlement, goes into the settlement and connects all of the pools in the settlement one after another. You only needed one flash flood to fill up all of the pools in the settlement, which is a good thing because in any given year you might only have one or two flash floods.

On the plateau to the east of the settlement is a large cemetery that consists of approximately 1,100 graves. We are standing on top of the tower, looking east we see the area where the plateau is located, if we walk up to the top of the plateau, we can see it here. We can actually walk up and see, here is a sign that says "cemetery" and some of the excavated graves. De Vaux excavated a relatively small number of graves in this cemetery, 46 of the graves out of approximately 1,100, and found a couple of very interesting things.

Most of the graves in the cemetery are located on the plateau immediately to the east of the settlement with scattered graves then located on the hills to the north, the east, and the south. In the main part of the cemetery and on the hills to the north and the east, all of the graves are lined up in neat rows, and all of the bodies are oriented, laid with the same orientation, with the feet facing north and the head facing south. In the southern part of the cemetery though, and to the south of Wadi Qumran, the graves are more randomly oriented with many of them oriented east/west.

All of these graves are what we call, in archaeological terms, individual inhumations. What does that mean? That simply means that they buried the whole body. They did not cremate it. They buried the bodies in a manner that is very similar to the way we bury our bodies today in the sense that they dug a trench in the ground six feet deep, took the body, wrapped it in a shroud, maybe placed it in a wooden coffin, put it at the base of the trench, sealed that off with mud, bricks, or stones, filled the trench in back with dirt, and then erected a headstone to mark the site of the grave. At Qumran actually, in addition, they actually put a stone by the feet and piled some stones one top of the grave.

So the graves are actually similar to the way that we bury our dead today. In addition to the fact that many of the graves seem to be oriented in a particular way with this north/south orientation, de Vaux found that in the main part of the cemetery and in the hills to the north and the east where the graves are all oriented north/south, the feet facing north, that in the main part of the cemetery, all but three of the excavated burials consisted of adult men. The three exceptions were adult women, no children or infants at all. Whereas, in the southern part of the cemetery where the graves are more randomly oriented, there were large numbers of women and children.

What we know now but de Vaux did not know at his time is that those burials to the south with the large numbers of women and children in the random orientation, those are relatively recent, i.e. modern Bedouin burials that have nothing to do with the settlement at Qumran. If we exclude them from our picture, as we should, we are left with an admittedly small excavated sample but a very interesting sample which suggests that the community at Qumran consisted overwhelmingly of adult men, and that this therefore was not an ordinary community consisting of families.

This picture goes along with information that we have about this sect from other sources which we will talk about together with the information from the Dead Sea scrolls in our next lecture.

The Dead Sea Scrolls and the Essenes
Lecture 16

> The Qumran sect, the Essenes, were an exclusive community, whereas with Jesus, we see just the opposite. We see an inclusive point of view, where everyone is welcomed to become a member of this group. In my opinion, then, we must distinguish between Jesus and his movement on the one hand and the Essenes on the other hand and show not only similarities between them but also very important and philosophical differences in their practices and in their way of life.

In this lecture, we consider how the Dead Sea Scrolls relate to the archaeology of Qumran and what they tell us about the community that lived there. The Dead Sea Scrolls are basically a library of religious literature. About one-quarter of them are copies of the Hebrew Bible. We have represented at Qumran examples of all of the books of the Hebrew Bible except for Esther (which may have simply not been preserved). These copies of the Hebrew Bible are by far the earliest that have been found, and they actually represent several versions of the Hebrew Bible that were later replaced by a standardized version called the Masoretic text. There are also a few fragments of the **Septuagint**, the ancient Greek translation of the Hebrew Bible.

Other kinds of works represented include a **Targum**, or Aramaic translation of the Hebrew Bible (Aramaic being the everyday language of the Jews); a **Pesher**, or commentary on a book of the Hebrew Bible; apocryphal works, such as Tobit and Ecclesiasticus; and so-called pseudepigrapha, such the book of Jubilees and the book of Enoch. Finally, we have works that can be described as sectarian; that is, they describe the beliefs and practices of the group that lived at Qumran. Examples of these sectarian works include the Damascus document, the war scroll, the community rule or manual of discipline, and perhaps, the temple scroll.

The sectarian scrolls identify the initial leader or founder of this sect as a figure called the Teacher of Righteousness. His main opponent was a figure referred to as the Wicked Priest. The sectarian scrolls also tell us that some members of this sect were married, had families, and lived in towns and villages around the country, including Jerusalem, but some members went to live apart in the desert (for example, at Qumran).

To become a member of this sect was not easy. There was no private property. Full admission was open only to unblemished adult males (that is, those without physical or mental handicaps, a criterion for the priesthood). Although not all members came from priestly families, all full members lived a priestly lifestyle. Why would anyone choose to live this sort of lifestyle? The appeal was apocalyptic expectation. This sect anticipated the end of days, when there would be a war between the forces of good and evil. They called themselves the Sons of Light; everyone else, including all the other Jews, were the Sons of Darkness.

Other peculiarities of this sect include their belief in predeterminism—the idea that God preordains everything, including the moral makeup of an individual—and their anticipation of two Messiahs. To the usual royal Messiah of Israel descended from David, they added a second priestly Messiah descended from Aaron—not surprising considering the priestly orientation of the sect. ■

Important Terms

Pesher: A type of biblical commentary or interpretation that was popular at Qumran.

Septuagint: Ancient Greek translation of the Hebrew Bible.

Targum: Ancient translation of the Hebrew Bible into Aramaic.

Questions to Consider

1. What is the relationship of the Qumran community to the Essenes?

2. Do you think Jesus was an Essene?

The Dead Sea Scrolls and the Essenes
Lecture 16—Transcript

Now that we have talked about the archaeology of the site of Qumran, let us consider how the Dead Sea scrolls relate to the archaeology and what they tell us about the community that lived at Qumran. First of all, let me clarify by saying that when I use the term "Dead Sea scrolls," I am using it to describe the 900 plus scrolls that were found in the eleven caves surrounding Qumran. These scrolls represent the library of the community that lived at Qumran. I use the word library to indicate that there was a deliberate process of selection involved in terms of what kinds of literature were included in this collection and what types of literature were not. Specifically what we have here is a collection of Jewish religious literature. There are no historical works. For example, 1 and 2 Maccabees are not represented among the Dead Sea scrolls. There are no personal documents: deeds to land, marriage contracts, personal correspondence. Instead, all of the scrolls reflect types of ancient Jewish religious literature.

What do we have represented among these works of Jewish religious literature? First of all about one-quarter of the copies of the Dead Sea scrolls are copies of the Hebrew bible. That is what many of you might refer to as the Old Testament. We have represented at Qumran examples of all of the books of the Hebrew bible except for the book of Ester. It is not clear whether Ester was originally represented by a copy that was not preserved or whether it was never there to begin with, but we do have copies of all of the other books in the Hebrew bible represented at least by one copy, and in some cases by multiple copies. These copies of the Hebrew bible are important because they are by far the earliest copies of the Hebrew bible that have even been found.

Until the discovery of the Dead Sea scrolls, the earliest copies of the Hebrew bible that we had dated are to the 9th and 10th centuries A.D. The Dead Sea scrolls date mostly to the 2nd and 1st centuries B.C., some of them a little earlier, some of them a little later. They take us back much closer to the time when the Hebrew bible was actually edited and written down, and we can then compare the copies of the biblical text that we have at Qumran with the copies of the biblical Hebrew text that we have today and see whether any changes have been made over the course of the centuries. I know what you are wondering. Have any changes been made? The answer is actually yes and no, and here is the reason why. The text to the Hebrew bible that we use today is called the Masoretic text, a Hebrew word which means the traditional text. It is the same standardized text that is used everywhere. That is, you can go anywhere in the world today, open a copy of the Hebrew bible, and you will find the same identical text, but this was not always the case. In antiquity, in the time of Qumran, there were different variants of the biblical Hebrew text that circulated among the Jewish population. By variants I mean not copies that varied widely from each other, but they did vary sometimes in word order sometimes in a sentence here or a sentence there being omitted or added, and so these variant copies circulated among the Jewish population.

It was not until after the time of Qumran, after 70 A.D. that Judaism decided that there should be one standardized authoritative version of the biblical Hebrew text in circulation, and when that happened, all of the other variant texts ceased to be copied and therefore disappeared. What is so important about the Dead Sea scrolls from Qumran is that we have represented copies of the proto Masoretic text, the text that is basically the basis for the texts that we used today, but also copies of variant text that were not preserved because they went out of use centuries ago.

In addition to copies of the Hebrew bible, we have a few fragments from Qumran of the Septuagint. The Septuagint is the ancient translation of the Hebrew bible into Greek, a translation that was apparently was made in the Hellenistic period, and that translation into Greek serves us the basis for the Catholic text, the Catholic translation of the Hebrew bible, which is based on the Greek not on the Hebrew; whereas, the protestant Old Testament is based on the Hebrew text. I should mention parenthetically that contrary to popular reports, there are no examples of New Testament found at Qumran.

In addition to copies of the Hebrew bible and a few fragments of the Septuagint, we have other examples of works related to the Hebrew bible from Qumran. These include a kind of work that is usually referred to as a Targum. A Targum is a translation of the Hebrew bible into Aramaic because by the time of Qumran, by the time of Jesus, the Jewish population in Judea spoke Aramaic as their everyday language, and they needed to have the bible translated for them into Aramaic. So we have copies of these Aramaic translations represented among the Dead Sea scrolls. We also have a kind of work at Qumran that is call Pesharim, or Pesher is the singular in Hebrew. A Pesher is a commentary on or interpretation of a book of the Hebrew bible. Famous example of Pesharim from Qumran would include the Pesharim Habakkuk, a commentary on the book of Habakkuk, one of the twelve minor prophets, and a Pesher Nahum which we already discussed in relation to Alexander Jannaeus.

There are also works from Qumran that are sometimes as described as apocrypha. By apocrypha, I mean works that are included in the Catholic canon of sacred scripture but not in the Jewish or Protestant canons. Examples of apocrypha from Qumran would include the book of Tobit and Ecclesiasticus or the wisdom of Ben Sira, and we have works from Qumran that can be described as pseudepigrapha. This is an extremely mushy category of literature basically referring to Jewish religious works that were not included in the Catholic canon of sacred scripture or in the Jewish and Protestant canons, but sometimes were preserved in the canons of other churches such as the Ethiopian church. Examples of pseudepigrapha from Qumran would include the Book of Jubilees and the Book of Enoch.

Finally, we have works from Qumran that can be described as sectarian. By sectarian I mean works that describe the beliefs and practices of the sect that lived at Qumran and which deposited the scrolls in the nearby caves. Examples of sectarian works would include the Damascus document, the war scroll, the community rule or manual of discipline and maybe the temple scroll. These sectarian scrolls, these sectarian scrolls, tell us about this sect. They give us some of the information that we already discussed including that this was a sect that was originally founded by and at least initially led by dispossessed sadici priests that apparently formed sometime around the middle of the 2nd century B.C., and these works give us a lot of other information about the sect. They tell us for example that the original leader or perhaps refounder of the sect is a figure who they refer to as the teacher of righteousness.

One of the peculiarities of the Dead Sea scrolls is that almost always when a real person, a real historical figure is mentioned, they are mentioned not by their real name but by a nickname. For example, the teacher of righteousness, the Wicked Priest, the lion of wrath, the Man of Lies, and one of the games that scholars play is trying to identify these nicknamed figures with known historical figures. If you have ever come across any theories that identify the Teacher of Righteousness with Jesus, James, John the Baptist, or anyone else in the circle of Jesus, these theories are certainly wrong because these scrolls that refer to these figures were composed well before the time of Jesus. In fact, there can be little doubt that the Teacher of Righteousness was one of these dispossessed Zadokite priests. How do we know this? We know, because his name tells us so. His name Teacher of Righteousness, Morah Hasidic in Hebrew, is a pun on Morah Hatzadik, the high priest, the teacher of the Zadokites. So the Teacher of Righteousness was undoubtedly one of these dispossessed Zadokite priests, which one exactly, we simply do not know for sure.

The scrolls tell us that the initial leader or founder of this sect was a figure they referred to as the Teacher of Righteousness. His main opponent is a figure who they refer to as the Wicked Priest. The sectarian scrolls also tell us about members of this sect. They tell us that some members of this sect were married and had families and lived in towns and villages around the country including in Jerusalem, but some members went to live apart in the desert. That is, some members practiced desert separatism. Qumran was one such desert community. Whether there were any others we do not know because no archaeological remains have ever been identified of any other such settlement.

To become a member of this sect was not easy. First of all, full admission was not open to everyone. Full admission was open only to unblemished adult males. By unblemished I mean you could have no physical or mental handicaps. You had to be a perfect unblemished adult male in order to apply for admission to the sect. Once you applied for admission, you then had to undergo a period of initiation that lasted between two to three years. During the course of the period of initiation, you went through a successive series of stages. During the course of initiation, at some stage you gave up your personal possessions to the community because this community practiced the pooling of possessions.

Each stage of admission, if you were admitted, symbolized the attaining of a higher and higher of level of Jewish ritual purity, until finally if you were admitted as a full member at the end, you were living your everyday life at the same level of ritual purity required for priests officiating in the Jerusalem temple. Although not all members came from priestly families, all full members lived a priestly lifestyle, so this was a priestly community living without a temple. It is hard to describe how difficult this lifestyle was. It meant that if you were a full member, you were living your life according to this sect's interpretation of Jewish law which was generally speaking stricter than that of other groups. It meant that you were observing Jewish ritual purity laws at their highest level on an everyday basis, which meant for example that you could eat and drink nothing but the pure food and drink of the sect. Why would anybody choose to live this sort of lifestyle? You would choose to live this way if you thought that the end of days was at hand and only you were going to be saved, and that is exactly what this group believed.

This was an apocalyptic sect that anticipated the eminent arrival of the end of days, and they believed that when the end of days arrived there would be a 40-year-long war between the forces of good and the forces of evil. They were the forces of good. They called themselves the sons of light. Everyone else including all the other Jews were the sons of darkness. One of the peculiarities of this sect is that they believed in predeterminism. Everything is preordained by God, and by the way, not only all future events are preordained by God but your personal makeup as an individual, how many parts of you are good and how many parts of you are evil, that is preordained by God. In other words, there is no human free will at all, and so this 40-year-long apocalyptic war is preordained by God, and the outcome of the war is preordained by God, victory for the sons of light. This victory then would usher in a Messianic era. Another one of the peculiarities of this sect is that they anticipated the arrival of not one but two Messiahs. To the usual royal Messiah of Israel descended from David, they added a second priestly Messiah descended from Aaron, this is not surprising considering the priestly orientation of the sect.

Who was this sect? A lot of times you read about them or hear about them referred to as Essenes, but nowhere in the Dead Sea scrolls is the word

"Essene" ever mentioned, at least not by that name. Instead, we hear about Essenes from contemporary outside sources. That is from people who lived at the time Qumran existed but were not members of the sect. Our most important sources on the Essenes are Flavius Josephus, the Jewish historian who lived in the 1st century A.D. Pholo Judaeus, the Jewish philosopher who lived in Alexandra in Egypt in the late 1st century B.C. and 1st century A.D., and Pliny the Elder, the same Pliny, who wrote natural history and died when Mount Vesuvius erupted in 79. These authors all describe a Jewish sect called the Essenes with beliefs and practices very similar to what we read about in the Dead Sea scrolls and reflected in the archaeology of the site of Qumran, and so many scholars identified the Essenes with the group at Qumran based on the testimony of these outside authors.

Furthermore, Pliny has a very interesting passage describing the Essenes. He is the only one of our ancient authors who actually places the Essenes as living on the shore of the Dead Sea to the north of Ein Gedi and so many scholars, including myself, identify the Qumran community with the Essenes described in our ancient sources. Some scholars argue that the Essenes should not be identified with the community that lived at Qumran. One of the problems they point out is that the word "Essene" is never mentioned in the Dead Sea scrolls. We only read about Essenes in these outside historical sources. In my opinion, that argument is not decisive. There are a couple of reasons that could explain why Essenes are not mentioned in the Dead Sea scrolls. For example, some scholars have pointed out that Josephus, Philo, and Pliny wrote or came down to us in Greek and in Latin; whereas, the majority of the Dead Sea scrolls are written in Hebrew with a smaller number in Aramaic. One possibility is that word "Essene" does occur in the Dead Sea scrolls but by a Hebrew or Aramaic term that was then translated or rendered as "Essene" in Greek and Latin.

For example, some scholar have said maybe the word Hasid, the Hebrew word meaning "pious one" was rendered Essene, Essenne in Greek and in Latin, or maybe the word Osay, which in Hebrew, means the doers i.e. those who observe Jewish law maybe that was rendered Essene. One possibility is that Essene does occur in the Dead Sea scrolls but by a term that was then translated a little differently into Greek and Latin. Some scholars have pointed out maybe Essene does not occur in the Dead Sea scrolls because

Essene was a term that was used by outsiders to refer to this sect, whereas they never referred to themselves as Essenes, just as the Pharisees did not call themselves the Pharisees. For example, the members of this sect refer to themselves by other names such as the sons of light, the sons of Zadok, the members of the Yahad; that is the community. So maybe Essene does not occur in the Dead Sea scrolls because it was outsiders who used it to refer to them, not they themselves. So the fact that Essene does not occur in the Dead Sea scrolls is not necessarily decisive for arguing against the identification of the community that lived at Qumran as Essenes.

If we take a little bit closer look at Pliny's passage we see something else. Pliny emphasizes that the members of this sect consisted entirely of adult men. He says, "they were a people unique in its kind and admirable beyond all others in the whole world without women and renouncing love entirely." Then he says, "owing to the throng of newcomers. The people is daily reborn in equal number; indeed, those whom wearied by the fluctuations of fortune, life leads to adopt their customs, stream in in great numbers." In other words, Pliny indicates that members of this sect were not married, they were adult celibate men, and that the sect maintained itself or sustained itself by drawing in new people all time, new members all the time. Our other sources, Josephus and Philo, also suggest that the Essenes where a sect that consisted of adult celibate men, and this has been the subject of a lot of discussion again among scholars who disagree about the identification of this sect at Qumran, the sect associated with the Dead Sea scrolls with the Essenes, and what is the problem here? Well there are several problems.

If we look at the Dead Sea scrolls and specifically at the sectarian literature, we will see that nowhere in the sectarian literature among the Dead Sea scrolls is adult male celibacy mandated. In fact, it's quite to the contrary. Many of the sectarian scrolls, such as the Damascus document for example, legislate for marriage, childbirth, divorce, suggesting in fact that members of this sect were married and had families, so how do we then reconcile that with the testimony of our ancient authors, and let us now remember too the picture that we got from the cemetery at Qumran where we saw that the excavated graves consist overwhelmingly of adult males with only three adult women and no children represented. How do we then reconcile all of this testimony? Some scholars do it by claiming well the community that lived at Qumran and was associated with the Dead Sea scrolls were not Essenes. Josephus, Philo, and Pliny were describing another group that was adult celibate male but not the Qumran community.

In my opinion actually again, the different kinds of testimony can be reconciled. First of all, we cannot just compare the testimony of Josephus, Philo, and Pliny on the one hand with the testimony of the Dead Sea scrolls on the other without being critical, because these are very different kinds of literature. The Dead Sea scrolls, the sectarian scrolls, represent the literature that was used internally by the sect that contains its legislation, the rules for everyday life; whereas, Josephus, Philo, and Pliny are writing for very different kinds of audiences, and let us think for a minute now in particular about Josephus and Philo.

Josephus and Philo were Jewish authors living in a Diaspora context, at least Josephus certainly was by the time he wrote his works; he is writing at the end of his life in Rome. Philo is in the Diaspora the whole time; he is in Alexandria in Egypt. There are living in a Greco-Roman world where Jews are a minority, and Josephus and Philo both are attempting in their works to show that whatever Greek and Roman culture have to offer in terms of philosophy and lifestyle, Judaism did it first and Judaism does it better. In other words, that Judaism is superior to anything that the Greeks and Romans have to offer. That is basically what Josephus and Philo are trying to do, and this explains why Josephus and Philo spent so much time talking about the Essenes who were a very small and marginal group relative to the other groups in Judea at this time, but they spent a lot more time talking about the Essenes in detail because the Essenes fit their agenda.

The Essenes are an example of a Jewish group that could be described as living the Greco-Roman philosophical ideal. What was the Greco-Roman philosophical ideal? It was that you live your life in sort of an ascetic lifestyle denying yourself physical pleasures including marriage, and instead devote your life to study, and this is basically what the Essenes did, and therefore Josephus and Philo highlight them. What is the problem here? The problem is well how do we still reconcile this with the fact that from the Dead Sea scrolls we learn that at least some members of this sect were married and had families. How do we reconcile this fact? Let's think about this for a minute. First of all, only adult men, unblemished adult men, could become full members of this sect. Why was that? It's because they were living a priestly lifestyle. Every full member lived his everyday life as if he was a priest officiating in the Jerusalem temple. Only unblemished adult men could serve as priests in the Jerusalem temple.

Yes, there were women in this sect. There were women who either married into the sect, and married members, full members, or were born into the sect but, women could not obtain the same status, the same level of full membership as men could because by definition women could not serve as priests in the Jerusalem temple. There were women in the sect for sure, and some members were married for sure, but the role of women in the sect was certainly not the same as the role of men. By the way, members of this sect who were women, who either were married to full members or were children of full members were expected to live their life according to Jewish law just like every other Jewish woman was.

Let's think about priests in the ancient Jerusalem temple. The priests who served in the ancient Jerusalem temple were not celibate. They were married and had families and lived around the country, and they served in the temple in rotations, what is called courses. So they would leave their families for a couple of weeks, go to Jerusalem, serve their rotation in the temple, and then go home. While they were in the temple serving, they had no contact with their families because of purity concerns. Because of purity laws, they had no contact with their families during the time they served in the Jerusalem temple. That was the case for an ancient Jewish priest serving in the Jerusalem temple.

Let's zip back to Qumran, what do we have? We have a community where every full member is living his everyday life as if he was a priest officiating in the Jerusalem temple. What I think is going on is that some full members practiced what we might call occasional celibacy, and like the priests in the Jerusalem temple, would leave their families for certain periods, and it may be that even though it not mandated by Dead Sea scrolls, some members may have practiced permanent celibacy, and it is this group which is practicing occasional and perhaps permanent celibacy that is highlighted by our ancient sources, by Josephus and Philo and then picked up by Pliny, because it serves their purposes of illustrating that there is a Jewish sect, a Jewish group that is living the philosophical ideal of the Greco-Roman world.

What was Jesus' relationship then to the Essenes? Most people are interested in the Essenes and the Dead Sea scrolls because they think that the Dead Sea scrolls tell us something about Jesus and think that Jesus might have been a member of the Essene sect. Let me first of all categorically say that is a mistaken impression, and I want to explain why, and I hope that now having gone through the archaeology of Qumran and talked about the Dead Sea scrolls that you can understand the problems with this point of view.

It is true that there are similarities between Jesus and his movement and what we read about in the Dead Sea scrolls and among the Essenes. The similarities include the practice of having communal meals, the pooling of possessions, the dualism between light and dark, and most significantly I think the fact that these were apocalyptic movements that anticipated the eminent arrival of the end of days. In my opinion, many of the similarities between Jesus' movement and the Essenes stem from the fact that these were both apocalyptic movements but what is important to remember is that in the late Second Temple period in Judea we had various groups of movements that if you take any two of them at any given moment, will have similarities. They are all Jewish groups, which means that they are all living according to Jewish law, and sometimes according to the same practice and interpretation of Jewish law, but what distinguishes them are their differences of interpretation and practice on specific points of Jewish law. In other words if you take any two groups there are going to be similarities and differences. If we take the Essenes and Pharisees, there will be similarities and differences. If we take the Essenes and Jesus' movement, there will be similarities and differences and so on.

What then are the sum of key differences between Jesus and his movement and the Essenes? First of all, there's this idea of predeterminism. Certainly unlike at Qumran, we do not find this idea among Jesus and his movement that everything is preordained by God and that there is no human free will at all. That is a big difference. Another difference is that at Qumran there was an anticipation or an expectation that there will be two Messiahs, and I should mention also that nowhere in the Dead Sea scrolls is Jesus ever mentioned.

In my opinion, however, there are two really, really, really big differences between Jesus and his movement on the one hand and the Essenes on the other. The first has to do with the observance of purity laws. The community that lived at Qumran took to the extreme the observance of Jewish purity laws. Every full member lived his everyday life observing Jewish purity laws more strictly than everybody else, and observing the purity laws that applied to the priests which were again stricter than for everybody else. Whereas, with Jesus we see pretty much the opposite. We see Jesus going out of his way to come into contact with the most impure and marginal members of Jewish society whether they were women with a hemorrhage or a menstrual period, lepers, corpses.

In other words, Jesus goes out of his way to come into contact with the sorts of people who no member of the Qumran sect would have come into contact with, and by the way I should say that I do not believe that Jesus advocated abolishing the observance of biblical Jewish purity laws. I think however that he was against the expansion of the observance of those laws beyond the boundaries of the temple cult. That by the way is a debate that I think distinguished many of these different groups from each other, as to what extent is it necessary to observe the purity laws outside the temple cult.

Another big difference between Jesus and the Essenes, or Jesus and the Qumran community, is an exclusive versus inclusive point of view. As I mentioned, it is very difficult to become a member of the Qumran community. First of all, full membership is not open to everyone, and once you have applied for membership, you have to undergo a long and rigorous period of initiation, and not everybody passed that period of initiation. So the Qumran sect, the Essenes, were an exclusive community; whereas, with Jesus we see just the opposite. We see an inclusive point of view where everyone is welcomed to become a member of this group. In my opinion then, we must distinguish between Jesus and his movement on the one hand and the Essenes on another hand and show not only similarities between them, but also very important and philosophical differences in their practices and in their way of life.

Finally, was John the Baptist an Essene? Could some of the similarities between Jesus' movement and the Essenes stem from John the Baptist? We do not know for sure. If there is any one figure in early Christianity who might have been an Essene at some point, it is John the Baptist because of course he is wandering around the area where Qumran is located at the time Qumran existed. He is the son of a priest, and of course he is obsessed with ritual emersion in water, with what becomes known as baptism, and he is living an ascetic lifestyle. His diet is very simple. His clothing is very simple, so it may be that at some point John the Baptist was a member of the Essene sect, or at least had some direct contact with them, but by the time we hear about him, and by the time he dies, he certainly not a member of his sect, because his practices and his diet and his clothing are all very different from what characterizes the Essene movement.

In our next lecture what I would like to is turn to look at some of our archaeological evidence for the everyday life of members of the Qumran sect.

The Life of the Essenes
Lecture 17

> Josephus was writing like other ancient Greek and Roman authors to educate but also to entertain his readers. Like other ancient Greek and Roman authors, Josephus typically focuses on things that are exotic, that make them different from everyone else. ... The reason Josephus singles out the toilet habits of the Essenes is because their toilet habits were different from everyone else's.

In this lecture, we'll look at some of the archaeological evidence that sheds light on the everyday life of members of the sect at Qumran and relate it to some of my own research on the archaeology there.

The full and final archaeological report by the excavators of Qumran was never published, but in 1994, a large volume that contains photographs and raw field notes was issued. I was invited to write a review of it. In searching the book for something that would interest readers, I found a description of a room with a pit dug into its dirt floor and one doorway opening to a ritual bath. This pit was filled with layers of dirty, smelly soil and had been identified as a toilet. I was intrigued—a toilet at Qumran? But after researching toilets in the Roman world, I became convinced that this identification was correct.

If indeed this is a toilet at Qumran, do we have any information from our literary sources about the toilets and toilet habits of this sect? Yes, in fact, there are three such sources: the war scroll, the **Temple Scroll**, and the writings of Josephus.

The war scroll, concerned with the 40-year-long apocalyptic war at the end of days, contains a passage that mandates the placement of toilets relative to war camps. In the temple scroll, which describes this sect's ideal temple and ideal Jerusalem, there is also a mandate for the placement of the toilets relative to the city. They are to be further than a Sabbath day's journey from the city (apparently, toilets weren't to be used on the Sabbath) and enclosed in roofed rooms with a pit dug into the floor. This description closely matches what we have in the archaeology of Qumran. The toilet at Qumran is a pit that was dug into the dirt floor of a room that was completely enclosed and was roofed over.

Interestingly, Josephus says that the Essenes didn't use the toilet on the Sabbath. He also says that a new member of this sect had to find a private spot in the desert, dig a hole, cover himself with his mantle while defecating, bury the result, then wash himself. This sect had a very modern Western concern with toilet modesty and privacy, unlike any other group in the Roman world. This description in Josephus perfectly complements what we read in the temple scroll and what we see at the Qumran site. And Josephus also seems to suggest, because these people washed afterward, that this sect considered defecation to be ritually polluting, an attitude unique among the Jews. I do not think it is a coincidence, therefore, that the only doorway in the room with the toilet at Qumran opens onto a ritual bath.

> **Interestingly, Josephus says that the Essenes didn't use the toilet on the Sabbath.**

The toilet room at Qumran offers a wonderful display of intersection of information from varied sources. ■

Important Term

Temple Scroll: A work found at Qumran that describes an ideal future city of Jerusalem and temple.

Questions to Consider

1. What do archaeology and literary sources (e.g., the Dead Sea Scrolls, the writings of Josephus) teach us about the lifestyle and beliefs of the Qumran community?

2. What do you think is the importance of the Dead Sea Scrolls?

The Life of the Essenes
Lecture 17—Transcript

We've spent a lot of time so far talking about the archaeology of Qumran and the Dead Sea Scrolls, and the identification of this sect as the Essenes. What I'd to do now is look at some of our archaeological evidence that sheds light on the everyday life of members of this sect. I'd like to relate this to some of my own research on the archaeology of Qumran.

The first thing that I have to mention is that although the scandals about the Dead Sea Scrolls are long over—the Dead Sea Scrolls are now fully published and have been fully accessible to the public for well over a decade—that is not the case with the archaeological material from de Vaux excavations at Qumran. de Vaux died in the early 1970s without ever having published a full and final scientific report on his excavations at Qumran. He did publish a number of preliminary reports and a sort of synthetic overview, but he never published a scientific archaeological report. Until now, that material, which has been inherited by successive generations of archaeologists at de Vaux's home institution, the Ecole Biblique. Until now, that material has never been published, and is still in the hands of the Ecole Biblique. No one, including myself, has access to that material without permission of the archaeologists at the Ecole Biblique.

I actually think that there is still a big scandal about Qumran and that is the lack of publication of the material from de Vaux's excavations. Having said that, in 1994, a volume was published on de Vaux's excavations by the current archaeologists at the Ecole Biblique—by a man named Jean-Baptiste Humbert. Together with another archaeologist, Alain Chambon, they published a very large volume that contains photographs from the time of de Vaux's excavations and de Vaux's raw field notes. This is, of course, the first step—hopefully—in a process towards final publication.

When that report was published in 1994, I was invited to write a review of it. I was very happy to be invited to review it because it meant that I received the volume for free, so I didn't have to pay for it. But, the bad news was then I had to actually read it and write a review of it. If you've ever read notes from an archaeological excavation, you know that there can be nothing that's dryer or more boring. Reading through de Vaux's notes, you know, we excavated through 10 centimeters of dirt mixed with stones and a few potsherds.

As I read through this volume, in order to write a review of it, what was always at the back of my mind? What sort of valuable information can I extract from this volume that was never published previously, and that will be interesting to readers of this review? I combed through de Vaux's field notes and finally found something very, very interesting and important in a room on the eastern side of the settlement. In this room, which de Vaux called Locus 51, de Vaux describes finding a pit dug into the dirt floor of this room. The room with this pit has one doorway. It opens south onto the miqveh, the ritual bath with the earthquake crack that we talked about originally in our tour of the site of Qumran.

de Vaux describes this pit as a pit that was dug into the dirt floor of the room. It had a circle of stones around the top and a terracotta pipe sunk into it. The photographs of this pit—which are from a volume with photographs from the time of the excavation—show it very clearly. In fact, what appears to be a ceramic jar is not a jar at all. In fact, it's the dried mud lining of the pit. When the pit was dug, they dug it into the dirt floor. In order to keep the sides of the pit from collapsing, they lined it with mud. The mud then caked and hardened. What the photographs from the time of excavation show then is de Vaux having dug away from around the outside of the pit, leaving just the dried, caked-mud lining with the terracotta pipe set down into the middle of it.

In this volume that was published in 1994, de Vaux describes this pit as being filled with layers of dirty, smelly soil. He identifies it as a toilet. I was intrigued—a toilet at Qumran? Was De Vaux correct, in fact, in identifying this installation as a toilet? I set out to try and find out. The logical thing to do would be to analyze soil samples from the pit to see if, in fact, it was a toilet. But, I have no access to the excavated material from Qumran. Even if I did, I find it doubtful that de Vaux would have saved soil samples for analysis, since he excavated back in the early 1950s. That was not an option. The next best option was to do research on toilets in the Roman world to see whether this pit fits the profile of an ancient toilet.

I began to do research on toilets in the Roman world. Very quickly I came across a very interesting kind of toilet called a Roman luxury latrine. It turns out that there have even been books written on these kinds of toilets. Roman luxury latrines are perhaps the most famous kind of ancient toilet. They are found all throughout the Roman world. I happen to show an example from the Scholastica baths at Ephesus. But, toilets like this are found all around the Mediterranean. How did Roman luxury latrines operate? Basically, Roman luxury latrines are usually attached to a bath house, that is, usually they are part of a bath house.

The way that they worked was that the Romans would bring in a constant source of running water by way of aqueduct. The water in the aqueduct then would be channeled through the various rooms in the bath house. After having gone through all of the other rooms in the bath house, it would then be channeled in an underground channel along the sides of the room of the latrine. You have an underground channel running along the walls. Built over the channel was a row of stone or wooden seats. The holes in the seats then allowed the waste to fall down into the channel with the water below. The channel with the water would then carry the waste away from the bath house.

Roman luxury latrines are very interesting. For our purposes, for the purposes of Qumran, they're really not all that relevant. This is because, in order to have this kind of toilet facility, you have to have a constant stream of running water being brought into the latrine. We don't have that at Qumran. There is no constant source of running water. For the purposes of understanding the Qumran toilet, Roman luxury latrines are really not all that helpful. But, there actually is a couple of things about Roman luxury latrines that are pertinent to our discussion.

Of course, the thing that strikes most modern Westerners automatically, when we look at Roman luxury latrine, is the fact that you have rows of seats side-by-side without any toilet privacy. As many as sixty people could sit side-by-side, in full view of each other, in a Roman luxury latrine without any problem at all. What Roman luxury latrines illustrate is the fact that the modern Western notion of toilet privacy did not exist in the ancient Roman world. People simply sat in full view of each other in these latrines.

Another interesting thing—not really relevant to Qumran—to notice about luxury latrines is the fact that, at the base of the seats, there is a channel cut into the pavement. What was that channel for? There are a couple of things—probably to carry off spillage and many scholars think the channel was used for a stream of water that held sponges on sticks. This was because, in the Roman world, there was no toilet paper. What did you do when you finished using the latrine? You would take a sponge on a stick that was then dunked into that water in the channel and you used it to wipe yourself off. When you were done, you put it back into its place. This is an example of what is probably the height of toilet luxury in the Roman world, these Roman luxury latrine installations. But again, for our purposes at Qumran, they're really not all that relevant.

I found, as I was doing my work, my research on toilets in the Roman world, a lot of interesting little tidbits. First of all, I found that a lot of people didn't have access to toilet facilities. That is, people wandered around and there wasn't always a Roman luxury latrine necessarily in the area. You didn't have access to other built toilet facilities. What I found is that, in the ancient world, it was very common for people to literally relieve themselves anywhere. When I say anywhere, I mean anywhere. I found examples of shops at Pompeii where the shopkeepers wrote on the outside of the shop, "Don't go here." I found examples of Roman laws trying to prohibit people from relieving themselves in other kinds of public places. What this indicates by the way, again, is that there was no concept of toilet privacy in the Roman world.

What did you do if you were in a house and you had to use the toilet? Many houses in the ancient world were not equipped with toilet facilities. People would use, well, the analogy would be a chamber pot. They would take, for example, the bottom part of a jar or something like that and they would use that. Then, they would toss the contents out onto the streets below. The streets were used for emptying the contents of chamber pots.

If you've ever been to ancient cities like Pompeii, you may have noticed that the curbs of the sidewalks are very high above the street. In fact, they're so high that you actually have stepping stones going across the street. Did you wonder why you have high curbs with stepping stones? Now you know why. By the way, having high curbs with stepping stones is a big improvement over not having high curbs with stepping stones, which is why cities like Pompeii were considered among the more advanced cities in the ancient world.

We do have examples of houses in the Roman world that have built toilets inside of them. When we do have houses with built toilets, what do these toilets look like? One of the best examples that I've found of a built toilet facility is not from the Roman world. It's from Iron Age Jerusalem, from our House of Achiel in the City of David. It dates to around 600 B.C. It's a very similar type of toilet facility to what we find in Roman houses because toilet technology did not change in the intervening centuries.

What do these sorts of built toilet facilities look like when a house actually has one? Basically, what it consists of is a pit that is dug into the dirt floor of a room. Set above that pit, we have a stone or a wooden toilet seat with a hole in it. When the pit, which is a cesspit, became filled, a manure merchant would be called to come and empty the contents of the pit. The contents of the pit were then sold to be used as fertilizer in the agricultural fields. I like to say, by the way, that if we could actually be transported back 2,000 years in time, we would first of all be bowled over by the odorama. I doubt that most of us would survive even a week because we lack immunity to the diseases that were circulating because of practices like this.

When we have built toilet facilities in Roman houses, they look very similar to what we find at Qumran. It was a cesspit dug into the floor of the room that had a stone or a wooden seat above it. What we're missing at Qumran is the seat. I actually think that de Vaux may have found the seat because, in his field notes, he describes finding in the next room over a square block of stone pierced by a hole. He didn't know what it was. There is no picture of this block of stone, so I've never seen what it looks like. But, from the description, I think he may have actually found the toilet seat at Qumran. After doing this research on toilets in the Roman world, I became convinced that de Vaux was correct in identifying the pit at Qumran as a toilet.

That raises the next interesting question. If indeed this is a toilet at Qumran, do we have any information from our literary sources about the toilets and toilet habits of this sect? I started to do research on that and very quickly found that yes, we do. We have three sources that talk about the toilets and toilet habits of the sect—number one, we have the War Scroll; number two, the Temple Scroll; and number three, Josephus.

I'm not going to look at the passage from the War Scroll, except to describe it a little bit. The War Scroll, of course, is the scroll that describes the 40-year-long apocalyptic war at the end of days between the forces of good and forces of evil, the sons of light and the sons of darkness. There is a passage in the War Scroll that mandates the placement of the toilets relative to the war camps. We have that reference there. But, what I do want to do is focus on the description in the Temple Scroll.

First of all, what is the Temple Scroll? The Temple Scroll is a document which may or may not be a sectarian composition. That is, we are not sure whether the Temple Scroll was composed by members of this sect, or simply used by them. Even if it wasn't composed by members of the sect, it certainly was authoritative at Qumran because it is represented among the Dead Sea Scrolls by multiple copies. The Temple Scroll is a document which describes this sect's ideal temple and ideal Jerusalem—not a heavenly temple, not an apocalyptic temple, but what Jerusalem and the temple will look like in the future when they're in control.

The scroll is written in a very particular way. It is written as though God is speaking. This is coming out of the mouth of God. What better way to give something authority than to have God telling you to do it? The scroll is so detailed in its description of this ideal future city of Jerusalem that even the placement of the toilets relative to the city of Jerusalem is mandated. We're going to look at the passage. I want you to note that, in this scroll, the word toilet, the Hebrew word toilet, is hand or a place for a hand. The term hand or place for a hand is actually a term that comes from Deuteronomy. When they were writing this scroll, they took that term from a passage in Deuteronomy.

Let's now read what the scroll says about the toilets in this future city of Jerusalem. It says, "And you shall make them a place for a hand to which they shall go out, to the northwest of the city." In this ideal future city of Jerusalem, the toilets are to be located outside the city and to the northwest of the city. "Roofed houses with pits within them, into which the excrement will descend." Notice, the toilets here are to be built toilet facilities consisting of an enclosed roofed room with a pit dug into the floor and the excrement then is to go down into the pit, "so that it will not be visible at any distance from the city, three thousand cubits."

Notice a couple of very interesting things about this. The toilets are to be enclosed so that you cannot see them from outside. If somebody is using the toilet, they will be within an enclosed facility. There is a concern that the toilets will not be visible at any distance from the city, so they're to be in a secluded location. They are supposed to be not just outside the city and to the northwest of the city, but at a distance of 3,000 cubits. Now, 3,000 cubits—a cubit is approximately the length from the tip of my elbow to the tip of the fingers. As Yigael Yadin, who published this scroll, noted, a distance of 3,000 cubits places the toilets outside the Sabbath limits. What does that mean? That means that that is farther than you are allowed to walk on the Sabbath according to biblical Jewish law. That's right. You couldn't reach the toilets on the Sabbath. What did they do? I don't know. It doesn't say what they did. I'm just reporting what it says.

It's very, very interesting; we also have a passage from Josephus that describes the toilet habits of the Essenes. You know what? As peculiar as it looks to us that they didn't go on the Sabbath, Josephus remarked on exactly the same thing. He starts out, in his description of the toilet habits of Essenes, by saying, "On the Sabbath they do not even go to stool." He thought that was pretty odd too. Josephus here is going to give a fairly long and detailed description of the toilet habits of the Essenes. This is actually pretty interesting. Why does Josephus provide a long and detailed description of the toilet habits of the Essenes? It's not as obvious as it may seem. As odd as it looks to us that in the Roman world up to 60 people could go to a Roman luxury latrine, sit side by side, and do it in full view of each other, there is not a single ancient Roman author that describes that.

Why does Josephus describe in detail the toilet practices of the Essenes? Josephus was writing like other ancient Greek and Roman authors to educate, but also to entertain his readers. Like other ancient Greek and Roman authors, Josephus typically focuses on things that are exotic, that make them different from everyone else. Josephus and other ancient Roman authors do not describe the typical practice of going in full view of each other on a Roman luxury latrine because they took that for granted. The reason Josephus singles out the toilet habits of the Essenes is because their toilet habits were different from everyone else's. One of the things that made them different was the fact, as he starts out by saying, that they don't go on the Sabbath. That was different, even from all of the other Jews. Then Josephus goes on to further describe their toilet habits. What does he say? "On other days they dig a trench a foot deep with a mattock—such is the nature of the hatchet which they present to neophytes." In other words, when you became a new member of this sect, you were presented with a little hatchet so that you could dig your own little pit. By the way, in cave 11 at Qumran, de Vaux found an iron pick, which he identified as possibly one of these picks that was presented to neophytes.

He says, on other days when you have to go what did they do? They would take the pick that they were given when they became a neophyte and they would dig a trench in the ground, a pit into the ground, "—and wrapping their mantles about them, that they may not offend the rays of the deity, sit above it." They go, they dig their little pit in the ground, and then they wrap their mantle about them and sit above it. Then he says, "They then replace the excavated soil in the trench. For this purpose they select the more retired spots. And though this discharge of the excrements is a natural function, they make it a rule to wash themselves after it, as if defiled."

Let's take apart this little passage here in Josephus because it's very, very interesting. First of all, he's describing what they do on other days, not on the Sabbath. He says they take their little pick and dig a hole in the ground. They then squat. Then, after they're done, they fill it back in with dirt. They wrap their mantle about them while they're going. He says they select retired spots. On the one hand, the description that we have here in Josephus looks different from what we just saw in the Temple Scroll, but I actually think these two sources are complimentary. The Temple Scroll is describing what built, that is, permanent, toilet facilities, should look like in this future city of Jerusalem. It's very interesting to notice that the description in the Temple Scroll very closely matches what we have in the archaeology of Qumran. This is because the toilet at Qumran is a pit that was dug into the dirt floor of a room in a room that was completely enclosed and was roofed over. The description in the Temple Scroll actually matches very closely the archaeological remains of the toilet that we have at Qumran. It's apparently referring to that kind of built toilet facility.

Josephus, on the other hand, is describing what appears to be a very different practice, but I think it's not exactly so. Josephus here is not describing what the Essenes do when they have access to a built toilet facility—why not? It's because that's like what everybody else does if you have access to a built toilet facility, you use the built toilet facility. What Josephus is singling out here as different is what this sect did when they did not have access to built toilet facilities. What did everybody else do when they didn't have access to built toilet facilities? We saw—they simply went anywhere. That is not the case with this sect. Instead of just going anywhere, they go to pains to find a remote, secluded spot, dig a pit in the ground, and wrap their mantle about them that they may not offend the rays of the deity.

In other words, this sect—and this is Josephus is singling out as so odd—had a very modern Western concern with toilet modesty and toilet privacy. There were no other groups in the Roman world that had such a concern. That's why Josephus is singling it out for description. Notice that this perfectly complements what we read about in the Temple Scroll where built permanent toilet facilities must be enclosed, roofed facilities—which we also see in the archaeology at Qumran. When they did not have access to built permanent toilet facilities, members of this sect, unlike everyone else, sought out a remote spot, dug a pit in the ground, and wrapped their mantle about themselves. Notice too that, in both the Temple Scroll and Josephus, there is a concern that the excrement must go down into a pit, be hidden, and buried inside a pit.

Josephus ends his passage in a very, very interesting manner. He says, "And though this discharge of the excrements is a natural function, they make it a rule to wash themselves after it, as if defiled." Why is this so interesting? It suggests, what Josephus seems to suggest here, is that this sect considered defecation to be a ritually polluting activity. Why is this interesting? In normative Rabbinic Judaism, that is, the Judaism that became eventually normative—that we still observe today—defecation and excrement are not connected with ritual impurity. In fact, there are rabbis who argue that it's quite to the contrary, that these acts are connected with purity, rather than ritual impurity. In other movements, sects, and groups in Judaism, including the prevailing type of Judaism that is observed until today, there is no connection between excrement, defecation, and ritual impurity. This group differed, therefore, from all other Jews in considering defecation to be a ritually polluting activity. Therefore, what Josephus is describing here is that, after using the toilet, they then immersed themselves in a ritual bath in order to purify themselves.

I do not think it is a coincidence, therefore, that the only doorway in the room with the toilet at Qumran opens onto that miqveh, that ritual bath with the earthquake crack running through it. What I think is that we see, reflected in the archaeology of Qumran, is this very same principle that Josephus raises in his description of the Essenes. This sect differed from everyone else in their toilet practices and concern with toilet modesty and toilet privacy. They differed from all other Jews even in considering defecation and excrement to be a ritually polluting activity.

What we have here, in looking at the toilet at Qumran, is a very interesting insight into the everyday life of this community. It's a community with habits so peculiar that they even differed from everyone else in the way that they used the toilet. What we have here, with this example of the toilet at Qumran, is a wonderful display of intersection of information from our outside sources. In this case, it's Josephus, the Dead Sea Scrolls, and the archaeology of the site of Qumran.

From Roman Annexation to Herod the Great
Lecture 18

> Augustus reportedly remarked, "It is better to be Herod's pig than his son." This is actually a pun in Greek because the words "pig" and "son" are very close. ... It also suggests, by the way, that Herod observed the biblical dietary laws and didn't eat pork. It's better to be Herod's pig than his son, because you're safer; he won't kill you.

The sectarian settlement at Qumran was established during the Hasmonean period and continued through the Roman takeover and the reign of Herod the Great. How did this very important transition from the Hasmonean period to the reign of Herod come about? When civil war broke out between the two sons of Salome Alexandra, both of them turned to Rome for help. The Romans then simply came in and took over the country.

The Romans took apart the Hasmonean kingdom, leaving the older son of Salome Alexandra, the high priest Hyrcanus II, in control only of areas with concentrations of Jews or Judaized non-Jews: Judea, Galilee, Idumaea, and Peraea. How was this area with the large Jewish population administered? Hyrcanus II, the high priest, received the title ethnarch of the Jews, but Antipater, an Idumaean Jew, was titled procurator. Antipater, the son of Antipas, is best known to us as the father of Herod the Great. Herod and his older brother Phasael assist Antipater in administering this territory.

> **In 40 B.C., Syria and Palestine were suddenly overrun by the great power to the east, the Parthians.**

In 40 B.C., Syria and Palestine were suddenly overrun by the great power to the east, the Parthians. With this invasion came a son of Aristobulus II, Mattathias Antigonus, who took over the country. He captured Hyrcanus II and Phasael. Antigonus bit off the ear of Hyrcanus II so that he could no longer serve as high priest; Phasael committed suicide; and Herod fled the country after depositing his family at the Hasmonean fortress of **Masada**.

He went south to the Nabataean kingdom to ask for help because his mother was a Nabataean. When his request was refused, he made his way to Egypt, where Cleopatra greeted him in magnificent manner, hoping that he would help her regain Palestine for the Ptolemaic kingdom. Uninterested, Herod sailed to Rome.

When Herod appeared before the Roman Senate, the influence of Mark Antony moved the Senate to appoint Herod the king of Judea and give him some forces to fight Mattathias Antigonus and the Parthians. He spent three years fighting Mattathias Antigonus and the Parthians; eventually, the Romans got involved, and in 37 B.C., Jerusalem fell after a siege. There was great slaughter in the city, and the Romans carried Mattathias Antigonus off to Mark Antony, who beheaded him. It was unprecedented for the Romans to execute captive kings, but Antony believed it necessary so that the Jews would accept Herod.

Herod was now able to govern the kingdom he'd been given. After the defeat of Cleopatra and Mark Antony by Octavian in 31 B.C., the kingdom even expanded. Herod convinced Octavian that he would be loyal to the emperor, and he eventually ruled as far north as the Golan Heights and into Syria.

However, Herod knew that many Jews didn't like or trust him. His family was also trouble: He had at least nine wives, and they jockeyed for position throughout his life, trying to influence who his successor would be. Herod's suspicions led to a great deal of family bloodshed, including the deaths of his favorite wife, the Hasmonean Mariamne, and that of his oldest son. In fact, Herod eliminated a large number of his own household, and it may be this bloody reputation that underlies the famous story of the massacre of the innocents reported in Matthew. ■

Important Term

Masada: Herodian fortified palace by the southwest shore of the Dead Sea.

Questions to Consider

1. Why would Augustus have remarked, "I would rather be Herod's pig than his son"?

2. Do you think Herod was really as horrible as our ancient sources portray him?

From Roman Annexation to Herod the Great
Lecture 18—Transcript

The sectarian settlement at Qumran was established during the Hasmonean period. It continued to be occupied through the period when the Romans come in and take over the country and through the reign of Herod the Great.

What I'd like to do now is turn to consider this very important transition from the Hasmonean period to the reign of Herod. How does this all come about? Our transition actually starts with the death of Salome Alexandra, who, as you may recall, had two sons—Aristobulus II, the younger son, and Hyrcanus II, the older son. Hyrcanus had served as the high priest when Salome Alexandra was queen of the Hasmonean kingdom.

With the death of Alexandra, a civil war broke out over the succession to the throne between her two sons. Ordinarily, in dynastic succession, what should happen is the older son becomes king. But, Aristobulus, the younger son, was much more energetic and ambitious than his older brother. A war develops between them over who's going to become the next king. Both of them then turned to an outside power for help. The outside power, of course—at this point we're in the middle of the 1st century B.C.—is Rome, which already was expanding its control into the Eastern Mediterranean. Both brothers turned to the Romans for help.

What the Romans then do is simply come in and take over the country. This occurs in the year 63 B.C. The annexation of the Hasmonean kingdom was done by a very famous general in Rome at the time whose name was Pompey. Parenthetically, I would point out that, at this period, middle of the 1st century B.C., what you have going on in Rome is a series of civil wars. They are followed by the division of rule between very powerful generals, as the late republic is beginning to break up. Pompey, one of these powerful generals in Rome at this time, comes in, in 63, and simply takes over. He annexes the Hasmonean kingdom.

When the Romans come in and take over the Hasmonean Kingdom, what do they do? They rightfully suspect that the Hasmoneans will not be loyal to them. Therefore, they remove the Hasmoneans pretty much from control.

They dismember, take apart, the Hasmonean kingdom. Basically, what they do is leave the high priest in control only of areas with concentrations of Jews. That would be Judea, Galilee, Idumaea, and Peraea. Peraea is the territory on the eastern side of the Jordan River and the eastern side of the Dead Sea. These are areas that were either Jewish or had been Judaized during the Hasmonean period. Those areas with those high concentrations of Jews were left under the control of Hyrcanus II, the high priest.

One of the things that the Romans wanted to do was to strengthen the non-Jewish, the Hellenized elements in Palestine. They did this then by detaching the most Hellenized cities and forming them into their own independent league. This league of cities—originally numbering 10, but not always numbering 10—became known as the Decapolis. Of course this, league of 10 Hellenized cities called the Decapolis is known from the New Testament. The Decapolis cities included, for example, Beth-Shean or Scythopolis—which is to the south of the Sea of Galilee today in the Jordan valley—and the cities of Pella and Abila, which are in the area of Jordan today on the other side of the Dead Sea and the Jordan River.

The Decapolis cities then were put under the administration of a newly established province in Rome, the province of Syria. Basically, what we have is the area where there are high concentrations of Jews being under the administration of the Jewish high priest. But, the most Hellenized parts of the country, in the north, are detached and put into a league of their own which is under the administration of the Roman province of Syria.

How is this area with the large Jewish population administered? Hyrcanus II, the high priest, is given the title ethnarch of the Jews. This basically means he's sort of like a local Jewish ruler or administrator of the Jews. The governor was a man named Antipater. He was given the title procurator. Who exactly was Antipater? Antipater was an Idumaean Jew whose father had been named Antipas. Antipater, the son of Antipas, is best known to us because he was the father of Herod the Great. What we have here is a very interesting succession. In the Hasmonean period, an Idumaean named Antipas had been forcibly converted to Judaism by the Hasmonean kings. His son, Antipater, becomes procurator on behalf of the Romans—governor on behalf of the Romans—in this heavily Jewish district with Hyrcanus II as high priest. Antipater was then assisted in administering this territory by his two sons, Herod and Phasael. This then is the picture that we have in these very heavily Jewish territories after the Roman annexation in the year 63 B.C.

In 40 B.C., the picture is upset by an outside event that is a little bit unexpected for us. In 40 B.C., Syria and Palestine were overrun by a people called the Parthians. Who were the Parthians? The Parthians were basically the successors of the Ancient Persians, way out to the east in the area of Iran. As the Romans had increased and expanded their control over territories further and further through the eastern Mediterranean, they began to get closer and closer to the Parthians. There was a constant series of wars, pretty much, conflicts between the Parthians to the east and the Romans throughout this period. In 40 B.C., the Parthians overran Syria and Palestine. What happens with the Parthian invasion? One of the successors of the Hasmoneans, the son of Aristobulus II, whose name is Mattathias Antigonus, comes in and takes over the country. He captures Hyrcanus II and Phasael. Phasael, Herod's older brother, commits suicide.

What happens with Hyrcanus II? Josephus tells us that Mattathias Antigonus pulls a Mike Tyson on Hyrcanus. Here is what Josephus says.

> Antigonus himself bit of Hyrcanus's ears with his own teeth, as he fell down on his knees to him, so that he might never be able upon any change of affairs to assume the high priesthood again, for the high priests who officiated were to be perfect and without blemish. (War 1.270)

Remember we talked about this at Qumran? In order to be a high priest in the Jerusalem temple, you had to be an unblemished adult male. Mattathias Antigonus bites off Hyrcanus' ears so that Hyrcanus can never again serve as high priest—basically getting Hyrcanus out of the way as any potential future threat.

What happens to Herod in 40 B.C.? Hyrcanus is disfigured. Phaesael, Herod's older brother, commits suicide. What happens to Herod? Herod flees the country in a very, very interesting way. He flees south to Idumaea.

Remember, Herod's family on his father's side of the family was Idumaean. He flees south to Idumaea. He goes to Masada, on the shore of the Dead Sea, where there is a Hasmonean fortress. There, he leaves his family, holed up for safekeeping. Then, he goes south to the Nabataean kingdom.

Why did Herod go to the Nabataean kingdom? Although Herod was Jewish on his father's side of the family through forced conversion and therefore Idumaean—he was Idumaean-Jew on his father's side of the family—Herod's mother was not Jewish. She was a Nabataean. Thus, Herod, in 40, goes down to the Nabataean kingdom and asks the Nabataean king for help. When the Nabataeans refused to help Herod, what does he do? He then makes his way to Egypt. What happens when he gets to Egypt? As Josephus says, Herod was greeted with a magnificent reception from Cleopatra, who hoped to entrust him with the command of an expedition which she was preparing.

We're now in 40 B.C. What is happening? Cleopatra's in Egypt. This, by the way, is Cleopatra VII. Cleopatra is going to be a very key figure for us. Cleopatra was a descendent of the Ptolemys. Like the Hasmonean kingdom, by this point, the Ptolemys had also been absorbed by Rome. Cleopatra, as a descendent of the Ptolomys, apparently wanted to revive Ptolemaic independence. She wanted to revive an independent Ptolemaic kingdom. Not only that, but remember that back in the 3rd century B.C., Palestine had been under the rule of the Ptolemys. Cleopatra has her sights on the same territory that Herod has been administering. Thus, they have a conflict of interest here. Herod gets to Egypt. Cleopatra greets him with a magnificent reception and offers to assist him. Herod, however, didn't trust Cleopatra—rightfully so, by the way. Therefore, he refuses her offer of assistance and sets sail from Egypt for Rome.

When Herod gets to Rome, what's happening in Rome? We're, again, in 40 B.C. At this point, Rome is being ruled by a triumvirate—a coalition of three men. Eventually, this triumvirate, this coalition of three men, will be reduced to two very important figures: Mark Antony and Octavian. Octavian later becomes known as Augustus. Eventually, Mark Antony will become the ruler of the eastern half of the Roman Empire, setting up his base of administration in Egypt. Octavian will become the ruler of the western half of the lands of Rome.

We're in the year 40 B.C. One of these very powerful men who's now ruling Rome is Mark Antony. When Herod gets to Rome, he goes before the Roman senate. It was through the influence of Mark Antony that the Roman senate then agrees to appoint Herod the King of Judea. That is, they give him literally the title King of Judea. They give him some forces and send him back to Palestine to fight Mattathias Antigonus and the Parthians.

It's 40 B.C. and Herod then goes back to Judea. He is now officially King of Judea on behalf of the Romans' client king. The first thing, of course, that he has to do is fight Mattathias Antigonus and the Parthians. He spends three years, until the year 37 B.C., waging a war. At this point, the Roman province of Syria and the Decapolis cities to the north were under the administration of a Roman official called a legate. A legate is a high-ranking Roman official who is high ranking enough to be able to command a legion. The highest ranking Roman official in this area at this point is the legate based in Syria—specifically based in Antioch—who commands one or more legions. It is this legate who is going to now help Herod to fight against Mattathias Antigonus and the Parthians. As Josephus says, "Now Antony entrusted Syria to Sosius (the legate of Syria) with instructions to aid Herod. ... And so Sosius sent two legions ahead to Judea to assist Herod, and himself followed with the greater part of his army." (Ant. 14:447)

You know, Herod wasn't a legate, so he couldn't command a legion. In order to have the assistance of a legion, the legate had to come down from Syria, which is what happens. Sosius, the legate, assists Herod in this war that Herod is now going to be waging for the next three years. This war goes on for three years until finally 37 B.C. when Jerusalem falls after a siege. Josephus describes in very graphic terms the fall of Jerusalem with the massacre of the inhabitants as follows:

> Soon every quarter was filled with the blood of the slain, for the Romans were furious at the length of the siege, while the Jews on Herod's side were anxious not to leave a single adversary alive. And so they were slaughtered in heaps, whether crowded together in alleys and houses or seeking refuge in the temple; no pity was shown either to infants or the aged, nor were weak women spared. (Ant. 14:480)

There's a massacre in Jerusalem in 37 B.C. After a siege, the city falls. What happens to Mattathias Antigonus? Mattathias Antigonus surrenders and then begs for mercy, begs for his life, and Josephus also describes this. "Then Antigonus, without any regard to his former or to his present fortune, came down from the citadel and threw himself at Sosius' feet. Without pitying him at all upon the change of his condition, he [Sosius] laughed at him, at Antigonus, beyond measure and called him Antigone." Notice the mocking, the pun, here. Antigone is the female form of the name Antigonus. He mocked him as if he was a woman—you're not behaving bravely like a man, groveling for your life here. Thus, he mocks him and calls him Antigone. Yet, he did not treat him like a woman by letting him go free. He put him into bonds and kept him in custody.

"Then Sosius dedicated a crown of gold to God and withdrew from Jerusalem, leading Antigonus away in chains to (Mark) Antony." Then, what's very, very interesting is that Josephus tells us that, in the end, Mark Antony had Antigonus executed. Josephus says, "Then the ax brought to his end one who still had a fond desire of life and some vain hopes of it to the last, but who, by his cowardly behavior, well deserved to die by it." (War 1:353, 357)

It's very interesting also—Josephus actually tells us that the beheading of royalty by the Romans was something that was not usual. Here is what Josephus says, "Mark Antony then became the first Roman who decided to behead a king, since he believed that in no other way could he change the attitude of the Jews so that they would accept Herod." (Ant. 15:9) Basically, according to Josephus, Mark Antony does something very unusual. Instead of simply taking Antigonus into captivity, he has him beheaded. This is because he believed that only in that way would the Jews accept Herod as client king on behalf of the Romans.

We're now in 37 and Herod is able to actually start governing the kingdom that he's been given. One of the problems that Herod has throughout his reign is the fact that Hasmoneans are now part of his household. Why is this a problem? This is because Herod, in many ways, was a usurper to the throne. He was, first of all, half Jewish on his father's side of the family, through forced conversion. That's one thing.

But, more importantly, he was not part of the Hasmonean line. He was not part of the Hasmonean dynasty. He did try to marry his way into the Hasmonean dynasty to gain legitimacy in the eyes of the Jews—although, as we'll see, that didn't work. But, he always struggled against the fact that many Jews did not accept Herod as a legitimate king. Throughout his reign, Herod feared a Jewish revolt against him because he knew that many Jews didn't like and trust him. Part of the problems that Herod had came from within his own household because there were Hasmoneans in his own household. Among the people who wanted to see a Hasmonean dynasty restored and independence from the Romans, were, of course, members of the Hasmonean family.

Who were these Hasmoneans who were part of Herod's household? The foremost one was one of his wives. One of Herod's wives was a Hasmonean woman named Mariamne. We hear a lot about her. We also hear a lot about her mother, whose name was Alexandra. One of the important things, by the way, to know about Herod is that he had wither 9 or 10 wives, depending on how you read Josephus. Anyone who has 9 or 10 wives has problems—not just because they have 9 or 10 wives, but they also have 9 or 10 mothers-in-law. That's exactly one of the things that Herod had a problem with. What was the problem? The problem was jockeying for position within Herod's household. This is because, for the most part, these women—the mothers and their daughters—didn't really care how much Herod liked them or not. What they were concerned about was who Herod was going to designate as his heir or successor—who was going to succeed Herod to the throne. If you have that many wives, mothers, and children, you can imagine there's going to be a lot of internal jockeying going on for positioning.

Unfortunately for Mariamne, she actually was Herod's favorite wife. He loved her best of all. She apparently was a very beautiful woman and Herod was madly in love with her. This was unfortunate because Herod therefore was also insanely jealous of her. He believed that, because she was so beautiful and he was so insanely in love with her, that everybody else also wanted her.

One of the problems, in addition to Herod's love for Mariamne, was the fact that Alexandra, Mariamne's mother, continually schemed about jockeying the Hasmoneans back into control. One of the things that Alexandra did, very early on, to try and make this come about was to position Mariamne's brother in the position of high priest. Mariamne had a younger brother whose name was Aristobulus III. Alexandra wanted Aristobulus III to be high priest, because, of course, this was a very important position. It could potentially develop into something else. Herod, as you can imagine, did not want Aristobulus III to be high priest because he saw Aristobulus III as a potential threat. Eventually, Alexandra actually contacts Cleopatra. Because of her pressure and contact with Cleopatra, Herod reluctantly made Aristobulus III the high priest.

This actually ended up badly for Aristobulus III. What happens? Aristobulus, who at this time is a 17-year-old young man, appears as high priest at the Feast of Tabernacles in Jerusalem. Josephus describes what happens.

> Aristobulus was a youth of 17 when he went up to the altar to perform the sacrifices in accordance with the Law, wearing the ornamental dress of the high priests and carrying out the rites of the cult, and he was extraordinarily handsome, and taller than most youths of his age, and in his appearance, he displayed to the full the nobility of his descent.
>
> And so there arose among the people an impulsive feeling of affection toward him. ... Being overcome, they gradually revealed their feelings, showing joyful and painful emotion at the same time, and they called out to him good wishes mingled with prayers, so that the affection of the crowd became evidence, and their acknowledgement of their emotions seemed too impulsive in view of their having a king. (Ant. 15:1–52)

In other words, this event plays right into Herod's worst fears—that Aristobulus III is going to be so popular that this is going to threaten Herod's position as king of Judea. What does Herod do? Almost immediately, Herod gives instructions to have Aristobulus put to death. This happened in one of the swimming pools in the palace at Jericho. The main Hasmonean and Herodian winter palaces were located at the oasis at Jericho, a nice, warm location not too far from Jerusalem. In one of the swimming pools there,

Herod gives orders to have Aristobulus III drowned. Here is how Josephus describes it:

> For although he (Herod) had given him the high priesthood at the age of 17, he killed him quickly after he had conferred that dignity upon him.
>
> When Aristobulus had put on the holy vestments and had approached the altar at a festival, the multitude in great crowds fell into tears. Thereupon the youth was sent by night to Jericho, and was plunged there by the Gauls, at Herod's command, in a pool until he drowned. (War 1:437)

Herod eliminates Aristobulus III, the younger brother of Mariamne.

While all of this is going on, there are other things going on outside, in the Roman Empire, that are going to affect Herod. First of all, in 36, 37—in that winter—Cleopatra VII, who's down in Egypt, married Mark Antony. At this point, Mark Antony had set up his base of administration in Egypt. It's in Egypt that Mark Antony meets and falls in love with Cleopatra. They get married. Once Cleopatra was married to Mark Antony, she was able to capitalize on her ambitions.

Remember, her ambitions include trying to revive the Ptolemaic kingdom. She has her sights set on the same territory that has been given to Herod. Little by little, Cleopatra gets Mark Antony to give her pieces of Herod's territory. Eventually, Cleopatra received from Mark Antony the Decapolis cities, most of the Palestinian coast, the balsam plantations at Jericho—which were very lucrative—and the eastern shore of the Dead Sea. Of course, Herod couldn't do anything about this. Remember, it was through the influence of Mark Antony that Herod had been appointed King of Judea. Ironically, what's happening at this point is that Herod's greatest threat is coming from his big supporter Mark Antony. He can't do anything about it.

All of this changes in the year 31 B.C. with a battle called the Battle of Actium. Eventually, tensions between Mark Antony and Octavian reach the point where they fight a big battle, a naval battle, off the coast of Greece. In this battle, the Battle of Actium, the forces of Mark Antony and Cleopatra were decisively defeated by the forces of Octavian. Subsequently, Mark Antony and Cleopatra go back to Egypt, where they both commit suicide. Octavian then become sole ruler of all of the lands of Rome. A few years later, in 27 B.C., he is given the title of Augustus by the Roman senate.

The Battle of Actium is very important for Herod because Herod had been appointed King of Judea through the influence of Mark Antony. After the Battle of Actium, the last thing that you want is to be associated with Mark Antony in any way. Herod, realizing this, immediately, after the battle of Actium, goes to the island of Rhodes to meet with Octavian. What Herod does, when meeting with Octavian, is basically to say, listen, we all know that I was appointed King of Judea because of my friendship with Mark Antony. But, he says, and this is what Josephus tells us, he says, "Do not be concerned with whose friend I was, but with how loyal a friend I was." Basically, what Herod says is, if you give me a chance, I will prove to you that I will be just as loyal as I was to Mark Antony.

Herod is so persuasive that not only does Octavian reconfirm Herod as King of Judea, but he actually increases the size of his kingdom. Eventually, Herod then rules over a very substantial kingdom that included not just those core areas of Judea, Samaria, Idumaea, Galilee, and Peraea, but also territories going far into the north, far into the area of the Golan Heights and Syria.

Before Herod left for Rhodes to meet with Octavian, he placed Mariamne and Alexandra under guard in one of his fortresses. After he returned from Rome, Herod suspected that Mariamne had had an affair with her guard. What does he do then? He gives orders to have her put to death. But, after Herod has Mariamne put to death, he has second thoughts. In fact, according to Josephus, he's actually haunted by Mariamne. He imagines that he sees her, even though she's dead. He goes through this delusional period. What happens then? While Herod is in this sort of delusional period, Alexandra takes advantage of this situation and gains control of the Jerusalem garrison. When Herod hears that, he has Alexandra executed. Notice that, by this point, Herod has had executed Alexandra, Mariamne, and Aristobulus III.

Before Mariamne was put to death, she bore Herod five children. Two of them are very important because they were sons, sons whose names were Alexander and Aristobulus. Herod sent them to Rome in order to be educated. This, by the way, is a very interesting thing. It was very common in these royal families to send your kids to Rome to be properly educated. Herod sends them, at a very young age, to Rome to be educated. In the year 17 B.C., these two sons, Alexander and Aristobulus, return to Jerusalem. Herod then arranges marriages for them.

Because they were Hasmonean princes, Herod's non-Hasmonean relatives, including his other wives and their children, were jealous of these two princes. They start to mount a campaign of slander against these two princes. Herod believes the slander. In the year 12 B.C., Herod denounces the two princes, Alexander and Aristobulus, before Augustus. He has them taken into prison, accusing them of treason. In the year 7 B.C., he has them strangled at Samaria Sebaste. In fact, just five days before Herod died, in the year 4 B.C., he also had his oldest son, the son of his first wife, executed because of a perceived threat.

Augustus reportedly remarked about Herod, "It is better to be Herod's pig than his son." This is actually a pun in Greek because the word pig and son are very close—hus and huios. This, by the way, suggests that, if Augustus really said this, he knew Greek well enough to pun in Greek. It also suggests, by the way, that Herod observed the Biblical dietary laws and didn't eat pork. It's better to be Herod's pig than his son, because you're safer; he won't kill you.

The fact of the matter is that Herod eliminated, as we've seen, large numbers of members of his own household. It may be this which underlies the famous story of the massacre or slaughter of the innocence reported in Matthew, where we read:

> After Jesus' birth in Bethlehem of Judea during the reign of King Herod, astrologers from the east arrived one day in Jerusalem inquiring, 'Where is the newborn king of the Jews? We observed his star at its rising and have come to pay him homage.' At this King Herod became greatly disturbed, and with him all Jerusalem...Once

Herod realized that he had been deceived by the astrologers, he became furious. He ordered the massacre of all the boys two years old and under in Bethlehem and its environs, making his calculations on the basis of the date he had learned from the astrologers.

Many scholars believe that there is little or no historical basis to the story of the slaughter of the innocence. There are various problems with it, including problems of chronology which don't work. That is the date of Herod's death versus the date of Jesus' birth, for example, astrological problems. There is also the fact that we simply don't have any evidence from any other sources for an episode like this. Probably what we have here is some sort of a legend that arises with the kernel of truth in this legend apparently being the fact that it was known that Herod had slaughtered many members of his own family, many members of his own household, including his very own sons. When we look at the slaughter of the innocence, what we're probably looking at is something that's an embellishment of the reputation that Herod had for being so ruthless that he even massacred his own sons.

Maps

Map of Ancient Near East (3rd to 1st millennium B.C.)

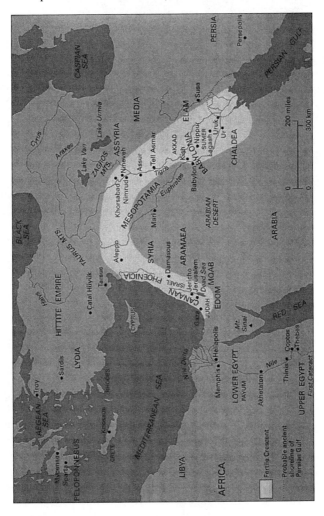

Topographic Map of Jerusalem

Administrative Division of Palestine in the Persian Period (6th to 4th centuries B.C.)

Map 2: PERSIAN PALESTINE
Samaria — Provincial Capital
T) — Town belonging to Tyre
S) — Town belonging to Sidon

Map of Palestine in the Biblical and Post-Biblical Periods (1st millennium B.C.)

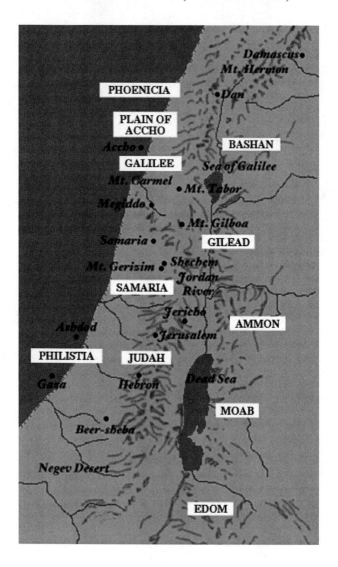

Timeline

B.C.

c. 1200 .... Moses dies; the Israelite tribes enter Canaan and settle in the hill country.

c. 1000 .... Death of Saul and establishment of the kingdom of David.

c. 950 .... Solomon builds the First Temple on Jerusalem's Temple Mount.

c. 920 .... Solomon dies; the United Kingdom splits into Israel (north) and Judah (south).

8th century .... Period of the prophets Isaiah, Amos, Hosea, and Micah.

722 .... Kingdom of Israel falls to Assyria.

701 .... Assyrians invade Judah, destroy Lachish, and besiege Jerusalem (under King Hezekiah).

641/40–610/09 .... Reign of King Josiah and the period of the Deuteronomistic reform.

c. 625–580 .... Activity of the prophet Jeremiah.

586 .... Kingdom of Judah falls to Babylonia; destruction of Solomon's Temple and beginning of the Babylonian Exile.

516	The Second Temple is consecrated.
c. 450	Ezra and Nehemiah in Jerusalem.
332	Alexander conquers Palestine.
323	Alexander dies.
301	Final division of Alexander's empire, with Seleucus in Asia Minor and Syria and Ptolemy in Egypt; Palestine comes under Ptolemaic rule.
198	Palestine comes under Seleucid rule.
167	Antiochus IV Epiphanes outlaws Judaism and dedicates the Jerusalem temple to Olympian Zeus, sparking the Maccabean revolt.
164	Antiochus IV rescinds his edict outlawing Judaism; the Jerusalem temple is rededicated to the God of Israel, but the Maccabean revolt continues.
c. 150–140	Maccabees establish an independent Jewish kingdom ruled by their descendants (the Hasmoneans); in the decades that follow, the Hasmoneans increase the size of their kingdom through territorial expansion.
c. 100	A sectarian community settles at Qumran (site associated with the Dead Sea Scrolls).

63	Romans annex the Hasmonean kingdom.
40	Parthians invade Syria-Palestine; Herod flees to Rome and is appointed king of Judea.
37	Herod defeats the last successor to the Hasmonean throne.
31	Octavian defeats Marc Antony and Cleopatra at the Battle of Actium; afterwards, reconfirms Herod as king of Judea and increases the size of his kingdom.
4	Herod dies and his kingdom is divided among three of his sons; Jesus is born around this time.

A.D.

6	Herod's son Archelaus is deposed and replaced by the Romans with low-ranking governors (prefects), who establish their base of administration at Caesarea Maritima.
26–36	Pontius Pilate is Roman prefect; executes Jesus.
37–44	Rule of Herod Antipas I, grandson of Herod the Great and his Hasmonean wife, Mariamne.

44–66	All of Palestine is placed under the administration of low-ranking governors (procurators).
62/63	James the Just (brother of Jesus) is executed by the Jewish Sanhedrin in Jerusalem; Paul is executed in Rome.
66	Outbreak of the First Jewish Revolt against Rome.
67	Galilee is subdued by the Romans and Josephus surrenders to the general Vespasian.
68	The sectarian settlement at Qumran is destroyed; the community flees, depositing the Dead Sea Scrolls in the nearby caves.
69	Vespasian becomes Roman emperor; leaves his son Titus in charge of subduing the revolt.
70	Jerusalem falls to the Romans and the Second Temple is destroyed.
73/74	Masada falls after a siege.
2nd–3rd centuries	Period of rabbinic Judaism.
115–117	Diaspora Revolt (during the reign of Trajan).
132–135	Second Jewish Revolt against the Romans (Bar-Kokhba Revolt) (during the reign of Hadrian).

313	Constantine and Licinius issue the Edict of Milan, legalizing Christianity.
324	Constantine establishes Constantinople (formerly Byzantium) as the new capital of the Roman Empire.
395	Roman Empire splits into two halves, west and east; the east becomes the Byzantine Empire.
527–565	Reign of the Byzantine emperor Justinian.
614	Sasanid Persian conquest of Palestine.
634–640	Muslim conquest of Palestine.
661–750	Umayyad dynasty rules Palestine.
750	Abbasid dynasty replaces the Umayyads, and the capital of the empire is moved from Damascus to Baghdad.
1800	Beginning of Western exploration of Palestine.
1914–18	World War I and the collapse of the Ottoman Empire.
1948	The British Mandate ends, Palestine is partitioned, and the State of Israel is established.

Glossary

Aelia Capitolina: Name given by Hadrian to his rebuilt city of Jerusalem, combining his name (Publius Aelius Hadrianus) and Capitoline Jupiter, the new patron deity.

agora: An ancient marketplace or forum consisting of a large, open, paved space surrounded by public buildings.

al-Aqsa: Arabic for "the farthest spot"; the name of the mosque on the Temple Mount, built by the Umayyad caliph Abd al-Malek or his son al-Walid.

ancient Near East: Modern Middle East.

Antiochia: Name given to Jerusalem by the Seleucid king Antiochus IV Epiphanes (175–164 B.C.) after he refounded it as a polis.

Antonia: Fortress built by Herod the Great at the northwest corner of the Temple Mount.

Apocrypha: Books included in the Catholic canon of sacred scripture but not in the Jewish and Protestant canons (examples: Tobit and Ecclesiasticus).

Arch of Ecce Homo: Hadrianic triple-arched gateway marking the entrance to a forum, identified in Christian tradition as the spot from which Pontius Pilate displayed Jesus to the crowds.

Asherah: A name possibly designating the ancient female consort of the God of Israel.

Asia Minor: Modern Turkey.

Assyria: Ancient empire based in the northern part of Mesopotamia (modern Iraq).

Avdat (a.k.a. **Oboda**): Nabataean city in the central Negev desert.

Baal: National deity of the Canaanites/Phoenicians.

Babylonia: Ancient empire based in the southern part of Mesopotamia (modern Iraq).

Barclay's Gate: A small Herodian gate leading from the Tyropoean Valley into the Temple Mount.

baris (a.k.a. **Qasr el-Abd**): Building at Tyros described by Josephus, made of stone and decorated with carved animals.

Bar Kathros: Name of a priestly family inscribed on a stone weight from the Burnt House.

Bar-Kokhba Revolt: The Second Jewish Revolt against Rome (132–135 C.E.).

basilica: Roman public hall consisting of a rectangular building with rows of columns inside to support the roof.

Battle of Chaeronea (338 B.C.): Philip II of Macedon unites Greece under his rule.

baulk (a.k.a. **balk**): A bank of earth left standing between the excavated squares in an archaeological dig.

Ben-Hinnom Valley: Encircles Jerusalem's Western Hill on the west and south.

Beth Alpha: Site of an ancient synagogue in the Jordan Valley, near Mount Gilboa.

Bethar: The last fortress of the Second Jewish Revolt to fall to the Romans and the site where Bar-Kokhba died.

bulla: A clay sealing.

Burnt House: A house in the Jewish Quarter excavated by Nahman Avigad that yielded vivid evidence of the Roman destruction of A.D. 70, including human remains.

Caesarea Maritima: The old coastal town of Straton's Tower, rebuilt by Herod and renamed in honor of Augustus.

Capernaum: Village on the northwest shore of the Sea of Galilee that was the center of Jesus's Galilean ministry.

cardo: North-south street in a Roman city.

Cave 4 at Qumran: Yielded fragments belonging to more than 500 different scrolls.

Cave of Horror and Cave of Letters: Caves in Nahal Hever in which Jewish refugees from Ein Gedi hid from the Romans and died; the caves were excavated by the Israeli archaeologist Yigael Yadin.

Chorazin: An ancient Galilean Jewish village very close to Capernaum.

Church of the Sisters of Zion: Convent located today on the north side of the Via Dolorosa, inside of which are the Struthion pools, Lithostratos pavement, and Arch of Ecce Homo.

City of David: Eastern Hill; Lower City.

columbarium (pl. **columbaria**): Caves or structures with rows of small niches in the walls, apparently used for raising pigeons and doves.

Constantinople (modern Istanbul): The former city of Byzantium, which Constantine rebuilt and made the capital of the Roman Empire.

contubernium: A group of eight Roman legionaries.

cuneiform: Ancient script made by making wedge-shaped impressions into a raw clay tablet.

Dagon: National deity of the Philistines.

Damascus Gate (Arabic, **Bab el-Amud**: the Gate of the Column): The main gate in the north wall of Jerusalem's Old City.

Decapolis: A league constituted by the Romans of the most Hellenized cities in Syria, including Beth-Shean (Scythopolis), Pella, and Abila.

decumanus: East-west street in a Roman city.

denomination: A legitimate religious group.

Deuteronomistic reform: Reform instituted by Josiah in 622 B.C. that eliminated the worship of other gods and centralized the cult of the God of Israel in the Jerusalem temple.

Ebernari: The Persian satrapy that included Judea.

Edomites: The Iron Age inhabitants of the area southeast of the Dead Sea.

Ein Gedi: An oasis on the western shore of the Dead Sea that was the site of an ancient Jewish village.

elders: Jewish communal leaders during the Babylonian Exile.

Essenes: A Jewish sect described by such ancient authors as Flavius Josephus, Philo Judaeus, and Pliny the Elder, members of which apparently lived at Qumran.

es-Suk: The largest columbarium cave at Marisa.

Gamla (a.k.a. **Gamala**): A large Jewish village or town in the southern Golan Heights that was destroyed by the Romans during the First Jewish Revolt (A.D. 67).

Gerasa: One of the Roman Decapolis cities; modern Jerash in Jordan.

Gihon spring: Jerusalem's only perennial source of fresh water.

glacis: In general, a plastered mound of earth piled around a town, with a fortification wall on top; a rampart.

Hammath Tiberias: Town to the south of Tiberias on the Sea of Galilee with the remains of an ancient synagogue.

hand (a.k.a. **place of a hand**): The Qumranic term for a toilet.

Hanukkah: Jewish holiday commemorating the rededication of the Jerusalem temple to the God of Israel in 164 B.C.

Hanukkah menorah: Nine-branched candelabrum used in the celebration of Hanukkah.

Hasmoneans (a.k.a. **Maccabees**): Priestly family from the town of Modiin that led a Jewish revolt against Antiochus IV Epiphanes and ruled the kingdom founded after the revolt.

Hebrew Bible: Roughly corresponds with the Old Testament.

Hegira (a.k.a. **Hejira**): Muhammad's flight from Mecca to Medina (A.D. 622).

Hellenistic: The period beginning with Alexander's conquests.

heresy: A doctrine of which we disapprove.

Herm: A stone pillar with the head of Hermes, usually erected at the entrance to an ancient Greek marketplace (agora).

Herodium (a.k.a. **Herodion**): A fortified palace near Bethlehem that is Herod's final resting place and memorial to himself.

hippodrome: Course for horse-and-chariot races.

horreum (pl. ***horrea***): Warehouse.

House of Ahiel: A four-room Israelite house of the 8th–7th centuries on top of the glacis in the City of David.

Hulda Gates: Two sets of Herodian gates in the southern wall of the Temple Mount that were the main thoroughfares for pilgrims.

Idumaea: The southern part of the former kingdom of Judah, inhabited after 586 B.C. by the descendants of the Edomites (Idumaeans).

Iraq el-Amir: A site located between Jericho and Amman that was the capital of the Tobiads in the early Hellenistic period; ancient Tyros.

Ituraeans: Native population of the Golan, forcibly converted to Judaism by the Hasmoneans.

James ossuary: An ossuary bearing an Aramaic inscription (all or part of which might be a modern forgery) that reads, "James son of Joseph brother of Jesus."

Jason's Tomb: A Hasmonean period rock-cut tomb in western Jerusalem.

Jebusites: The original (Bronze Age) population of Jerusalem.

Jewish Antiquities: Josephus's massive history of the Jewish people, beginning with creation (completed c. A.D. 93–94).

Jewish War: Josephus's seven-volume account of the First Jewish Revolt against Rome, ending with the fall of Masada (completed c. A.D. 80).

Jordan Valley: The valley between the Sea of Galilee (north) and Dead Sea (south) through which the Jordan River flows.

Jotapata (a.k.a. **Yodefat**): Last fortress in Galilee under Josephus's command to fall to the Romans.

Ketef Hinnom: The site of a late Iron Age cemetery on the northwest slope of Jerusalem's Ben-Hinnom Valley; one of the tombs in the cemetery contained a silver amulet inscribed with the priestly benediction.

The Khazneh: Most famous rock-cut tomb at Petra, reached at the end of a narrow canyon called the Siq, probably the tomb of the Nabataean king Aretas IV (time of Jesus).

Khirbet Qazone: A large Nabatean cemetery on the southeast side of the Dead Sea.

Kidron Valley: Separates the Mount of Olives from the Temple Mount and the City of David.

Kuntillet Ajrud: Eighth-century Israelite cultic site in Sinai.

Lachish: Important city in the southern part of the kingdom of Judah, destroyed by the Babylonians in 701 B.C.

legate: A high-ranking governor in the Roman administration who could command a legion.

Levirate marriage: Biblical law requiring a man to marry his brother's widow if his brother was childless.

Lithostratos pavement: Stone pavement of a Hadrianic forum in Jerusalem overlying the Struthion pools; identified in the Christian tradition as the spot where Pontius Pilate sentenced Jesus to death.

loculus (pl. **loculi**; Hebrew, *kokh*, pl. *kokhim*): Niche cut into the wall of a burial cave to accommodate a single inhumation (whole body).

Machaerus: Herodian fortified palace in Peraea (eastern side of the Dead Sea).

Madaba Map: Mosaic floor of circa A.D. 600 in a church in the town of Madaba (Jordan), decorated with a map of the Holy Land as it appeared at that time.

Magdala (Hebrew, **Migdal**; Greek, **Tarichaea**): Jewish town on the Sea of Galilee that was the home of Mary Magdalene.

Marisa (Hebrew, **Maresha**; Arabic, **Tell Sandahannah**): Main city in Hellenistic-period Idumaea, inhabited by Idumaeans and Hellenized Sidonians.

martyrium: A site associated with a martyr (someone who gave witness to the truth of Christianity).

Masada: Herodian fortified palace by the southwest shore of the Dead Sea.

Mausoleum at Halicarnassos: Monumental tomb of King Mausolus of Caria (c. 350 B.C.) at modern Bodrum on the southwest coast of Turkey.

medinah (pl. **medinot**): Smaller administrative districts within Persian satrapies.

menorah: Seven-branched candelabrum in the Jerusalem temple.

Merneptah stele: Monumental stone inscription of the pharaoh Merneptah, which contains the first reference to the people "Israel" (1209 B.C.).

Mesha stele: Inscribed stone found in Jordan that records Mesha's revolt against one of the Omride kings in the mid-9th century.

Mesopotamia: In Greek, literally means "the land between the rivers," referring to the Tigris and Euphrates rivers; a territory that corresponds roughly with modern Iraq.

miqveh (pl. ***miqva'ot***): Jewish ritual bath, used for repeated immersion in observance of biblical purity laws.

Moabites: Iron Age inhabitants of the area south of Ammon and north of Edom.

Mount Gerizim: Sacred mountain of the Samaritans, overlooking biblical Shechem (modern Nablus).

Nabataeans: An Arab people who created a kingdom in the area of modern Jordan, the Negev, and the Sinai from the mid-2nd century until A.D. 106.

Nahal Hever: Canyon to the south of Ein Gedi.

Nea (New) Church: Church dedicated to Mary the Mother of God (Greek: Theotokos), built by Justinian at the southern end of Jerusalem's main cardo.

nefesh: From the Hebrew for "soul"; a monumental marker, often in the shape of a pyramid, marking the site of a rock-cut tomb.

Nemrut Dagi: A burial tumulus in eastern Asia Minor that is the final resting place of a local king and that might have been a source of inspiration for Herod's tomb at Herodium.

Nicanor's Gate: A gate donated to the Herodian temple by a wealthy Jew named Nicanor of Alexandria.

Nicanor's Tomb: Tomb on Mount Scopus of the Alexandrian man who donated a gate to the Jerusalem temple.

Omrides: Dynasty that ruled the biblical kingdom of Israel, founded by Omri and including his son Ahab.

opus reticulatum (a.k.a. **reticulate work**): Bricks used in Roman concrete construction, laid in a net-like pattern.

ossuaries: Small lidded containers, which in Jerusalem are made of the local stone, used to contain remains removed from loculi.

Palestine: Modern Israel, Jordan, and the Palestinian territories (ancient Canaan).

patera: Handled bowl for pouring liquid offerings (libations).

Pentateuch: Torah; Five Books of Moses.

Persia: Roughly, modern Iran.

Pesher: A type of biblical commentary or interpretation that was popular at Qumran.

Pesher Nahum: A Dead Sea Scroll that refers to Demetrius's attempt to take Jerusalem and to Alexander Jannaeus's crucifixion of his Pharisaic opponents.

Petra: Capital of the Nabataean kingdom, located to the southeast of the Dead Sea in modern Jordan.

Pharisees: Jews of the Late Second Temple period who were moderately prosperous and known for their strict observance of Jewish purity laws.

Philistines: People of Aegean origin who settled the southern coast of Palestine in the early Iron Age.

Phoenicians: The Iron Age inhabitants of modern Lebanon, descendants of the Bronze Age Canaanites.

pilaster: Square column engaged in a wall.

polis: A Greek or Greek-style city.

Pool of Siloam: Pool for storing water from the Gihon spring, at the southern tip of the City of David.

praetorium: Living quarters of the Roman commander.

prefect/procurator: Low-ranking governors who administered Herod's former kingdom after his sons died or were removed.

principia: Camp headquarters.

Pseudepigrapha: Jewish religious works of the Late Second Temple period that were not included in the Catholic, Jewish, or Protestant canons of sacred scripture (examples: Enoch and Jubilees).

Qumran: Ancient settlement by the northwest shore of the Dead Sea, surrounded by caves in which the Dead Sea Scrolls were found.

rabbi: Originally, a Hebrew term of respect for someone learned in biblical Jewish law ("my master").

repository: Pit in a rock-cut tomb to collect remains of burials.

Robinson's Arch: A monumental Herodian gate supported on arches that led from the Tyropoean Valley into the area of the Royal Stoa on the Temple Mount.

Roman luxury latrine: A sophisticated type of Roman toilet, usually attached to a bath house, with rows of seats above a water channel that carried the waste away.

Rotunda: The circular structure in the Church of the Holy Sepulcher that enshrines the tomb of Jesus.

Royal Stoa (a.k.a. **Royal Basilica**): Large public hall built by Herod at the southern end of the Temple Mount.

Russian Alexander Hospice: Building to the east of the Church of the Holy Sepulcher, belonging to the White Russian church, that contains the remains of Hadrian's western forum and the original Constantinian Church of the Holy Sepulcher.

Sadducees: Elite Jews (upper-class priests and aristocracy) of the Late Second Temple period.

Samaria: Capital of the northern kingdom of Israel and, later, the name of the surrounding district, as well.

Samaritans: Descendants of the population of the former kingdom of Israel who claimed descent from the old Joseph tribes (Ephraim and Manasseh).

Sanhedria tombs: Rock-cut tombs in the northern Jerusalem neighborhood of Sanhedria.

satrap: Governor of a Persian satrapy.

satrapy: Enormous administrative districts within the Persian Empire.

scabbard chape: The reinforced metal tip of a sword sheath.

Sebaste (a.k.a. **Sebastos**): Greek for "Augustus"; name given by Herod to Samaria and to the harbor at Caesarea.

sect: A group characterized by separation and exclusivity.

sectarian works: Works that describe the beliefs and practices of the Jewish sect that lived at Qumran (examples: Damascus Document, Community Rule [Manual of Discipline], War Scroll).

"seekers of smooth things" (Hebrew, *dorshay halakot*): Term used in the Dead Sea Scrolls to denote Pharisees. It is a pun on the Hebrew *dorshay halakhot*, meaning "those who seek the law".

Sepphoris: Major city in Galilee in the time of Jesus, only four miles from Nazareth; rebuilt by Herod Antipas.

Septuagint: Ancient Greek translation of the Hebrew Bible.

sheqel: Ancient Jewish coin (originally a weight).

shofar: Ram's horn blown during ceremonies on the Jewish high holidays.

Sidonians: Natives of the Phoenician city of Sidon (in modern Lebanon).

Siwa: Oasis in the Egyptian desert with an oracular shrine dedicated to Zeus Ammon.

Solomon's Stables: A later name given to the underground arches built by Herod to support his extension of the Temple Mount to the south.

Solomon's Temple: First Temple.

soreg: Low stone fence surrounding the temple building on top of the Temple Mount, into which were set Greek and Latin inscriptions prohibiting non-Jews from entering on pain of death.

stratigraphy: The accumulation of layers (strata) in an archaeological site.

Struthion pools: Originally, pools in the open moat to the north of the Antonia fortress, later covered by Hadrian.

Sukkot (a.k.a. **Feast of Tabernacles**): One of the three Jewish pilgrimage holidays to the Jerusalem temple.

synagogue (Hebrew, *beth knesset*): Jewish assembly hall.

Syria-Palestina: The new name given to the province of Judea after the Bar-Kokhba Revolt.

Talpiyot tomb: A rock-cut tomb in the southern Jerusalem neighborhood of Talpiyot, in which were found several ossuaries inscribed with names corresponding to figures mentioned in the New Testament.

Targum: Ancient translation of the Hebrew Bible into Aramaic.

tel (a.k.a. **tell**): Artificial mound.

Tel Dan stele: Monumental stone inscription of the mid-9th century mentioning the House of David (the dynasty founded by King David).

temenos **wall**: Wall surrounding a sacred enclosure.

temple: The house of a deity.

Temple Scroll: A work found at Qumran that describes an ideal future city of Jerusalem and temple.

Tenth Legion: The Roman legion that participated in the siege of Masada.

Theodotus inscription: Dedicatory inscription of a Jerusalem synagogue antedating A.D. 70.

Tiberias: New capital city built by Herod Antipas on the shore of the Sea of Galilee, named in honor of the emperor Tiberius.

Tobiads: A Judean dynasty that governed the district of Ammon in the Persian and Hellenistic periods.

Tomb of Bene Hezir: Tomb at the foot of the Mount of Olives in Jerusalem that belonged to the priestly family of Bene Hezir.

Tomb of the Kings: The family tomb of Queen Helena of Adiabene, who converted to Judaism in the mid-1st century C.E. and moved from Syria to Jerusalem.

Tomb of Zachariah: A solid, rock-carved cube adjacent to the Tomb of Bene Hezir in Jerusalem that apparently served as its *nefesh* (marker).

Torah Shrine: Structure holding the Torah scrolls in a synagogue.

tribunal: Podium or dais on which a Roman commander could stand to review and address his troops.

triclinium: Dining room.

tsinnor: Biblical Hebrew word perhaps referring to the Warren's Shaft system in the City of David.

Tulul Abu al-Alayiq: Herodian Jericho; the site of the Hasmonean and Herodian palaces, on the banks of Wadi Qelt.

Tyropoeon Valley (a.k.a. **Central Valley**): Literally, Valley of the Cheesmakers; separates the Temple Mount and the City of David from the Western Hill.

Umayyads: The first Muslim dynasty (A.D. 661–750).

Umm el-Amed: Rock-cut tomb in northeast Jerusalem with walls cut in imitation of Herodian-style masonry.

Via Dolorosa ("Way of Sorrow"): The route walked by Jesus from the point where he was sentenced to death by Pontius Pilate to the place where he was crucified and buried (today enshrined within the Church of the Holy Sepulcher).

Wadi Daliyeh: Site of a cave in a riverbed near Jericho, in which Samaritan families who rebelled against Alexander the Great took refuge.

Warren's Shaft: Along with the Siloam Channel and Hezekiah's Tunnel, one of three ancient water systems of Jerusalem.

Western Hill: Upper City.

Wilson's Arch: A Herodian bridge connecting the Temple Mount with the Western Hill.

window wall: Interior wall in Galilean village houses pierced by windows to let light and air into rear rooms.

Yahud: The Persian medinah of Judea.

YHWH: Name of the God of Israel.

Yotvata: The site of a late Roman fort in Israel's southern Arava.

Zadokites: Descendants of Zadok, high priest in the time of Solomon.

Biographical Notes

Abd al-Malek (646/647–705): The Umayyad caliph who built the Dome of the Rock (A.D. 696) on Jerusalem's Temple Mount (Arabic: al-Haram al-Sharif).

Alexander and **Aristobulus** (fl. 1st century B.C.): Sons of Herod the Great by Mariamne; strangled to death on Herod's orders in 7 B.C.

Alexander the Great (356–323 B.C.): Son and successor of Philip II of Macedon, defeated the Persian king Darius III and created a vast empire stretching from southern Russia and northern India through Egypt and Asia Minor. Alexander's conquests mark the beginning of the Hellenistic period.

Alexander Jannaeus (r. 103–76 B.C.): Hasmonean king who married his brother's widow (Salome Alexandra) and was known for his cruelty and disregard for the observance of Jewish law. Josephus and the Pesher Nahum from Qumran report that he had 800 Pharisaic opponents crucified while dining with his concubines.

Alexandra (fl. 1st century B.C.): Mariamne's mother; an ambitious woman who attempted to maneuver the Hasmoneans back into power and was executed on Herod's orders in 28 B.C. after she moved to take over the Jerusalem garrison.

Antiochus IV Epiphanes (r. 175–164 B.C.): A Seleucid king whose rededication of the Jerusalem temple to the Greek god Olympian Zeus led to the outbreak of the Maccabean revolt.

Antipas (late 2nd–early 1st century B.C.): An Idumaean who was forcibly converted to Judaism by the Hasmoneans and was the grandfather of Herod the Great.

Antipater (c. 100–43 B.C.): Son of Antipas and father of Herod the Great; served as governor of Judea for the Romans from 47 B.C. until he was murdered.

Antipater (fl. 1st century B.C.): Herod's oldest son by his first wife, Doris; was executed by Herod just five days before Herod himself died (4 B.C.).

Aristobulus I (d. 103 B.C.): Son and successor of John Hyrcanus I (134–104 B.C.); a Hellenizer and the first Hasmonean to adopt the title "king."

Aristobulus III: Mariamne's younger brother (grandson of Hyrcanus II and Aristobulus II); served briefly as high priest before being drowned in a swimming pool at Jericho on Herod's orders in 35 B.C.

Athanasius Yeshua Samuel (1907–1995): Patriarch of the Syrian Orthodox Church in Jerusalem who purchased four of the seven scrolls from Cave 1 from Kando.

Avigad, Nahman (1905–1992): Israeli archaeologist who conducted excavations in Jerusalem's Jewish Quarter after 1967.

Bar-Kokhba (d. A.D. 135): Nickname for the leader of the Second Jewish Revolt, meaning "son of a star" and, thus, reflecting messianic expectations; his real name was Simeon Bar Kosiba.

Bliss, Frederick (1859–1937): British archaeologist who excavated Marisa in 1900 with Robert Macalister.

Cestius Gallus (fl. 1st century A.D.): The Roman legate of Syria at the outbreak of the First Jewish Revolt (A.D. 66); suffered a humiliating defeat at the hands of the Jewish rebels.

Cleopatra VII (70/69 B.C.–30 B.C.): A descendant of the Ptolemies who was the lover of Julius Caesar and later married Mark Antony; she was a rival of Herod the Great and coveted his kingdom. After being defeated by Octavian at the battle of Actium in 31 B.C., Antony and Cleopatra returned to Egypt and committed suicide.

Constantine I (after A.D. 280?–337): Roman emperor who issued the Edict of Milan in A.D. 313 legalizing Christianity; he built the first Christian churches, including the Church of the Holy Sepulcher in Jerusalem and the Church of the Nativity in Bethlehem.

Cyrus (a.k.a. **Cyrus the Great**; 590/580 B.C.–c. 529 B.C.): Persian king who repatriated the Judean exiles and granted permission for the construction of the second Jerusalem temple.

Darius III (d. 330 B.C.): King of Persia from 336 to 330 B.C.; defeated and replaced by Alexander the Great and subsequently murdered by his own men.

David (fl. 10th century B.C.): The eighth and youngest son of Jesse, from the tribe of Judah, David succeeded Saul as king of Israel and ruled the United Kingdom for 40 years, from c. 1010 to 970 B.C. He conquered Jerusalem and made it the capital of his kingdom. David also brought the Ark of the Covenant to Jerusalem. He was succeeded to the throne by his son Solomon.

Demetrius III (r. c. 95–88 B.C.): Seleucid king and opponent of Alexander Jannaeus.

Eleazar Ben-Yair (fl. 1st century A.D.): The leader of the Jewish rebels at Masada (A.D. 66–73), who according to Josephus, persuaded the rebels to commit mass suicide rather than surrender to the Romans.

Ennion (fl. 1st century A.D.): A glass maker from Phoenicia who signed some of his vases, one of which was discovered in a Herodian mansion in Jerusalem's Jewish Quarter.

Ezra (fl. mid-5th century B.C.): Scribal leader of Persian Judea (Yahud); he was sent by the Persian king to oversee the implementation of Jewish law (Torah) as the law of Yahud.

Flavius Josephus (a.k.a. **Josephus ben Mattitiyahu**; A.D. 37–c. 100): Jewish leader and later historian put in charge of the district of Galilee on behalf of the Jews at the time of the First Jewish Revolt. After surrendering to the Romans, Josephus became a client of the Roman imperial family (the Flavians); he spent the rest of his life in Rome, where he wrote a series of history books on the First Jewish Revolt and the history of the Jews, as well as an autobiography. He provides valuable information about the Essenes and is our only ancient source on the siege of Masada.

Flavius Silva (fl. 1st century A.D.): The commander of the Roman troops during the siege of Masada (A.D. 72/73 or 73/74).

Gemaryahu son of Shaphan (dates unknown): Israelite name impressed on a bulla from the City of David, apparently the same scribe mentioned in Jeremiah 36:10.

Herod Agrippa I (A.D. 10–44): Grandson of Herod the Great and Mariamne and a childhood friend of Gaius Caligula; ruled Herod's former kingdom from A.D. 37/41 to 44.

Herod Antipas (21 B.C.–A.D. 39): Herod's son and successor, who ruled Galilee and Peraea (the territory on the eastern side of the Jordan River and Dead Sea) from 4 B.C. to A.D. 39 Known for having beheaded John the Baptist.

Herod Archelaus (22 B.C.–c. A.D. 18): Herod's son and successor, who ruled Judea, Samaria, and Idumaea from 4 B.C. to A.D. 6.

Herod Philip (20 B.C.–A.D. 34): Herod's son and successor, who ruled the mostly Gentile territories of Gaulanitis, Trachonitis, Batanea, and Panias from 4 B.C. to A.D. 33/34.

Herod the Great (73/4–4 B.C.): In 40 B.C., the Romans appointed Herod client king of Judea. Herod was unpopular among the Jewish population because of his cruelty and because he was not a member of the Hasmonean dynasty (the native Jewish royal family). In archaeological circles, Herod is known as the single greatest builder in the history of the land of Israel, having changed the face of the country with his massive projects, including the reconstruction of the Second Temple in Jerusalem.

Herodias (d. A.D. 39): Granddaughter of Herod the Great; she divorced Herod Philip in order to marry his half-brother, Herod Antipas; their marriage was condemned by John the Baptist on the grounds that it was prohibited by biblical law.

Hezekiah (r. c. 715–c. 686 B.C.): King of Israel during the Assyrian invasion of the southern kingdom of Judah at the end of the 8th century B.C.

Hippicus (fl. 1st century B.C.): A friend of Herod the Great, after whom Herod named one of the three towers at the northwest corner of Jerusalem's Western Hill.

Hippodamus of Miletus (c. 500 B.C.): Ancient Greek architect credited with developing a grid plan for cities (a "Hippodamian town plan").

Hyrcanus (d. 175 B.C.): Tobiad governor in the early 2nd century B.C. who built Tyros (Iraq el-Amir); he committed suicide when Antiochus IV Epiphanes became king.

Jesus of Nazareth (c. 7 B.C.–33 C.E.): Charismatic teacher and prophetic figure who was the leader of a Jewish sect in Galilee, was crucified by the Romans, and is believed to be the messiah by his followers (Christians).

Jezebel (d. 843 B.C.): Phoenician wife of Ahab, king of Israel (r. 872–851); condemned by the prophet Elijah and reviled by biblical authors for having introduced the cult of the Canaanite god Baal into Samaria.

John Hyrcanus I (c. 175–104 B.C.): Hasmonean ruler (134–104 B.C.) who was Simon's son and successor; he conquered Idumaea and territories in Transjordan, forcibly converting the native populations to Judaism. He also conquered Samaria and destroyed the Samaritan temple on Mount Gerizim.

John Hyrcanus II (d. 30 B.C.): Older son of Salome Alexandra. He served as high priest (76–40 B.C.) under Salome Alexandra and became embroiled with his brother Aristobulus II in a civil war over the succession to the throne after their mother's death.

John son of Levi of Gischala (a.k.a. **Gush Halav**; fl. 1st century A.D.): Leader of a rebel band at the time of the First Jewish Revolt against the Romans and bitter enemy of Josephus. He was captured by the Romans in Jerusalem in A.D. 70 and sentenced to life in prison in Rome.

Jonathan (d. 142 B.C.): One of Mattathias's sons, who assumed leadership after the death of Judah Maccabee in 160 B.C. and became ruler of Judea; he died through an act of treachery in 142 B.C.

Josephus: *See* **Flavius Josephus**.

Josiah (r. c. 640–609 B.C.): King of Judah at the end of the 7th century B.C. who instituted the Deuteronomistic reform, eliminating the worship of other gods and centralizing the cult of the God of Israel in the Jerusalem temple.

Judah Maccabee (d. 161/160 B.C.): Third son of Mattathias and military leader of the Jewish revolt against Antiochus IV Epiphanes. Under his leadership, the Jerusalem temple was returned to the Jews and rededicated to the God of Israel (164 B.C.), an event commemorated by the Jewish holiday of Hanukkah.

Justinian (483–565): Byzantine emperor from A.D. 527 to 565. He built the St. Sophia in Constantinople and carried out a reconquest of the Roman Empire; he also built the Nea Church (New Church of Mary, Mother of God) in Jerusalem.

Kando (fl. 20th century A.D.): Cobbler in Bethlehem who, in 1947, purchased the seven Dead Sea Scrolls found by the Bedouin in Cave 1 at Qumran. He sold four of the scrolls to Athanasius Yeshua Samuel, the Patriarch of the Syrian Orthodox Church in Jerusalem, and the other three scrolls to Eleazar Lipa Sukenik.

Kenyon, Kathleen (fl. 20th century A.D.): British archaeologist who worked in Palestine in the mid-1960s, including conducting excavations in Jerusalem and Jericho.

Macalister, Robert (1870–1950): Irish archaeologist who worked in Palestine in the early 20th century and excavated in Jerusalem and at Marisa.

Manassah (fl. 4th century B.C.): Brother of the Jewish high priest Jaddua; he became the first high priest in the Samaritan temple (c. 332 B.C.).

Mariamne (c. 57–29 B.C.): Herod's Hasmonean wife, mother of Alexander and Aristobulus; beloved of Herod but executed on his orders on a charge of infidelity.

Mattathias (d. c. 167 B.C.): Patriarch of the Hasmonean clan, whose opposition to the ban imposed by Antiochus IV Epiphanes on the practice of Judaism sparked the outbreak of the Maccabean revolt in 167 B.C.; he died shortly thereafter.

Mattathias Antigonus (fl. 1st century B.C.): Hasmonean set up on the throne after the Parthian invasion of Palestine in 40 B.C.; defeated and killed by Herod in 37 B.C.

Menahem (fl. 1st century B.C.): An Essene mentioned by Josephus as having foretold to Herod that he would one day be king.

Mesha (dates unknown): King of Moab who rebelled against the Omrides, as commemorated in a victory stele from ancient Dibon (in Jordan), c. 850 B.C.

Nehemiah (fl. 5th century B.C.): A high-ranking Judean in the Persian administration who was sent by the Persian king to be governor of Yahud from 446 to 424 B.C. and oversaw the rebuilding of Jerusalem's city walls.

Octavian (63 B.C.–A.D. 14): Roman ruler who was given the title Augustus in 27 B.C. and ruled until his death in A.D. 14. After the Battle of Actium in 31 B.C., Octavian reconfirmed Herod as client king of Judea and increased the size of his kingdom.

Omar (fl. 7th century A.D.): An elected caliph, during whose administration Jerusalem surrendered to the Muslims (A.D. 638).

Omri (fl. 9th century B.C.): Ruler of the northern kingdom of Israel (r. 884–872) who moved the capital to Samaria and established the Omride dynasty; father of Ahab.

Petrie, William Flinders (1853–1942): A British archaeologist who conducted the first stratigraphic archaeological excavations in Palestine (at Tell el-Hesi in 1890).

Phasael (fl. 1st century B.C.): Younger son of Antipater and brother of Herod; committed suicide during the Parthian invasion of Palestine in 40 B.C. Later, Herod named one of the three towers at the northwest corner of Jerusalem's Western Hill in his memory.

Philo Judaeus (b. 15–10 B.C., d. A.D. 45–50): A Jewish philosopher from Alexandria in Egypt, who applied allegorical interpretation to the Hebrew Bible; he is one of our sources of information on the Essenes.

Pliny the Elder (a.k.a. **Gaius Plinius Secundus**; A.D. 23–79): Roman author, naturalist, philosopher, and naval commander known for his massive work, *Natural History*. Pliny died during the eruption of Mount Vesuvius. He is one of our sources of information on the Essenes and the only one who indicates their geographical location (by the Dead Sea).

Pompey (106–48 B.C.): Roman general who entered the Jerusalem temple and annexed the Hasmonean kingdom (63 B.C.).

Pontius Pilate (d. A.D. 36): Roman prefect of Judea from A.D. 26 to 36; during his administration, Jesus was crucified.

Ptolemy I (Soter) (c. 365–c. 283): One of Alexander's generals who established a kingdom in Egypt (the Ptolemaic kingdom).

Salome Alexandra (139–67 B.C.): Wife of Aristobulus I and, later, his brother Alexander Jannaeus; she ruled the Hasmonean kingdom after Jannaeus's death.

Sanballat I: Governor of Samaria in the second half of the 5th century B.C. and a contemporary of Nehemiah.

Sanballat III: Governor of Samaria at the time of Alexander the Great's conquest (332 B.C.); established a Samaritan temple on Mount Gerizim.

Seleucus I (c. 355–281 B.C.): One of Alexander's generals who established a kingdom in Asia Minor and Syria (the Seleucid kingdom).

Shiloh, Yigal (1937–1987): Israeli archaeologist who conducted excavations in the City of David in the 1970s.

Simon (d. 134 B.C.): The youngest of Judah's brothers, he ruled the Hasmonean kingdom after Jonathan's death in 142 B.C.

Simon bar Giora (fl. 1st century A.D.): Leader of a rebel band during the First Jewish Revolt; he was captured by the Romans during the siege of Jerusalem in A.D. 70 and was executed in Rome.

Solomon (r. c. 970–930 B.C.): Son of David and successor to the throne of the United Kingdom. Solomon is renowned for his wisdom; his many wives; his political and commercial alliances with Hiram, king of Tyre, and with the queen of Sheba; and for having established the First Temple on Jerusalem's Temple Mount.

Sosius (fl. 1st century B.C.): Legate of Syria who assisted Herod in his battle against Mattathias Antigonus in 37 B.C.

Sukenik, Eleazer Lipa (1889–1953): Israeli archaeologist and biblical scholar (and father of Yigael Yadin) who purchased three of the seven scrolls from Cave 1 from Kando; apparently, the first scholar to identify the Qumran sect with the ancient Essenes.

Titus (A.D. 39–81): Vespasian's older son, he was put in charge of taking Jerusalem (A.D. 70) after his father was proclaimed emperor; succeeded his father to the throne.

Vaux, Roland de (1903–1971): French archaeologist and biblical scholar affiliated with the École Biblique et Archéologique Française de Jerusalem. He excavated Qumran and explored the surrounding caves between 1951 and 1956 and identified Qumran as the settlement of a Jewish sect (apparently the Essenes) that deposited the Dead Sea Scrolls in the nearby caves.

Vespasian (A.D. 9–79): General sent by Nero to quell the First Jewish Revolt; proclaimed emperor of the Roman Empire in A.D. 69 and established the Flavian dynasty.

Warren, Charles (1840–1927): Nineteenth-century British explorer of Jerusalem who discovered a water shaft that was part of Jerusalem's ancient water system. He later became London commissioner of police and investigated the murders by Jack the Ripper.

Yadin, Yigael (1917–1984): Israeli archaeologist, politician, and chief-of-staff of the Israeli army, who arranged for the purchase of the four Dead Sea Scrolls that were in the possession of Athanasius Yeshua Samuel. Later, Yadin excavated Herod's palaces atop Masada and explored the Bar-Kokhba caves in Nahal Hever.

Zadok (fl. 10th century B.C.): High priest in the time of Solomon, whose priestly descendants became known as the Zadokites.

Zedekiah: Last king of Judah (597–587/586 B.C.), who was taken captive to Babylonia in 586 B.C. The last thing he saw before the Babylonians blinded him was the execution of his sons; he died in Babylonian captivity.

Bibliography

Ahlström, Gösta W. *The History of Ancient Palestine*. Minneapolis: Fortress Press, 1993. A comprehensive survey of the history of Palestine from the Bronze Age to 586 B.C.

Avigad, Nahman. *Discovering Jerusalem*. Nashville, TN: Thomas Nelson, 1983. An excellent overview and popular account of ancient Jerusalem, focusing on the Western Hill (modern Jewish Quarter), where the author conducted excavations in the 1970s.

Avi-Yonah, Michael. *The Holy Land from the Persian to the Arab Conquest (536 B.C.–A.D. 640): A Historical Geography*. Grand Rapids, MI: Baker, 1977. An old but still valuable overview of the geographic divisions of the Holy Land in the post-biblical periods.

Bahat, Dan. *The Illustrated Atlas of Jerusalem*. New York: Simon and Schuster, 1990. A wonderful resource for the archaeological development of Jerusalem over time, richly illustrated.

Ben-Dov, Meir. *In the Shadow of the Temple: The Discovery of Ancient Jerusalem*. New York: Harper and Row, 1985. A popular account of Israeli excavations conducted to the south and west of Jerusalem's Temple Mount in the 1970s.

Berlin, Andrea M. "Between Large Forces: Palestine in the Hellenistic Period." *Biblical Archaeologist* 60.1 (1997), pp. 2–51. The best existing overview of the archaeology of Palestine in the Hellenistic period.

Bloch-Smith, Elizabeth. *Judahite Burial Practices and Beliefs about the Dead*. Sheffield: Sheffield Academic, 1992. An academic study of tombs and burial practices in the kingdom of Judah (before 586 B.C.).

Cline, Eric H. *From Eden to Exile: Unraveling Mysteries of the Bible.* Washington, DC: National Geographic, 2007. An authoritative and highly readable account of the archaeological evidence for various biblical (Old Testament) stories, such as Noah's Ark, the Ark of the Covenant, and the Exodus.

Cohen, Shaye J. D. *Josephus in Galilee and Rome.* Boston: Brill, 2002. A study that compares Josephus's works and his development as a historian.

Davies, Philip R., George J. Brooke, and Phillip R. Callaway. *The Complete World of the Dead Sea Scrolls.* London: Thames and Hudson, 2002. A general and nicely illustrated introduction to the world of the Dead Sea Scrolls.

Dever, William G. *Who Were the Early Israelites and Where Did They Come From?* Grand Rapids, MI: Eerdmans, 2003. A highly readable book by a senior archaeologist and expert, presenting his view on the origins of the early Israelites in light of the archaeological and biblical evidence. (Note: This book should be read in conjunction with that by Avraham Faust [below] because the two represent different yet current scholarly views on the origins of the early Israelites, written in a manner that is not overly specialized or technical.)

Eshel, Hanan. "The Bar Kochba Revolt, 132–135." In Steven T. Katz, ed., *The Cambridge History of Judaism*, vol. IV, *The Late Roman-Rabbinic Period.* Cambridge: Cambridge University Press, 2006, pp. 105–127. The most authoritative current overview of the Bar-Kokhba revolt.

Fagan, Brian. *In the Beginning: An Introduction to Archaeology.* Boston: Little and Brown, 1981. A basic introduction to archaeology, by a leading authority.

Faust, Avraham. *Israel's Ethnogenesis: Settlement, Interaction, Expansion and Resistance.* London: Equinox, 2006. An excellent overview of current scholarly debates on the origins of early Israel, focusing on the archaeological evidence and the author's point of view.

Finkelstein, Israel, and Neil Asher Silberman. *The Bible Unearthed: Archaeology's New Vision of Ancient Israel and the Origin of Its Sacred Texts.* New York: Free Press, 2001. A controversial but highly readable account of the archaeology of ancient Israel as it relates to the biblical account.

Friedman, Richard Elliott. *Who Wrote the Bible?* New York: HarperCollins, 1997. A fascinating and readable analysis of the complex sources of the Hebrew Bible.

Goldenberg, Robert. *The Origins of Judaism from Canaan to the Rise of Islam.* Cambridge: Cambridge University Press, 2007. A good, concise overview of the origins of the Jewish religion.

Goodman, Martin. *Rome and Jerusalem: The Clash of Ancient Civilizations.* New York: Alfred A. Knopf, 2007. An analysis of the events and causes leading to the outbreak of the First Jewish Revolt against Rome, by a leading authority.

Grabar, Oleg, and Benjamin Z. Kedar, eds. *Where Heaven and Earth Meet: Jerusalem's Sacred Esplanade.* Austin: University of Texas Press, 2009. A beautifully illustrated, recent volume focusing on the history and archaeology of Jerusalem's Temple Mount (al-Haram ash-Sharif) under Islam.

Green, Peter. *Alexander the Great and the Hellenistic Age: A Short History.* London: Weidenfeld and Nicolson, 2007. A brief historical survey of Alexander and his successors by a leading authority.

Hayes, John H., and Sara R. Mandell. *The Jewish People in Classical Antiquity: From Alexander to Bar Kochba.* Louisville, KY: Westminster John Knox, 1998. An authoritative history of the Jews in the Second Temple period.

Holum, Kenneth G., et al. *King Herod's Dream: Caesarea on the Sea.* New York: W.W. Norton, 1988. A richly illustrated and readable overview of the history and archaeology of Caesarea Maritima.

King, Philip J., and Lawrence E. Stager. *Life in Biblical Israel*. Louisville, KY: Westminster John Knox, 2001. Presents a wonderful picture of life in ancient Israel, blending archaeology and the Bible.

Kloner, Amos, and Boaz Zissu. *The Necropolis of Jerusalem in the Second Temple Period*. Leuven: Peeters, 2007. A catalogue of tombs—mostly rock-cut—surveyed by the authors in the Jerusalem area.

Levine, Lee I. *The Ancient Synagogue: The First Thousand Years*. New Haven: Yale University Press, 2000. A comprehensive overview of ancient synagogues, written by the leading authority in the field.

———, ed. *Ancient Synagogues Revealed*. Jerusalem: Israel Exploration Society, 1981. An old and somewhat outdated volume that nevertheless contains valuable chapters on Gamla and other early synagogues.

———. *Jerusalem, Portrait of the City in the Second Temple Period (538 B.C.–70 C.E.)*. Philadelphia: Jewish Publication Society, 2002. A comprehensive yet readable overview of the history and archaeology of Jerusalem in the Second Temple period.

Levine, Lee I., and Zeev Weiss, eds. *From Dura to Sepphoris: Studies in Jewish Art and Society in Late Antiquity*. Portsmouth, RI: Journal of Roman Archaeology Supplementary Series Number 40, 2000. A collection of specialized articles, including discussions of the iconography (figured decoration) of Palestinian synagogues.

Magness, Jodi. *The Archaeology of Qumran and the Dead Sea Scrolls*. Grand Rapids, MI: Eerdmans, 2002. An authoritative and readable overview of the archaeology of Qumran.

———. *Jewish Daily Life in Late Second Temple Period Palestine*. Grand Rapids, MI: Eerdmans, 2010. A study of aspects of Jewish daily life, including diet, clothing, Sabbath observance, toilet habits, and tombs and burial customs, drawing on a combination of literary information and archaeological evidence.

———. "Ossuaries and the Burials of Jesus and James." *Journal of Biblical Literature* 124.1 (2005), pp. 121–154. A discussion of the reasons for the introduction of ossuaries into Jerusalem's rock-cut tombs and an analysis of the Gospel accounts of the deaths and burials of Jesus and his brother, James, in light of archaeological and literary evidence.

Markoe, Glenn, ed. *Petra Rediscovered: Lost City of the Nabataeans*. New York: Harry N. Abrams, 2003. A catalogue with entries and illustrations that accompanied a recent museum exhibit.

Mazar, Amihai. *Archaeology of the Land of the Bible (10,000–586 B.C.)*. New York: Doubleday, 1990. A comprehensive and academic overview of the archaeology of the Holy Land in the Old Testament period.

McCane, Byron R. *Roll Back the Stone: Death and Burial in the World of Jesus*. Harrisburg, PA: Trinity Press International, 2003. A study of Jewish tombs and burial customs in the time of Jesus.

Netzer, Ehud. *The Architecture of Herod the Great Builder*. Grand Rapids, MI: Baker, 2008. A comprehensive overview and discussion of Herod's building program, by the leading authority.

———. *The Palaces of the Hasmoneans and Herod the Great*. Jerusalem: Yad Ben-Zvi, 2001. A richly illustrated and readable description of the palaces of the Hasmoneans and Herod, including Jericho, Masada, and Herodium.

Pollitt, J. J. *Art in the Hellenistic Age*. Cambridge: Cambridge University Press, 1993. A scholarly yet readable—and fascinating—analysis of the use of art for various purposes (e.g., religious, political) by Alexander and his successors.

Rajak, Tessa. *Josephus: The Historian and His Society*. London: Duckworth, 1983. A comprehensive study of Josephus by a leading authority.

Reed, Jonathan L. *Archaeology and the Galilean Jesus: A Re-examination of the Evidence*. Harrisburg, PA: Trinity Press International, 2000. A survey of archaeological remains and sites in Galilee in the time of Jesus.

Richardson, Peter. *Herod, King of the Jews and Friend of the Romans*. Minneapolis: Fortress Press, 1999. The best existing biography of Herod that is accessible also to non-specialists, including discussions of his building program.

Saldarini, Anthony J. *Pharisees, Scribes and Sadducees in Palestinian Society*. Grand Rapids, MI: Eerdmans, 2001. An old but still authoritative and highly readable analysis of sectarianism in Palestine in the Late Second Temple period.

Shanks, Hershel. *Jerusalem: An Archaeological Biography*. New York: Random House, 1995. A good, popular overview of Jerusalem's history and archaeology.

Silberman, Neil Asher. *Between Past and Present: Archaeology, Ideology, and Nationalism in the Modern Middle East*. New York: Doubleday, 1989. A fascinating analysis of the use of archaeology for nationalistic and religious purposes in the modern Middle East, highlighting such sites as Masada in Israel.

———. *Digging for God and Country: Exploration in the Holy Land, 1799–1917*. New York: Doubleday, 1982. A highly readable account of the rediscovery of the Holy Land by Western (European and American) explorers in the 19th century.

Tcherikover, Victor. *Hellenistic Civilization and the Jews*. Peabody, MA: Hendrickson, 1999. An old but still authoritative source on the history of the Jews in the Hellenistic period.

Tsafrir, Yoram, ed. *Ancient Churches Revealed*. Jerusalem: Israel Exploration Society, 1993. A collection of articles, some of which are synthetic studies and others on specific sites and churches in Palestine, including the Church of the Holy Sepulcher.

VanderKam, James C. *An Introduction to Early Judaism.* Grand Rapids, MI: Eerdmans, 2001. An authoritative introduction to early Judaism that includes discussions of relevant ancient literary works.

VanderKam, James C., and Peter Flint. *The Meaning of the Dead Sea Scrolls.* San Francisco: HarperSanFrancisco, 2002. A good, comprehensive introduction to the Dead Sea Scrolls.

Vermes, Geza. *The Complete Dead Sea Scrolls in English.* New York: Penguin, 2004. A collection of all of the Dead Sea Scrolls translated into English, with accompanying explanations and an excellent introduction, by one of the world's leading authorities.

Yadin, Yigael. *Bar-Kokhba: The Rediscovery of the Legendary Hero of the Last Jewish Revolt against Imperial Rome.* London: Weidenfeld and Nicolson, 1971. An old but still thrilling account of the Bar-Kokhba Revolt, focusing on discoveries made by the author in caves near the Dead Sea.

———. *Masada: The Momentous Archaeological Discovery Revealing the Heroic Life and Struggle of the Jewish Zealots.* New York: Random House, 1966. An old but still classic and thrilling account of the archaeology and history of Masada, written by an excavator of the site.

General Resources:

Levy, Thomas E., ed. *The Archaeology of Society in the Holy Land.* New York: Facts on File, 1995.

Meyers, Eric M., ed. *The Oxford Encyclopedia of Archaeology in the Near East.* New York: Oxford University Press, 1997.

Murphy-O'Connor, Jerome. *The Holy Land: An Oxford Archaeological Guide.* Oxford: Oxford University Press, 2008.

Stern, Ephraim, ed. *The New Encyclopedia of Archaeological Excavations in the Holy Land.* New York: Simon and Schuster, 1993; plus supplementary volume 5, 2008.

Journals:

Annual of the Department of Antiquities of Jordan (ADAJ)

Biblical Archaeologist (BA) (now renamed *Near Eastern Archaeology*)

Biblical Archaeology Review (BAR)

Bulletin of the American Schools of Oriental Research (BASOR)

Israel Exploration Journal (IEJ)

Journal of the American Oriental Society (JAOS)

Journal of Near Eastern Studies (JNES)

Levant

Palestine Exploration Quarterly (PEQ)

Online Resources:

Hebrew Bible online: http://www.mechon-mamre.org/e/et/et0.htm.

Josephus online: http://pace.mcmaster.ca/York/york/texts.htm.

The Orion Center for the Study of the Dead Sea Scrolls at the Hebrew University of Jerusalem: http://orion.mscc.huji.ac.il.

Philo online: http://www.earlyjewishwritings.com/philo.html.

Notes

Notes

Notes

Notes